Monica Correa Fryckstedt

Geraldine Jewsbury's *Athenaeum* Reviews: A Mirror of Mid-Victorian Attitudes to Fiction

UPPSALA 1986

Distributor:
Almqvist & Wiksell International
Stockholm

Printed with a grant from The Swedish Council for Research in the Humanities and Social Sciences.

The illustration on the dust-jacket:
photograph of Geraldine Jewsbury in Carlyle's House,
reproduced by permission of the National Trust.

Abstract

Fryckstedt, Monica Correa. Geraldine Jewsbury's *Athenaeum* Reviews: A Mirror of Mid-Victorian Attitudes to Fiction. Acta Univ. Ups. *Studia Anglistica Upsaliensia* 61. 163 pp. Uppsala. ISBN 91-554-1914-3.

This study examines the Victorian writer Geraldine Jewsbury's reviews of fiction, published anonymously in the *Athenaeum* between 1849 and 1880. Whereas scholars have drawn on her reader's reports to the publisher Bentley in order to illustrate mid-Victorian taste, her 2,300 reviews have hitherto been neglected. Her basic criterion in judging fiction was that a novel should both be entertaining and present a moral message. Consequently she shared the readers' taste for the moralistic domestic novels, which flourished in the 1850s, while she objected to the sensation novels, which came into vogue with the reading public in the 1860s. At a time when novels were largely written by and for women, Miss Jewsbury's notices furnish important evidence of the prejudices and predilections of a professional woman reader who, besides possessing an uncommon experience in judging novels, faithfully reflected the tastes of the vast reading public among the Victorian middle classes. In fact, her reviews give us an accurate picture of the entire mid-Victorian scene of fiction.

ISBN 91-554-1914-3
ISSN 0562-2719

Printed in Sweden 1986
Textgruppen i Uppsala AB

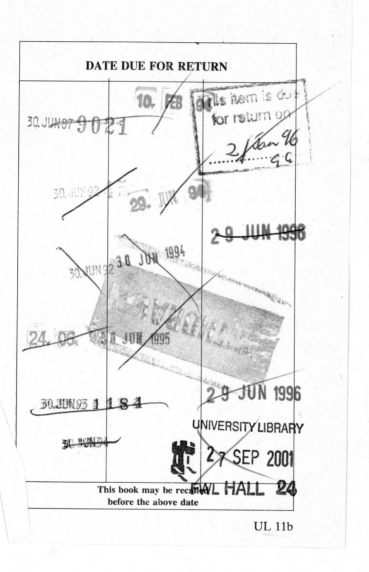

DATE DUE FOR RETURN

This book may be recalled
before the above date

UL 11b

For my father
J.C.M. Alvares Correa

Contents

Acknowledgements

I should like to express my sincere gratitude to the following persons and institutions without whose assistance this study would not have been completed.

Ms Joanne Hurst, Production Manager of the *New Statesman*, gave me permission in 1981 to consult the "marked file" of the *Athenaeum* and Ms Gillian Boyd kindly assisted me in locating the volumes in their basement strongroom.

Mrs Micheline Hancock, M.Sc., Librarian of Special Collections at the City University, London, generously spared the time for stimulating discussions about the *Athenaeum* when, in 1983, the "marked file" was moved to this library. Her interest in my project and her kind invitations to coffee in the Senior Common Room sustained me physically as well as morally.

Professor Jeanne Rosenmayer Fahnestock allowed me to borrow her Ph. D. thesis via Interlibrary Loan and to quote from it.

The National Trust permitted me to reproduce the photograph on the dust-jacket.

Dr Joanne Shattock, Victorian Studies Centre, the University of Leicester, patiently answered my queries about the *Athenaeum* and suggested ways of locating the office records of the periodical.

Dr J. A. Edwards, Keeper of Archives and Manuscripts at the University of Reading, and the staff of the National Register of Archives, London, assisted me in my attempts to unearth further material pertaining to the *Athenaeum*.

The courteous staff of the British Library facilitated my research in London. Uppsala University Library made this study possible by generously placing sixty volumes of the *Athenaeum* at my disposal for over a year and its Interlibrary Loan Section indefatigably obtained much-needed books.

The Department of English, Uppsala University, granted me a part-time leave of absence during the academic year 1984—85 which made it possible for me to write this study.

A travel grant from Hilda Kumlin's Fund at Uppsala University financed research in London.

The Swedish Council for Research in the Humanities and Social Sciences and Acta Universitatis Upsaliensis defrayed the expenses of publishing this book.

Professor Gunnar Sorelius, Uppsala University, kindly read the manuscript at a time when his workload was very heavy.

Mr D.A.H. Evans, University College, Dublin, checked the manuscript and suggested valuable stylistic improvements.

Colleagues at the English Department, Uppsala University—Arne Axelsson, Donald MacQueen, Hedda Friberg and Göran Rönnerdal—patiently initiated me into what at first seemed an unfathomable world—word processing.

Mrs Barbro Kinnwall's meticulous proof-reading excised many typographical errors.

In particular, I should like to thank my severest critic, my husband Olle, for offering perspicacious but ruthlessly frank comments which proved a challenge as well as a constant source of inspiration.

Our ten-year-old daughter Ulrika helped me to place my project in a salutary perspective by disrespectfully re-naming Geraldine Jewsbury—"Gelatine Gooseberry."

Uppsala, July 1986

M. C. F.

Introduction

That the mid-Victorian period was "the age of female novelists" is today a commonplace. Mrs Oliphant's well-known phrase[1] was but a reverberation of George Henry Lewes's protest in 1850 against women invading what he considered "our legitimate domain." Confronted with a massive encroachment upon his profession by a "multitudinous" group of female writers, becoming more successful every year, he asked in despair: "How many of us can write novels like Currer Bell, Mrs. Gaskell, Geraldine Jewsbury, Mrs. Marsh, Mrs. Crowe, and fifty others, with their shrewd and delicate observations of life?"[2] This "invasion" reached such proportions that in 1862 *Temple Bar* estimated that as many as two-thirds of all published novels were "by feminine hands."[3] The recognition of women novelists as a major factor in English fiction, the growing interest in the characteristics of their novels, the urge to differentiate between male and female traits in novels and speculation about what idiosyncrasies made women particularly apt at writing fiction were widely reflected in contemporary periodicals.[4] On the one hand, "lady novelists" were praised for their depiction of everyday incidents of domestic life, their rendering of pathos and sentiment, their character portrayal and their ability to tell a story. On the other hand, however, their novels were accused of lacking the breadth that arose from a man's wider range of experiences, of being devoid of "the

[1] [Margaret Oliphant], "Modern Novelists—Great and Small," *Blackwood's Magazine,* 77 (1855), 555.
[2] "Vivian" [George Henry Lewes], "A Gentle Hint to Writing-Women," *Leader,* 1 (1850), 189.
[3] R[obert] W. B[uchanan], "Society's Looking-Glass," *Temple Bar,* 6 (1862), 136.
[4] See for instance "The Lady Novelists of Great Britain," *Gentleman's Magazine,* 40 (1853), 18—25; [Richard Holt Hutton], "Novels by the Authoress of 'John Halifax,' " *North British Review,* 29 (1858), 466—81; "The Author of *Heartsease* and the Modern School of Fiction," *Prospective Review,* 10 (1854), 460—82; [G.H. Lewes], "The Lady Novelists," *Westminster Review,* NS 2 (1852), 129—41; [George Eliot], "Silly Novels by Lady Novelists," *Westminster Review,* NS 10 (1856), 442—61 and [W.R. Greg], "The False Morality of Lady Novelists," *National Review,* 8 (1859), 144—67.

broad intellectual framework of masculine novels" and of failing to evoke "the unseen side of character."[5] The range of women novelists being very wide, there was no consensus of opinion as to their achievement: while the *Gentleman's Magazine* hailed George Sand and Harriet Beecher Stowe as "most wonderful Consuelo" and "earnest, inspired, duteous, magnanimous 'Uncle Tom',"[6] William Rathbone Greg and George Eliot criticised the "false morality" of lady novelists, the latter condescendingly assorting them into the "mind-and-millinery species" and the "white neck-cloth species."[7] However, praise and censure alike acquire full significance only when seen as the expression of an all-pervasive and irrepressible need to appraise the legion of women's novels which flooded the English fiction market in the 1850s.

The ranking of women novelists in 1850 by somebody as perceptive and clear-sighted as Lewes is too significant to be ignored. Evidently he rated Geraldine Jewsbury highly, placing her directly after Charlotte Brontë and Mrs Gaskell and, two years later, he praised her "subtle and . . . deep observation of morals" and "manners," displayed in her novels *Zoë* (1845), *The Half-Sisters* (1848) and *Marian Withers* (1851) and prophesied a promising future for her.[8] The author of six novels and two children's books, Miss Jewsbury has, in spite of Lewes's prophecy, received relatively little attention as a novelist in our century.[9] What has attracted literary scholars in the last few decades, however, is her influential role as a publisher's reader for Bentley from 1858 to her death in 1880.[10] In 609 reports she discussed the acceptability of 808 manuscript novels, their probable audiences and potential profits, both serving the publisher's interest and acting as a guardian of morality and convention. At

[5] [Hutton], "Novels by the Authoress of 'John Halifax,' " *North British Review,* 29 (1858), 469 and 474.

[6] "The Lady Novelists of Great Britain," *Gentleman's Magazine,* 40 (1853), 19.

[7] [Eliot], "Silly Novels by Lady Novelists," *Westminster Review,* NS 10 (1856), 449 and 456—57.

[8] [Lewes], "The Lady Novelists," *Westminster Review,* NS 2 (1852), 140.

[9] Robert Lee Wolff, *Gains and Losses: Novels of Faith and Doubt in Victorian England* (London: Murray, 1977), pp. 402—05; Patricia Thomson, *George Sand and the Victorians: Her Influence and Reputation in Nineteenth-Century England* (London: Macmillan, 1977), pp. 132—33, 142—43; Jenni Calder, *Women and Marriage in Victorian Fiction* (London: Thames and Hudson, 1976), pp. 57—58; Elaine Showalter, *A Literature of Their Own* (Princeton: Princeton Univ. Press, 1977), pp. 97—98, 141.

[10] Jeanne Rosenmayer, "Geraldine Jewsbury: Novelist and Publisher's Reader." Part II "Work as a Publisher's Reader," pp. 310—679. Diss. London, 1970. I should like to thank Professor Rosenmayer Fahnestock for her permission to quote from her dissertation. Jeanne Rosenmayer Fahnestock, "Geraldine Jewsbury: The Power of the Publisher's Reader," *Nineteenth Century Fiction,* 28 (1973), 253—72; Royal A. Gettman, *A Victorian Publisher: A Study of the Bentley Papers* (Cambridge: Cambridge Univ. Press, 1960), pp. 194—213; Guinevere L. Griest, *Mudie's Circulating Library and the Victorian Novel* (Bloomington: Indiana Univ. Press, 1970), pp. 120—37; Showalter, *A Literature of Their Own,* p. 177; Linda Marie Fritschner, "Publishers' Readers, Publishers, and their Authors," *Publishing History,* 7 (1980), 45—100; R.C. Terry, *Victorian Popular Fiction, 1860—80* (London: Macmillan, 1983), pp. 31 and 39.

a time when Bentley employed several women readers, Geraldine Jewsbury was, as the historian of the publishing house states, the adviser "whose reports were sent out as models for other readers to emulate."[11] Although Fritschner describes her as a "hack" reader compared with the highbrow, "influential" Edward Garnett, who, at the end of the century, virtually discovered and "made" writers,[12] others point to her judgment of novels as unique evidence of the tastes of middlebrow readers: her reports thus provide new insights into mid-Victorian attitudes to what could and what could not be treated in novels. Griest draws on Miss Jewsbury's reports for her illustration of the prejudices that guided Charles Edward Mudie in his choice of novels for his Select Library; Showalter refers to them in her analysis of the sensation novel of the 1860s; Terry quotes from them in his discussion of the controversial Rhoda Broughton.[13] In other words, Geraldine Jewsbury's verdicts emerge as the epitome of conventional, middlebrow Victorian taste in novels, a taste which few novelists aspiring to win the favour of the reading public at large could afford to disregard.

In view of the credit given Miss Jewsbury as an experienced judge of fiction, it is surprising that her thirty-year career as a reviewer for the *Athenaeum* should only have been mentioned in passing.[14] The reason for this is, no doubt, the relative inaccessibility of her 2,300 reviews, which appeared anonymously between 1849 and 1880. Since the *Athenaeum* has not yet been indexed, the authorship of a particular contribution can only be established by going through, page by page, the volumes of the so-called marked file, i.e. the set in which the various editors wrote in the names of the contributors, sometimes in the margin, sometimes across the text itself. At a time when women were not only the dominant writers but also the chief readers of novels, publishers and editors naturally employed women as judges of the "light reading" intended for their sex. A novelist herself and a publisher's reader for Bentley, as well as Hurst and Blackett from 1860, Geraldine Jewsbury came to possess, as her biographer rightly claims, "a familiarity with current fiction such as few women

---

[11] Gettman, *A Victorian Publisher,* p. 194.

[12] Fritschner, "Publishers' Readers," pp. 47—48.

[13] Griest, *Mudie's Circulating Library,* pp. 120—37; Showalter, *A Literature of Their Own,* p. 177 and Terry, *Victorian Popular Fiction,* pp. 31 and 39.

[14] Professor Fahnestock, the scholar who has researched Jewsbury most extensively, pointed out in 1970 that "only her importance as the author of 1600 *Athenaeum* reviews over a period of thirty years . . . has yet to be assessed." *Nineteenth Century Fiction,* 28 (1973), 253. However, the figure 1,600 proves to be inaccurate: more than 2,300 reviews emanate from Miss Jewsbury. Her career as a reviewer is briefly referred to in Leslie Marchand, *The Athenaeum: A Mirror of Victorian Culture* (Chapel Hill: Univ. of North Carolina Press, 1941), p. 321; John Cordy Jeaffreson, *A Book of Recollections* (London: Hurst and Blackett, 1894), I, 313—15; Gettman, *A Victorian Publisher,* p. 194 and Susanne Howe, *Geraldine Jewsbury* (London: George Allen & Unwin, 1935), p. 95.

of her day could have equalled''[15] and, consequently, she was a valuable asset for the *Athenaeum* which aimed at a full coverage of the fiction of the day.

Since failing eye-sight forced Miss Jewsbury to devote herself, in the 1870s, almost exclusively to reviewing children's books, which were much shorter than the three-deckers intended for adults, most of her reviews of novels were written between 1850 and 1870. Her most active period as a reviewer coincided with a crucial period in the development of fiction. Mudie's Select Library, established in 1842, opened new premises in New Oxford Street in 1854 to be able to cater for a steadily growing reading public which for a guinea a year gained access to, among other books, the latest three-volume novels: in ten years (1853—62) Mudie added nearly 960,000 volumes to his stock, half of which were fiction.[16] Railway bookstalls, initiated by W.H. Smith in 1846, part issue publication, serialisation in periodicals and cheap reprints brought novels within the reach of new layers of society avid for light reading. Without exaggeration, one might claim also that the period 1850—1870 was the time when a theory of fiction began to emerge:[17] although only a handful of book-length studies of the novel appeared,[18] numerous important articles by G.H. Lewes, George Eliot, Walter Bagehot, Richard Holt Hutton, E.S. Dallas, Mrs Oliphant, Anthony Trollope and James Fitzjames Stephen vigorously discussed questions concerning the novel.

In their examination of Victorian fiction, literary scholars have of course used various approaches. The chronological one has resulted in Kathleen Tillotson's seminal study of novels of the 1840s and Michael Wolff's examination of the literature of 1859, recent monographs have rescued women novelists such as Ouida, Mrs Oliphant and Mary Elizabeth Braddon from oblivion and genre studies like Hughes' exploration of the sensation novel of the 1860s and Terry's informative book on popular fiction have greatly added to our knowledge of little known areas.[19] Modern scholars' attempts to read and to assess Victorian

---

[15] Howe, *Geraldine Jewsbury*, p. 95.

[16] Griest, *Mudie's Circulating Library*, p. 21.

[17] Richard Stang, *The Theory of the Novel in England 1850—1870* (London: Routledge & Kegan Paul, 1959) and Kenneth Graham, *English Criticism of the Novel 1865—1900* (Oxford: Clarendon Press, 1965).

[18] J.C. Jeaffreson, *Novels and Novelists from Elizabeth to Victoria* (London, 1858); David Masson, *British Novelists and Their Styles: Being a Critical Sketch of the History of British Prose Fiction* (Cambridge, 1859); G.L. Craik, *A Compendious History of English Literature*, 2 vols (London, 1861); James Hannay, *A Course of English Literature* (London, 1866) and Eneas Sweetland Dallas, *The Gay Science* (London, 1866).

[19] Kathleen Tillotson, *Novels of the Eighteen-Forties* (1954; rpt. London: Oxford Univ. Press, 1962); Michael Wolff, "Victorian Reviewers and Cultural Reponsibility" in *1859: Entering an Age of Crisis* eds. Philip Appleman, William A. Madden and Michael Wolff (Bloomington: Indiana Univ. Press, 1959); Eileen Bigland, *Ouida: The Passionate Victorian* (London: Jarrolds Ltd., 1950); Vineta and Robert Colby, *The Equivocal Virtue: Mrs. Oliphant and the Literary Market Place*

fiction with "Victorian eyes" have created an awareness of the undergrowth of minor fiction out of which the surviving masterpieces grew and placed them in a new perspective. It is with such a "contemporary" or historical approach that the present study would claim affinity. The appropriateness of adopting this method for an examination of mid-Victorian attitudes to fiction becomes obvious to anyone perusing Miss Jewsbury's *Athenaeum* reviews. For what strikes a modern reader is not only her remarkable familiarity with the various genres of novels co-existing with the main stream of domestic fiction, but, above all, her refusal, shared by many of her contemporaries, to rank novelists, to compartmentalise them into major and minor. The editorial juxtaposition in the *Athenaeum* of what *we* label major and minor should induce the modern reader to defer the accepted classification based on aesthetic grounds in order to see the complete literary scene at the time: in other words, to apply a historical rather than aesthetic perspective. We must not forget that to Miss Jewsbury and other reviewers, novelists like Mrs Craik, Mrs Oliphant, Charlotte Yonge, Julia Kavanagh, J.C. Jeaffreson, William Robinson, James Grant and Miss Braddon all seemed so full of talent that their novels provided acceptable alternatives to the intellectually demanding fiction of Meredith and George Eliot.

It may seem fruitless to devote a study to the reviews of one single contributor to the *Athenaeum*. That such an enterprise is justifiable, however, depends mainly on three factors. Indisputably, in the 1850s and 1860s, few reviewers, and no other woman reviewer, of the *Athenaeum* were as prolific as Geraldine Jewsbury: reviewing some 2,300 books, she acquired an unusual familiarity with mid-Victorian fiction. Although both Henry Fothergill Chorley and William Hepworth Dixon reviewed a larger number of "important" novels, no one, I would contend, was given such a mixture of novels to review for the *Athenaeum,* ranging from trash and nonsense via a host of mediocre books to future classics like *Adam Bede, Sylvia's Lovers* and *Barchester Towers.* Consequently her reviews furnish remarkable evidence of a highly trusted reviewer's attitudes to legions of known and unknown novels, to what emerges as nothing but an unusually full cross-section of Victorian fiction. Secondly Miss Jewsbury's reviews reflect a woman reader's views on fiction at a time when a large portion of it was written by and for women. The principal value of her reviews, however, lies in the fact that they mirror the preferences and prejudices of a middlebrow reader endowed with unusual expertise. For it was not the taste of the intellectual elite, like George Eliot, R.H. Hutton or E.S. Dallas, that guided Charles Edward Mudie in his choice of novels for his temple of fiction

(Hamden, Conn.: Archon, 1966); Robert Lee Wolff, *Sensational Victorian: The Life and Fiction of Mary Elizabeth Braddon* (New York: Garland, 1979); Winifred Hughes, *The Maniac in the Cellar: Sensation Novels of the 1860s* (Princeton: Princeton Univ. Press, 1980) and Terry, *Victorian Popular Fiction, 1860—80.*

in New Oxford Street; it was not a highbrow reader like George Meredith he had in mind when ordering hundreds of copies of the latest novels. On the contrary, it was for the vast reading public of conventional and conservative taste, anxious for wholesome, easily digestible fare, that he catered, a public which by and large shared the values reflected in Miss Jewsbury's *Athenaeum* reviews. Since Mudie's empire was indisputable and his refusal to circulate a book sufficed to ruin a new writer, his preferences became instrumental in shaping much of middlebrow fiction. There is no doubt that an exploration of Miss Jewsbury's reviews gives further insight into the taste of Mudie and his innumerable readers throughout the British Empire, the very taste that was the driving force behind the flourishing mid-Victorian fiction market.

This study is divided into seven chapters, the first two providing the necessary context in which Geraldine Jewsbury's reviews should be appraised. Chapter One surveys novel reading, the status of the mid-Victorian novel, its moral impact and subject range and the second chapter reviewing in the 1850s and 1860s, the position of the *Athenaeum* and Miss Jewsbury's connection with that journal. Chapters Three and Four are a thematic analysis of the reviews themselves: Miss Jewsbury's attitudes to morality, realism, plot, characterisation and subject matter will be dealt with. In my discussion I hope to illustrate how her judgments relate to those of other critics and how her reviews compare with those appearing in the competing literary weeklies, the *Spectator* and the *Saturday Review*. In Chapter Five her opinion of major novelists such as Trollope, George Eliot and Meredith will be explored. Chapter Six will focus on her criticism of "major" minor writers of domestic fiction in the 1850s and Chapter Seven will map her attitudes to the sensation novelists Mrs Wood, Miss Braddon and the "wicked" Ouida and Rhoda Broughton of the 1860s.

Chapter One
The Mid-Victorian Novel

The all-pervasive passion for reading and writing novels was seen by the *Saturday Review* as "one of the most important intellectual features of the age."[1] In 1859 David Masson estimated that about 3,000 novels had been published in England since *Waverley* (1814), and other mid-Victorians testified to the extraordinary flood of novels pouring over the country and forming part of the education of her literate population.[2] Not surprisingly, the *North British Review* claimed that no amusement was so "universal" as novel-reading and *Temple Bar* even regarded it as an obsession only a little less repulsive than dramdrinking.[3] In fact, by 1869 fiction had attained an empire which overshadowed all other kinds of literature.[4]

The importance of Miss Jewsbury's achievement as a reviewer depends largely on the status enjoyed by the novel and consequently the role attached to reviews of fiction. In 1849, when she submitted her first review to the *Athenaeum,* the novel was still regarded as an inferior genre, held in contempt by many and shunned by the evangelical middle class. Well into the 1860s the attitude to fiction remained vacillating: whereas the *National Review* contended in 1862 that "the novel belongs to a lower order of art than either narrative or dramatic poetry," the *Saturday Review* claimed the same year that "in the hands of some writers they [novels] have almost risen to the dignity of the drama and epic."[5] Contradictory as such statements are, there was, however, a consensus of opinion about the penetrating influence of fiction, exemplified by W.R. Greg's declaration in 1859:

---

[1] "Novel-Reading", *Saturday Review,* Feb. 16, 1867, p. 196.
[2] Masson, *British Novelists and Their Styles,* p. 213 and [Margaret Oliphant], "Novels," *Blackwood's Edinburgh Magazine,* 94 (1863), 168.
[3] [A.S. Kinnear], "Mr. Trollope's Novels," *North British Review,* 40 (1864), 369 and [Alfred Austin], "The Vice of Reading," *Temple Bar,* 42 (1874), 253.
[4] [R.H. Hutton], "The Empire of Novels," *Spectator,* Jan. 9, 1869, p. 43.
[5] "Mr. Charles Reade's Novels: *The Cloister and the Hearth,*" *National Review,* 14 (1862), 134 and "A Great Sensation," *Saturday Review,* March 8, 1862, p. 276.

It it not easy to over-estimate the importance of novels, whether we regard the influence they exercise upon an age, or the indications they afford of its character-istic tendencies and features. They come, indeed, under the denomination of "light literature;" but this literature is effective by reason of its very lightness: it spreads, penetrates, and permeates, where weightier matter would lie merely on the outside of the mind . . .[6]

Thus, ephemeral by nature, novels nevertheless seemed to have an immediate effect on the reading public. They were, in fact, felt to be one of the best indica-tions of the moral and intellectual condition of the nation and to "show the bent of a people's mind."[7] What struck Hannay, trying to survey English fic-tion in 1866, was the twofold interest attached to it: the quantity in which it was produced and the influence it exerted on public opinion.[8] This impact, universally credited to novels, lent considerable value to criticism of the genre, which came to constitute, in the eyes of the *National Review,* "a function of periodical literature as essential as the examination of the graver problems of politics."[9]

The empire of the novel was slow, however, to gain recognition. As late as 1870 Trollope deplored the prejudice which still existed against fiction and felt the need to vindicate his profession.[10] One of the reasons why this patronising attitude towards the genre lingered on was undeniably the masses of worthless novels that poured from the printing presses. This flooding of the market with trash had curious repercussions. Whereas in 1859 David Masson saw no signs that the novel was about to lose its popularity, predicting that "more and more of talent will flow into it,"[11] warning voices were raised in the 1860s. Lewes, for one, complained that "the vast increase of novels, mostly worthless, is a serious danger to public culture," and R.H. Hutton drew attention to the changing reading habits caused by the superabundance of fiction. Although novel reading, like all reading, was increasing among the less educated, "it is dying away," he stated, "among the more cultivated section of society" who "read only novels supposed to be exceptional."[12] Literary editor of the *Spec-tator* and joint editor of the *National Review,* Hutton was a perceptive judge of literature and his appreciation of the status of the novel in 1869 is significant:

[6] [W.R. Greg], "The False Morality of Lady Novelists," *National Review,* 8 (1859), 144.
[7] "Mr. Charles Reade's Novels," *National Review,* 14 (1862), 134.
[8] Hannay, *A Course of English Literature,* p. 233.
[9] "Mr. Charles Reade's Novels," *National Review,* 14 (1862), 135.
[10] Anthony Trollope, "On English Prose Fiction as a Rational Amusement" [1870] in *Four Lectures,* ed. Morris L. Parrish (London: Constable & Co., 1938), p. 94.
[11] Masson, *British Novelists and Their Styles,* p. 292.
[12] [G.H. Lewes], "Criticism in Relation to Novels," *Fortnightly Review,* 3 (1865), 354 and [Hutton], "The Empire of Novels," *Spectator,* Jan. 9, 1869, p. 43.

There is no evidence of a contempt of the old kind for novels, but of a d
of regard for them which makes itself visible in the decreasing attention they
mand in the reviews, a decrease which has been marked for some time e\
journals of a strictly literary kind. While George Eliot writes, the publicati\
a novel must every now and then be a literary event; but the book of the se
is more and more rarely a story. The production of stories . . . does not decr\
but the taste for them, and above all, the belief in them as important works, cer-
tainly does. (*Spectator,* Jan. 9, 1869, p. 43)

The craze for sensation novels in the 1860s was another reason for the decline
of the status of the novel. The tendency was, Hutton prophesied, that the novel
would eventually give way to the "news journal," for the reader avid for sensation, he claimed, "obtains in an evening paper, all that he obtains in an ordinary
novel" (*Spectator,* Jan. 9, 1869, p. 43).

The role of fiction as a former of behaviour patterns as well as the function
of the novelist were widely discussed in mid-Victorian England. That the moral
impact of a novel was crucial was a view Geraldine Jewsbury shared with many
of her contemporaries: Dinah Mulock Craik contended that "the modern novel
is one of the most important moral agents of the community,"[13] Trollope
believed that the novel had become "the former of our morals, the code by
which we rule ourselves, the mirror in which we dress ourselves,"[14] and James
Fitzjames Stephen noted that "the number of young people who take from them
[novels] nearly all their notions of life is very considerable."[15] Practised so
widely among the young, novel reading was felt to be instrumental in shaping
the future of the growing generation. To Greg the instances were
"numerous . . . in which souls trembling and hesitating on the verge of good
and evil have been determined towards the former by some scene of fiction
falling in their way."[16]

Once its moral function had been recognised, a novel assumed importance
in proportion to the moral lesson it imparted. Good and evil *per se* were not
so crucial as the way they were represented, and the acceptability of characters
such as fallen women, adulteresses and bigamists depended entirely on the artistic treatment, whether they were held up to the readers as warning examples
or presented as interesting women with a claim on their sympathy. The distinction between right and wrong required that the mid-Victorian novelists
rewarded virtue and punished vice. To Trollope's satisfaction, "the British
reading public is . . . averse to the teaching of bad lessons," and poor novels

[13] [D.M. Craik], "To Novelists and a Novelist," *Macmillan's Magazine,* 3 (1861), 442.
[14] Anthony Trollope, "Novel Reading," *Nineteenth Century,* 5 (1879), 26.
[15] F.S. [Sir James Fitzjames Stephen], "The Relation of Novels to Life," in *Cambridge Essays*
(London: Parker, 1855), p. 148.
[16] Greg, "The False Morality of Lady Novelists," *National Review,* 8 (1859), 146.

were not quite so bad if the lessons taught were "in the right direction."[17]

Trollope was not alone in believing that the novelist had to fill the offices of entertainer, teacher and clergyman alike. The *Quarterly Review* admitted that novels had usurped "a portion of the preacher's office," and the *Saturday Review* placed novels and sermons "on a footing somewhat similar."[18] When more people were felt to be influenced in their course of action from reading novels than from listening to sermons, and when the two genres constituted the only mental fare of a large portion of the population, the responsibility of the novelist both towards his craft and his readers became a focal issue. Criticising what she saw as the perilous morality conveyed in *The Mill on the Floss,* Mrs Craik forcefully emphasised the novelist's moral responsibility: since fiction reproduces life, she says, "he who dares to reproduce it is a Prometheus who has stolen celestial fire: let him beware that he uses it for the benefit of his fellow-mortals."[19] The greater the novelist, Mrs Craik argues, the greater damage he or she can work by inculcating unhealthy ideas:

> For he is not like other men, or other writers. His very power makes him the more dangerous. His uncertainties, however small, shake to their ruin hundreds of lesser minds . . . You are the very Prometheus, carrying the stolen fire. See that it does not slip from your unwary hands, and go blasting and devastating the world.[20]

In the 1850s the traditional subject matter of novels, love ending in marriage, began to lose its monopoly. Although Trollope's novels, portraying "love and matrimony as healthy domestic pleasure,"[21] were still taken as the yardstick against which the morality of fiction was measured, new trends slowly emerged: partly novels were increasingly used to ventilate opinions, whether on religious matters or social reform, partly a demand developed for a more epic scope in fiction. In 1859 David Masson urged that "breadth of interest" and the "ranging of the mind over a wide surface of the phenomena of human life" should form the territory of the novel.[22]

With the advent of sensation novels, however, in the 1860s, a vogue initiated by Wilkie Collins's *The Woman in White* (1860), the subject matter of fiction came under serious debate. By 1866 the "purely didactic or semi-religious novel" had, according to the *Saturday Review,* become "virtually obsolete"[23]; the morally edifying novels by Mrs Craik, Charlotte Yonge, Lady

---

[17] Trollope, "On English Prose Fiction as a Rational Amusement," pp. 110—11.
[18] [H.L. Mansel], "Sensation Novels," *Quarterly Review,* 113 (1863), 482 and "The Shadow of Ashlydyat," *Saturday Review,* Jan. 16, 1864, p. 82.
[19] [D.M. Craik], "To Novelists and a Novelist," *Macmillan's Magazine,* 3 (1861), 442.
[20] [D.M. Craik], "To Novelists and a Novelist," *Macmillan's Magazine,* 3 (1861), 443.
[21] "Novel-Reading," *Saturday Review,* Feb. 16, 1867, p. 196.
[22] Masson, *British Novelists and Their Styles,* p. 296.
[23] "Novels, Past and Present," *Saturday Review,* April 14, 1866, p. 439.

Georgiana Fullerton, Julia Kavanagh and Mrs Oliphant could no longer vie with the more thrilling products by Mrs Henry Wood, Miss Braddon, Ouida and Rhoda Broughton, and Trollope's charming heroines were swept aside by the wicked Lady Isabel Carlyle in *East Lynne* and the unmaidenly Nelly Lestrange in *Cometh up as a Flower*. With nostalgia Mrs Oliphant looked back in 1867 to the 1850s as a decade when novels were still free from "noxious topics" and were suitable for family reading.[24] In the 1860s passion and crime were let loose: spiced with bigamy, adultery, lost wills, mistaken identities and murder, the sensation novels portrayed women whose morals horrified critics like Mrs Oliphant:

> women who marry their grooms in fits of sensual passion; women who pray their lovers to carry them off from husbands and homes they hate: . . . who give and receive burning kisses and frantic embraces . . .—such are the heroines who have been imported into modern fiction.[25]

It is noteworthy, however, that while describing such illicit passions, novelists moved away from objectivity towards greater introspection, trying, as the *Saturday Review* stated in 1862, "to 'get inside' their subject—to throw themselves into the inner consciousness of the character represented, and show the motive springs of passion at war."[26] This new trend in fiction, which to many at the time seemed a morbid analysis of sentiments, pointed the way to a growing interest in the psychological side of fictional characters and anticipated, no doubt, novelists such as Henry James, Joseph Conrad and James Joyce.

[24] [Mrs. Oliphant], "Novels," *Blackwood's Edinburgh Magazine*, 102 (1867), 257.
[25] [Mrs. Oliphant], "Novels," *Blackwood's Edinburgh Magazine*, 102 (1867), 259.
[26] "A Great Sensation," *Saturday Review*, March 8, 1862, pp. 276—77.

Chapter Two
Mid-Victorian Reviewing, the *Athenaeum* and Geraldine Jewsbury

By 1850 the three quarterlies, the *Edinburgh Review,* the *Quarterly Review* and the *Westminster Review,* the arbiters of taste for most of the first half of the nineteenth century, had lost much of their influence. Their long-delayed articles, each of which was ostensibly a book review, no longer satisfied the demands of a growing reading public confronted with a torrent of new books and, consequently, their pre-eminence was successfully challenged by the weeklies, featuring shorter and prompter notices of literature.

When Geraldine Jewsbury began her career as a reviewer, the two principal English weeklies, focusing on book reviews, were the *Spectator* and the *Athenaeum,* both founded in 1828. Whereas the former, liberal in politics, was both a political and a literary journal, the conservative *Athenaeum* devoted itself, as the title page states, exclusively to "Literature, Science, the Fine Arts, Music and the Drama." However, with the establishment of the moderately conservative *Saturday Review* in 1855, the empire of the first two journals received a severe blow. Intellectually the most distinguished among contemporary weeklies, the *Saturday* made such rapid progress that its circulation passed that of the *Spectator* in 1857 and that of the *Athenaeum* in the 1860s.[1]

The various preferences and prejudices of the three leading weeklies in the 1850s and 1860s can be inferred from their reception of fiction.[2] In the first of the two decades the *Spectator's* favourite novelists were Thackeray and Charles Kingsley, but by the 1860s, when Richard Holt Hutton became its literary editor, George Eliot was praised as the greatest living English novelist. For

---

[1] J.D. Jump, "Weekly Reviewing in the Eighteen-Fifties," *Review of English Studies,* 24 (1948), 42.

[2] See Jump's two articles, "Weekly Reviewing in the Eighteen-Fifties" and "Weekly Reviewing in the Eighteen-Sixties," *Review of English Studies,* NS 3 (1952), 244—62; William Beach Thomas, *The Story of the Spectator 1828—1928* (London: Methuen & Co. Ltd., 1928), Ch. XIII; Merle Mowbray Bevington, *The Saturday Review 1855—1868* (New York: Columbia Univ. Press, 1941), pp. 153—202; Leslie Marchand, *The Athenaeum,* pp. 298—340.

nearly forty years Hutton's editorship impressed a stamp of homogeneity on the *Spectator*, and it became possible to consider the journal "as a kind of collective literary critic," favouring genius rather than art and placing imagination before the formal side of fiction.[3] Similarly, the *Athenaeum* acknowledged George Eliot's genius, while also praising Trollope for his characterisation and Meredith for his cleverness. In one respect, however, the *Athenaeum* differed sharply from its two rivals: its admiration for Dickens made it defend him in 1857 against the *Saturday* which felt that his "journalistic" novels were doomed to perish.[4] In spite of its peremptory dismissal of Dickens, the *Saturday* was by far the most advanced in its views of the three weeklies. Refusing to subscribe to the widespread opinion that no novels should be published except those fit for young ladies, it accepted the outspoken *Madame Bovary* (1857) and stated in a review of Meredith's *The Ordeal of Richard Feverel* (1859) that "there should be men's novels, if only it is understood at the outset they are only meant for men" (July 9, 1859, p. 48). Like the *Athenaeum,* as will be shown below, the *Saturday* showed interest in "the underworld of English letters": it examined fiction intended for the lower classes and showed an awareness of the disintegration of the reading public which had advanced far enough by the 1850s to attract the attention and concern of the upper middle classes.[5]

As a rule fiction was not widely reviewed outside the literary weeklies. But there were of course exceptions: "important" writers like Thackeray and Bulwer-Lytton were noticed by the quarterlies, the *Westminster* featured a "Belles Lettres" section, where astute critics like George Eliot and George Meredith in the mid-fifties reviewed the best novels of the quarter, and *Fraser's Magazine* published highly perceptive criticism of fiction. However, even in the literary weeklies, reviews of fiction did not occupy a very prominent place: whereas a book on history, theology, science, economic history or philosophy was a serious proposition, novels were still regarded as "light reading," and as such generally relegated to a section entitled "New Novels." Thus a review which opened an issue of the *Athenaeum,* spreading over two or three pages, hardly ever dealt with a novel. When it comes to minor fiction the *Athenaeum,* no doubt, provided the best coverage: its "Our Library Table" noticed, though sometimes very briefly, innumerable now forgotten novels and constitutes an invaluable record of large areas of fiction still awaiting exploration.[6]

---

[3] Richard A. Colby, " 'How It Strikes a Contemporary': The 'Spectator' as Critic," *Nineteenth Century Fiction,* 11 (1956), 183.

[4] Jump, "Weekly Reviewing in the Eighteen-Fifties," p. 50.

[5] Jump, "Weekly Reviewing in the Eighteen-Fifties," pp. 50—51.

[6] While searching for reviews of minor novels, I have found, on numerous occasions, that the *Athenaeum* reviewed a far larger number of novels than the *Spectator* or the *Saturday Review.* In fact, only the *Athenaeum* among the three weeklies could claim to mirror the vast scene of minor fiction.

What strikes a modern reader of mid-Victorian reviews is that they were longer than today's notices and that they appeared anonymously. Following the tradition of the quarterlies, both the *Athenaeum* and the *Spectator,* unlike the *Saturday,* published long extracts from the books reviewed, thus giving full samples of the wares. At a time when few could afford to buy three-volume novels at a guinea and a half, such extracts fulfilled a function by enabling the reader to form his own opinion about a book's quality before ordering it from the circulating library. Consequently, the reviewer operated as a mediator between writers and audiences and his reviews served as a guideline for readers among the torrent of new fiction that inundated the market. The role of the reviewers must therefore not be underestimated: they led the educated opinion of their day and were, indeed, as Jump claims, "the representative spokesmen of the public which they addressed."[7]

In the first half of the nineteenth century, the quarterlies and the weeklies preserved complete anonymity. But during the decades when Geraldine Jewsbury worked as a reviewer, the question of anonymous contributions versus signed ones came under serious debate. On the one hand, this anonymity gave each periodical a separate identity, an editorial consistency expressed by all its contributors, and it made reviewers subordinate their personal idiosyncrasies to the general standards of value propagated by the magazine in question. In an unsigned article, the editorial "we" lent a semi-oracular authority to the product. As Trollope said in his *Autobiography:* "An ordinary reader would not care to have his books recommended to him by Jones; but the recommendation of the great unknown comes to him with all the weight of the *Times,* the *Spectator,* or the *Saturday.*[8]

The ethical implications of anonymity, however, were obvious. Whereas a responsible reviewer would place the editorial policy above personal likes and dislikes, many gave way, under the veil of anonymity, to personal rancour and slander even in the respectable journals. The attack on anonymous reviews, initiated by Bulwer as early as 1833 in *England and the English,*[9] found its most outspoken channel in the neglected pamphlet *The 'Athenaeum' Exposed* (1863), published over the initials "S.A.B."[10] This publication draws attention to the damage done by *Athenaeum* reviewers to the reputation of numerous artists, whose only crime has been "that of having mistaken their own powers,

---

[7] Jump, "Weekly Reviewing in the Eighteen-Sixties," p. 261.

[8] Anthony Trollope, *An Autobiography* (1883; rpt. London: Oxford Univ. Press, [1947], p. 175.

[9] Oscar Maurer Jr., "Anonymity vs. Signature in Victorian Reviewing," *Studies in English,* 27 (1948), 20.

[10] Neither Maurer, in his discussion of the attack on anonymity, nor Leslie Marchand in his history of the *Athenaeum,* refers to this pamphlet in the British Museum.

and [who] would have been amply punished by being consigned, unnoticed, to oblivion."[11] Instead, slashing reviews, dismissal in a few lines of works based on extensive research, bring ruin to young artists. The power of the press is tremendous, the pamphlet contends, but that power is not wielded by great people, but by bullies who delight in finding fault and showing off their superiority. Written in all likelihood by someone criticised in the *Athenaeum,* the pamphlet caricatures an irresponsible reviewer:

> Coarse and ruthless, regardless of the feelings he wounds, or the injury he does, he indulges at once, by rude attacks and abuse, his own peculiar tastes and vulgar appetite for slander. Envious and malignant . . . his chief enjoyment is in depreciating and decrying others, and with the true spirit of a literary garrotter, he takes a mean advantage of the darkness of "anonymous" to publish what he would not dare to put his name to. (p. 15)

As we shall see, Miss Jewsbury also expressed herself about inferior novels in a scathing manner.

Many evils would, no doubt, have been checked by the abolition of anonymity. But as *The 'Athenaeum' Exposed* declared, "the pleasures of stabbing in the dark . . . and appearing to be something great . . . would not be easily parted with" (p. 15). In some respects, however, the 1860s were a turning point: the *Fortnightly Review* of 1865 started giving signatures for fiction and poetry as well as for reviews, and in the 1870s no new monthly magazine was published with anonymous articles.[12] Signatures, in their turn, gave rise to the "star system" of the seventies and eighties when journals sought to raise their profits by employing well-known writers. The weeklies, however, did not follow suit: the *Athenaeum,* the *Spectator* and the *Saturday* maintained rigid anonymity to the end of the century.

The review which employed Miss Jewsbury as a regular member of its staff for nearly a third of the nineteenth century was one of the most noteworthy disseminators of culture in Victorian England. Writing at the centenary of the *Athenaeum* in 1928, Edmund Blunden stated that it constituted "an authority on English civilization in the nineteenth century . . . and as a speculum of the literary world and the phases of taste during the Victorian age it is an extraordinary inheritance."[13] Not only was it so rich in obituaries that it furnished almost a full biographical survey of contemporary literature, but a perusal of the volumes for any one year suffices to put an attentive reader, as Kellett puts it, "abreast with the whole intellectual and aesthetic life of the time."[14] In

---

[11] S.A.B., *The 'Athenaeum' Exposed* (London, 1863), p. 2.
[12] Maurer, "Anonymity vs. Signature," pp. 5—6.
[13] Edmund Blunden, "Some Early Glories" in "The Athenaeum Centenary Supplement," *Nation & Athenaeum,* Jan. 21, 1928, p. 602.
[14] E.E. Kellett, "The Press," in G.M. Young, *Early Victorian England 1830—1865* (London: Oxford Univ. Press, 1934), II, 79.

many fields the *Athenaeum* was in advance of its times: it was quick to recognise the importance of the scientific discoveries of the day, it showed an open-mindedness to and understanding of foreign literature only rivalled by the *Foreign Quarterly Review* and the *Westminster*, and it provided a complete coverage of every cultural event unparallelled in other journals. Called "perhaps the most notable literary achievement of the Victorian age,"[15] it constituted, as Marchand claims, "the best single source of information concerning books published and their contents," providing modern scholars with hard-to-come-by bibliographical information of minor fiction by its regularly published "Lists of New Books."[16] The physical appearance, however, of an issue of the authoritative *Athenaeum* is hardly attractive to a modern reader: the three-column pages and the fine print, almost microscopic when it comes to extracts from books reviewed, are equally forbidding. Each issue, at first spanning sixteen pages, but in the 1860s as many as thirty-two, opens and closes with advertisements, a large part of which emanate from publishing houses. The body of the journal begins with long book reviews, between three and seven in number, continues with the sections "New Novels" and "Our Library Table", and features articles on science, geography, topical issues, fine arts, music and drama.

Launched on January 2, 1828, by James Silk Buckingham, the *Athenaeum* led a struggling existence until Charles Wentworth Dilke took over the editorship in 1830. Gradually he established the reputation of the weekly: by reducing the price from 8d. to 4d., by hiring a competent staff of critics and, most importantly, by openly declaring war on the system of puffery, he raised the circulation from 3,000 copies per week to 18,000.[17] This is how he announced his aim in the *Athenaeum* of June 4, 1831:

> It is a matter of notoriety that the principal literary papers are the mere *bellows* to the great publishing *forges*—and are used but to puff the *works* as they go on. The ATHENAEUM asserts, and will maintain, its independence. It is under the influence of no Publisher, and is in no way swayed by the *trade winds*, that carry all other craft along with them . . .[18]

Once the fairness and integrity of its reviews had been recognised, its reputation grew as the most trustworthy of the literary weeklies, whose judgement was not to be bought. The *Athenaeum* was thus a trendsetter in creating new standards of literary criticism, an organ whose statements were regarded "as reliable as

---

[15] Kellett, "The Press," p. 77.

[16] Marchand, *The Athenaeum*, p. 27 and Sara Keith, "The 'Athenaeum' as a Bibliographical Aid. Illustrated by 'Lady Audley's Secret' and Other Novels," *Victorian Periodicals Newsletter*, 8 (1975), 25—28.

[17] Marchand, *The Athenaeum*, p. 45.

[18] Quoted in "The Athenaeum Centenary," *Nation & Athenaeum*, Jan. 14, 1928, p. 559.

THE

ATHENÆUM

JOURNAL

OF

LITERATURE, SCIENCE, AND THE FINE ARTS.

FOR THE YEAR

1856.

LONDON:

PRINTED BY JAMES HOLMES, TOOK'S COURT, CHANCERY LANE.

PUBLISHED AT THE OFFICE, 14, WELLINGTON STREET NORTH, STRAND,
BY J. FRANCIS.

SOLD BY ALL BOOKSELLERS AND NEWSMEN IN TOWN AND COUNTRY.

AGENTS: FOR SCOTLAND, MESSRS. BELL AND BRADFUTE, EDINBURGH;—FOR IRELAND, MR. JOHN
ROBERTSON, DUBLIN;—FOR THE CONTINENT, MDE. BAUDRY, RUE BONAPARTE, PARIS.

MDCCCLVI.

a Government report"[19] and whose prestige surpassed that of the great quarterlies when Dilke gave up the editorship in 1846.

Although the proprietorship remained in the Dilke family for three generations, the editorship passed to T.K. Hervey in 1846. It was under his leadership that the *Athenaeum* took such a lively interest in social reform movements: the "Weekly Gossip" column discussed prison reform, the housing of the poor, the reform of the criminal laws, public parks, the slave trade and factory legislation and played a considerable part in arousing public awareness of these matters. While it was Hervey who took on Miss Jewsbury in 1849, William Hepworth Dixon was editor (1853—69) during her most active years. Under his editorship, however, the reputation of the *Athenaeum* declined steadily. It was hardly to his credit that much of the reviewing was given, as Marchand points out, to friends of authors, or that he reviewed at least half a dozen of his own books.[20] In spite of this loss of prestige during the fifties and sixties, the *Athenaeum* continued to be "the great literary authority among newspapers" whose position vied with that of *The Times* in its field.[21] That Dixon was popular among his staff, John Cordy Jeaffreson, novelist, critic and a close friend of Miss Jewsbury's testifies in his memoirs:

> No writer ever worked under a more genial and considerate editor than Hepworth Dixon. Whenever complaints against my reviews came to him from angry authors, he displayed the nicest care for my feelings in his way of calling attention to the wrathful letters; and, on the single occasion when I made a slip on an important matter of fact, he made light of the error, which the honourable practice of the *Athenaeum* required him to acknowledge and correct in the next issue . . . It was seldom that he gave me a hint of the way he wished me to review a book.[22]

Dr John Doran's brief interregnum in 1869 served as a transition to Norman Mac Coll's editorship which started in 1870. Under him, the *Athenaeum* soon recovered its prestige and became such an influential organ of literary criticism in the late Victorian era that at one time booksellers would not stock a book until they had read the review of it in the *Athenaeum*.[23] Again, the editor aimed at securing impartiality and at excluding favouritism.

Geraldine Jewsbury's connection with the *Athenaeum* began in an irregular and tentative way. In 1849 and in 1850 she only submitted one single review, in 1851 eleven and in 1852 and 1853 none. It was really not until 1854 that she

---

[19] Kellett, "The Press," p. 78.

[20] Marchand, *The Athenaeum*, pp. 78 and 80.

[21] H.R. Fox Bourne, *English Newspapers: Chapters in the History of Journalism* (London: Chatto & Windus, 1887), II, 313. See also A. Ellegård, "The Readership of the Periodical Press in Mid-Victorian Britain," *Victorian Periodicals Newsletter,* 13 (1971), 22.

[22] John Cordy Jeaffreson, *A Book of Recollections* (London: Hurst and Blackett, 1894), I, 167.

[23] Marchand, *The Athenaeum*, p. 89.

came to review fiction with any kind of regularity, becoming a permanent member of the staff. That year she was frequently allotted the entire "New Novels" section, and on August 26 her long review of a biography was placed at the opening of the issue. By 1861 Miss Jewsbury's reviews opened no less than three issues and she became more and more entirely in charge of the "New Novels." A yearly count of her reviews, showing that 1858—1860 were her peak years, is nevertheless deceptive.[24] For *one* review may mean anything from a three-line mention of an inferior novel to a seven-column review placed in a leading position. Also, after 1870, the fifty to ninety yearly reviews are mostly brief notices of children's books or Christmas books, some ten, or even as many as twenty, lumped together in a single review. Hence, her reviews of 105 books in 1854 are of far greater interest and constitute a more impressive achievement than, say, her reviews of 113 books in 1871.

A careful perusal of the appended checklist of Miss Jewsbury's reviews reveals interesting aspects of the Victorians' attitude to fiction. Surviving masterpieces such as *The Mill on the Floss* would be reviewed in the "New Novels" section, whereas now forgotten novels were given long separate notices; the review of *Adam Bede* (Feb. 26, 1859) received no more prominent a position under "New Novels" than did James Payn's now little known *The Foster Brothers* the following week, and Meredith's *The Ordeal of Richard Feverel,* though placed at the beginning of the "New Novels" section of July 9, 1859, had to struggle for the readers' attention in the company of the now forgotten Annie Keary's *Through the Shadows,* Lady Ponsonby's *A Mother's Trial* and Hamilton Aidé's *Confidences,* works by authors then sufficiently well-known to publish under the light disguise, so frequently adopted, of "By the Author of . . ." The year 1863 provides a curious case in point. Although George Eliot had then won recognition as perhaps the greatest of living English novelists, her *Romola,* not felt to be on a par with her earlier achievements *Adam Bede* and *The Mill on the Floss,* was reviewed on July 11 under "New Novels" together with novels by the prolific and well-known Frederick William

---

[24] Yearly count of Jewsbury's reviews:
The figures denote the number of books reviewed each year. However, for the last ten years, when she frequently reviewed ten or even twenty children's books in one review, the number of *reviews* is indicated within brackets.

1849	1	1861	79	1871	113 (18)
1850	1	1862	58	1872	75 (17)
1851	11	1863	88	1873	80 (14)
1854	105	1864	93	1874	72 (7)
1855	122	1865	73	1875	54 (6)
1856	147	1866	56	1876	49 (10)
1857	101	1867	69	1877	60 (9)
1858	119	1868	87	1878	68 (11)
1859	111	1869	110	1879	101 (10)
1860	126	1870	90	1880	15 (3)

Robinson and John Cordy Jeaffreson. It is noteworthy that in 1863 George Eliot's "tame" fare could not compete in popularity with Miss Braddon's sensation novels and the "wicked" Ouida's passionate romances, which had a higher market value and created a fervour among the readers that Eliot neither could nor desired to attain: Miss Braddon's *Eleanor's Victory* was honoured with a separate three-column review on September 19 and Ouida's *Strathmore* with two and a half columns on the fourth page of the July 29 issue.

Besides novels, Geraldine Jewsbury reviewed children's books, memoirs, biographies, histories, cookery books and books on household management, the servant question and the woman question. This study is solely concerned with what gave rise to the bulk of her reviews, namely fiction. What puzzles a modern reader struggling through her innumerable reviews, ranking from uninteresting and careless to highly perceptive ones, is the number of books covered. How could anyone, for instance, review eleven novels in one week— January 30, 1858—four novels and one book on women the following week and eight novels on February 13, 1858? That this could only have been managed by skipping and skimming is quite clear. Nonetheless, Miss Jewsbury reveals to Bentley that she was able to read the manuscript of a three-volume novel at one sitting carefully enough to show a knowledge of the entire plot.[25] This explains how she found time at the height of her career to report on some fifty or sixty manuscript novels a year to Bentley, in addition to reviewing over a hundred books for the *Athenaeum*.

Paradoxically enough, Miss Jewsbury's career as a reviewer both refutes and confirms Leslie Marchand's contention that in the 1850s books, assigned to friends of the author, were often unduly praised in the *Athenaeum*. It seems she was unable to secure favourable reviews for Bentley's books—that is at least the impression she wished to convey when writing to him on October 4, 1863, presumably in answer to complaints from this publisher who was also her employer. She emphasised the unbiased reviewing practices of the *Athenaeum*:

> As to the Athenaeum you are under a mistake if you think there is any *malice* or *favouritism* exercised—the ruling desire is to be *fair* . . . I can only say that the very severest and fault finding reviews *I* have ever experienced on my *own* books have been in the *Athenaeum* & yet the editor & Seven of the contributors are personal friends; but no books are committed, if it is known, either to friends or foes—but to strictly indifferent people.[26]

However, this policy of impartiality was not consistently kept up even in Miss Jewsbury's case. She was allowed to review no less than seven novels by John

---

[25] Jeanne Rosenmayer, "Geraldine Jewsbury: Novelist and Publishers's Reader," pp. 320—21.

[26] Brit. Mus. Add. MSS. 46,653. Letter by Geraldine Jewsbury to Bentley on 4 October, 1863. Quoted by Rosenmayer, p. 331.

Cordy Jeaffreson, her colleague and close friend, who considered her his "severest" as well as his "most discerning and sympathetic critic."[27] In view of this, it seems inconsistent that when applying for the favour of reviewing *The Letters of Mrs. Delaney,* which she had helped Lady Llanover to prepare for the press, she was *"peremptorily refused"* with the motivation that she was the latter's friend.[28]

Little is known of the London life of Geraldine Jewsbury, the Manchester spinster who made an overnight success in 1845 with *Zoë,* who moved to London in 1850 and became Jane Carlyle's best friend. A frequent guest in the Carlyles' home in Cheyne Row, she also became the intimate friend of John Cordy Jeaffreson's wife, "singular amongst fascinating women," as Jeaffreson states, "for being even more acceptable to her own than to the harder sex."[29] Jeaffreson's recollections of Miss Jewsbury add a few personal glimpses of her. No less "dear and precious" to his wife than to Mrs Carlyle, the Hepworth Dixons and the Dorans, she was "a consummate mistress of colloquial raillery," "witty and humorous," whose conversation was "finely satirical," character traits that are often revealed in her style as a reviewer.[30] With "spectacles and her reddish-blonde hair confined in a net," she was, as William Hepworth Dixon's daughter recalls, "a most attractive woman."[31] Living chiefly by her pen, Miss Jewsbury had to restrict her expenditure. But she had one weakness: always well dressed, "she was sumptuous in her raiment on occasions of state,"[32] hiring the smartest dressmaker. However, it was no doubt her conversational powers and personal charm that made this single woman a welcome guest at Mr Doran's dinner parties where she enjoyed the company of the Jeaffresons and the Hepworth Dixons among others.[33]

With a few exceptions, Geraldine Jewsbury, the reviewer, was veiled even from her contemporaries by the anonymity provided by the *Athenaeum.* It was a well-guarded secret that the slashing review of Thackeray's *Lovel the Widower* (Dec. 7, 1861, p. 758), the severest judgment to which his novel was subjected, stemmed from Miss Jewsbury. Similarly, the authorship of the negative review of Anne Thackeray's *The Story of Elizabeth* (April 25, 1863, pp. 552—53) was unknown to Thackeray himself.[34] The review was wrongly attributed to Jeaf-

[27] Jeaffreson, *A Book of Recollections* (London: Hurst and Blackett, 1894), I, 171.
[28] Brit. Mus. Add. MSS. 46,653. Letter of Geraldine Jewsbury to Bentley on 28 Dec. 1860. Quoted by Rosenmaye, p. 330.
[29] Jeaffreson, *A Book of Recollections,* I, 312.
[30] Jeaffreson, *A Book of Recollections,* I, 312.
[31] Ella Hepworth Dixon, *"As I Knew Them"; Sketches of People I Have Met on the Way* (London: Hutchinson & Co. Ltd., 1930), p. 14.
[32] Jeaffreson, *A Book of Recollections,* I, 311.
[33] Jeaffreson, *A Book of Recollections,* I, 154.
[34] Jeaffreson, *A Book of Recollections,* I, 315.

freson, who refused to take advantage of Dilke's permission to clear himself of the accusation and thus break the anonymity of the journal, since it would injure Miss Jewsbury. Not only did Thackeray speak of him as "a man who, in order to give him pain, had slapped his daughter's face,"[35] but as late as 1894 there were people who regarded Jeaffreson as the man who caused Thackeray pain in his last years. Bearing no grudge, therefore, to Geraldine Jewsbury, he numbered her among his new friends in 1863.[36] In contrast, her criticism of Rhoda Broughton's *Cometh up as a Flower* (April 20, 1867, p. 514) became so well-known that the authoress revenged herself by caricaturing Miss Jewsbury in her novel *A Beginner* published in 1894.

In spite of the editors' annotations of the names of the contributors in the so-called marked file, the identification of them involves certain problems. Besides nearly illegible handwriting, the practices of only giving surnames without initials and of cutting the sheets after the names had been inscribed, thus leaving, for instance, the cryptical "wsbury" instead of "Miss Jewsbury," consistute stumbling blocks, which can be partly overcome, however, by the help afforded by Marchand's seminal study of the *Athenaeum,* which thoroughly surveys the reviewers on the staff.

A glance through the marked file shows, first, that although the staff of the *Athenaeum* changed over the years, a core of contributors, such as Henry Fothergill Chorley, William Hepworth Dixon, Alan Cunningham, John Doran and Miss Jewsbury remained active over several decades. Taken on in 1831 thanks to the recommendation of Maria Jane Jewsbury, Geraldine's elder sister,[37] Chorley was the most prolific reviewer of fiction for more than thirty years. In the 1850s, however, many others shared the reviewing of fiction with him: Hepworth Dixon, T.K. Hervey, Cunningham, Doran. G.H. Lewes, H. St. John, Oxenford, Miss Jewsbury, Lady Eastwick, Mrs Gaskell, James Hannay, David Masson, J.C. Jeaffreson and Julia Kavanagh were on the staff. Miss Jewsbury's position was most prominent from 1854 to the early 60s when she reviewed a large number of novels by significant and popular novelists whose products were constantly in demand at Mudie's Select Library. Only surpassed in the number of reviews by Chorley, Dixon and perhaps Cunningham and Doran, she nevertheless came to review fewer important novels in the late 60s while a host of mediocre fiction deceptively kept up the yearly figure. The reason for this is, no doubt, that Geraldine Jewsbury did not change with the

---

[35] Jeaffreson, *A Book of Recollections,* I, 314.

[36] Gordon Ray, *Thackeray: The Age of Wisdom* (London: Oxford Univ. Press, 1958), p. 405.

[37] Monica Correa Fryckstedt, "The Hidden Rill: The Life and Career of Maria Jane Jewsbury," *Bulletin of the John Rylands University Library of Manchester,* 66 (1984), 177—203 and 67 (1984), 450—73.

520 THE ATHENÆUM N° 1487, Apr. 26, '56

us observe him when his feelings receive a painful shock, likewise at Munich:—

At the tables of the Café Tambori, which were ranged under the trees in the open air, sat gentlemen and ladies, Philistines and students, officers and artists, the learned and the laity,—or, at any rate, those whom I supposed to be such,—in a motley throng, nearly every one with a lighted cigar in his mouth and with a glass before him, filled with a fluid of unpleasant colour, the aspect of which was most unpromising. At first, I could not make out what the people were drinking; but when I asked for a cup of coffee, and one of these glasses was handed to me, the riddle was solved at once. Although the beverage was both cheap and faultless, I could not admire a fashion of drinking coffee, which was altogether new to me, nor could I come to any other conclusion than that this fashion was diametrically opposite to the simplest rules of gastronomy, and, on this account, was utterly indefensible. To the mere vulgar consumer it is, of course, indifferent in what sort of vessel his meat and drink are served, for he looks rather at the contents than the external cases; and, provided the former are good, he cares little for the rest. However, a more refined sense judges otherwise, and insists that, when we eat and drink, not only the palate, but the nobler organ, the eye, shall be considered. Now, to the eye nothing can be more agreeable than the aspect of a pellucid fluid; and it is unquestionably on this account that we prefer to drink clear wine out of glasses, and that the genuine gastronomer always holds the full transparent goblet to his eye before he touches the contents with his tongue. And, if the beverage has an odour or a *bouquet* in addition to its taste, he gratifies his nose likewise, and makes it a participator in his enjoyment.

A gentleman who has brought to such perfection the art of finding "sermons in stones" need not go so far as from Schaffhausen to Vienna to pick up materials for thinking. A half-hour's walk in any great town would answer the purpose.

NEW NOVELS.

The Ring and the Veil: a Novel. By James Augustus St. John. 3 vols. (Chapman & Hall.)—We are almost afraid of 'The Ring and the Veil.' It is written in a bold, triumphant style, that rides down criticism. But we must stand our ground as well as we can. The novel is entertaining—after a fashion. There is a constant bustle and excitement going on, keeping the reader in hopes of being told what it is all about,—but he never *is* told. There are many and deep mysteries of long standing; at least, they date long before the book begins. The hero starts by saying, that his life has been divided into three cycles,—with the first of which the readers have no concern,—and then he takes up his parable and falls at once into the midst of things. He is homeless, penniless, an outcast from society, standing at midnight in Kensington Gardens, where he purposes to sleep under the stars. Whilst preparing to lie down, he stumbles upon the mystery which is to be the first instalment of the second cycle in his life. Instead of sleeping out of doors, he is taken to a mean house in St. John's Wood, where he breaks a *two-days' fast* upon coffee and buttered toast. The next night he sleeps in a cart full of straw, and more mysteries meet him. After that, he goes to sing in the streets, where he meets with the people who are to influence the remainder of his days, as well as some mysterious enemy, who has blighted the beginning of them. It is, however, quite clear that it is not the hero's virtues which have brought him low:—if he is persecuted, as he dimly hints at this stage, he has done enough to deserve it. Although on the point of starvation, every woman who is introduced is spoken of in a tone of speculation, as to the probability or improbability of—what shall we say? seducing her! By his own account, he has brought all the women he has known to grief and shame: so that in the third cycle, when he begins to repent and to entertain a "virtuous passion" for a young woman destined to a convent, he celebrates his return to the paths of virtue with as much unction as if he were his own prodigal son. There is a running accompaniment of intriguing Jesuits, lost wills, forged deeds, attempts at abduction, and many touching difficulties of the social and economical kind. With all this, there is the total refusal on the part of the author to enter into any explanation to the reader, who is left almost as much in the dark at the end of the third volume as he was at the beginning of the first. The book is clever, and most readers who begin will follow it to the end; yet there is an odour of bad society about it, which, though overlaid with eloquent phrases and imposing philosophy, that will dispose them to call for "an ounce of civet, good apothecary," after closing the book.

Beyminstre. By the Author of 'Lena,' &c. 3 vols. (Smith, Elder & Co.)—This is a book we can cordially recommend to such of our readers as may be in search of a good novel:—it is clever and interesting, the two cardinal virtues of a novel. Alban, the hero, is an improvement on the fraternity of heroes. He is drawn with spirit and individuality. His qualities are not smoothed down to the perfectness which is *de rigueur* for the heroes and heroines of fiction. He is essentially a gentleman, not of the Sir Charles Grandison school—nor of the superior race of men who can act the part of providence on the shortest notice—men never at a loss for the wise thing to say, or the right thing to do. He is, on the contrary, full of defects; and, what is worse, he behaves in the worst possible manner to the heroine; yet, if the reader be of our opinion, he or she will forgive Alban as he is forgiven in the story, or as he would have been in real life,—for the excellence of the delineation lies in the fact that Alban would be recognized in real life by the likeness. Regina, the heroine, is very charming: she behaves well, but not too well to secure the reader's sympathies. All the other characters in the book partake of the nature of human beings: and the story itself, although slight, is well and firmly woven together. It is evident that both care and pains have been bestowed upon the work.

John Halifax, Gentleman. By the Author of 'The Head of the Family,' &c. 3 vols. (Hurst & Blackett.)—'John Halifax' is an improvement on the last novel by the same author. Of plot there is not much, but there is a design which is followed without haste and without weariness. John Halifax, the hero, is intended to be the type of a man who, from the lowest depths of destitution, works his way up to fortune and a position in society. There are many such men, more than the world ever heard of,—but John Halifax cannot be accepted as the type of such; he is too much idealized. A boy who begins by being a farm servant until he is fourteen, and who then is employed in a tan-yard to fetch the skins from market, might possess all the fine characteristics bestowed on John Halifax,—his self-reliance, his energy, his integrity, his passion for self-improvement,—but he would not—he could not—attain the bearing and manners of a fine gentleman; he could not by mere effort of self-culture attain the tone of good society. The real men who have raised themselves from nothing polish as they rise and as their intercourse with persons of breeding and education extends,—that is, if they have an innate refinement of their own, otherwise they remain coarse and unpolished at the end as at the beginning. Amongst the Orientals the conventional manners of the great and those of the meanest are of the same quality,—a water-carrier or a donkey-driver may dine with a Grand Vizier without shocking any of the external punctualities; but in England it is different, and John Halifax is made producible in a drawing-room without ever having seen any one better than himself! This is the mistake of the book; the authoress has been too anxious to make her hero perfect, and has by so doing thrown a fictitious rose-coloured tint over a character that could have dispensed with any such aid. The story is, however, interesting; the attachment between John Halifax and his wife is beautifully painted, as are the pictures of their domestic life and the growing up of the children. The strife between the two brothers when they discover they are each attached to the same object is vigorously drawn, and the conclusion of the book is beautiful and touching. There is a blind child, Muriel, very prettily done, but she might have died earlier with advantage to the book,—her part is too long drawn out. The friendship between John Halifax and Phineas Flecher is well managed, and opens a source of interest and emotion which we wonder is not oftener and more efficiently used in novels:—friendship has capabilities of interest quite as deep and as universal as love, only it requires more knowledge to handle it nobly and adequately.

OUR LIBRARY TABLE.

A New History of England: Civil, Political and Ecclesiastical. By G. S. Poulton. (Freeman.)—Mr. Poulton is a careless writer. Mistakes of all kinds abound in his book, from those of the press upwards. Any one inclined to pull a book to pieces on account of its inaccuracies and loose statements, half truth, half error, might make of this one a spectacle for gods and men. But no historical work that does not cite authorities deserves so much attention. Mr. Poulton is also extremely prejudiced, especially in matters relating to the Church. Against the Church of Rome he is ferocious. There is no end of the hard words he applies to it. He wholly denies its claim to be considered Christian. The Church of England since the Reformation fares but little better; he thinks it "quite as intolerant and anti-Christian." Of course, it is not only allowable, but essentially right and just, that every person should be free to state his views on all subjects. We by no means object to Mr. Poulton stating his; but careless misrepresentations and blind prejudices make poor history. Still, there is good in Mr. Poulton's book. His views are friendly to freedom; and occasionally he writes with a rough, manly vigour. If he would examine his authorities, and so far open his mind as to perceive that every question has two sides, he might do something which would be useful. He professes to write for "the masses," and not for "students." We cannot accept that as an excuse for carelessness. On the contrary, to mislead those who cannot inquire for themselves is a moral offence, comparable to leading the blind into a situation of danger.

Historical and Edifying Letters addressed to the Ladies of St.-Louis, by Madame de Maintenon: published for the first time from authentic Manuscripts, with Notes—[*Lettres, &c.*] By M. Th. Lavallée. (Paris, Charpentier.)—Admitting that Madame de Maintenon may have been the good woman she was reputed to be by those who formed her *suite* and were thrown under her patronage,—it may be asserted that few people have managed to make goodness less popular than the widow of Scarron, the "Solidity," who tried to make *Louis Quatorze* end his days respectably. We do not by this intend any criticism on her early story, nor to join the cry of those who have denounced her as a monster of ingratitude to Madame Montespan, feeling that in all such cases there must be a point to be stretched. It becomes a matter of terrible necessity, that those who will rise by the agency of dirty ladders have small choice, save afterwards to repudiate the stair-way. Cold hearted Madame de Maintenon no doubt was,—but her coldness in part belonged to the time and the events of her life. After, however, Madame de Maintenon had risen,—after she had succeeded in conciliating the authority of a married mistress with the virtue of a devotee, who, for no throne's sake, would imperil her soul,—she wrought out her life in a manner which, however amiable, engaging, and womanly it may seem to her parasites, was at heart and at root hollow, unsympathetic, self-occupied, and self-occupying. That there is always danger mixed up with philanthropic effort, is a fact which should discourage no one, still less be reckoned for in a grudging spirit. The young, in their necessity for wholesale idolatry, will not admit the existence of human weakness as possible to their heroes. But the neglects and inequalities which belong to an absorbed and pre-occupied enthusiast—the forgetfulness of home duties, that great schemes of mercy and bounty may be pro-

A page from the so-called marked file of the *Athenaeum*.

times: while her moralistic outlook on fiction was identical with the editorial policy of the magazine in the 1850s, her rigid standards may have become an anachronism in the 1860s when the craze for sensation novels threatened to drown the mainstream of domestic fiction.

Chapter Three
Morality and Fiction

Geraldine Jewsbury saw herself as a mediator between authors and readers, as an experienced pilot guiding the public through the maze of new novels available from the circulating libraries. Clearly she had Mr Mudie and his customers constantly in mind: "those searching library catalogues," she writes, "may send for" Mrs Hubback's *The Old Vicarage* "without fear of disappointment" (May 10, 1856, p. 584) and on one occasion she urged them not to order the disappointing novel *Dharma,* for "few readers sending to Mudie for a new book would expect to receive a three-volume novel inculcating admiration of the doctrines of Buddhism" (June 10, 1865, p. 777).

It is noteworthy that Miss Jewsbury attempted to provide each novel, each product, with a label, indicating for what category of readers it was suitable and what degree of intellectual effort was required in order to enjoy it. We can easily infer what "tame" fare was concealed by her recommendation that a novel was "safe reading," or fit "to circulate in families with perfect confidence" (Jan. 25, 1868, p. 127). Familiar with the demands of the vast reading public, she recognised that much of the fiction was written merely to fulfil ephemeral purposes. Many a novel, like Amelia B. Edwards's *Hand and Glove,* made "good railway reading" (June 19, 1858, p. 783) or would do "to beguile the time in a railway-carriage" (June 16, 1855, p. 704). Just as a modern television viewer may watch an intellectually demanding play by Beckett one day only to watch pure entertainment the following day, the Victorians tended to look for different kinds of novels for different occasions. Thus Miss Jewsbury's phrases "good railway reading" or "sea-side reading" denote exciting novels making few claims on the reader's attention or intellect. She was not slow, however, to declare when a novel was so intellectually demanding that it would hardly be a popular circulating library book. Julia Wedgwood's *Framleigh Hall* belonged to this category, written for the appreciation of "those readers who care for a higher class of reading" (Aug. 21, 1858, p. 232).

At a time when "no boy or girl undertakes an hour's journey by railroad without investing a preliminary shilling at the book-stall," as *Fraser's* claimed in 1860,[1] it became an important part of the reviewer's task to foster a taste for good, "healthy" novels. Miss Jewsbury's basic concern was a novel's moral-didactic qualities: on her scale of values necessary to make up a good novel she rated highest its ability "to leave an influence for good." Thus *Romola,* which she did not find "entertaining," was still praised as a work of art, since it instilled in the readers " 'the joy of elevated thoughts' " (July 11, 1863, p. 46). If Miss Jewsbury took a novel's healthy morality for granted, she also insisted that it was indispensable for a good novel to be entertaining. This quality was important enough for her to condone many shortcomings, since a reader who was entertained and thrilled, she argued, suspended his criticism until he had finished the volumes and disregarded improbable incidents on account of the book's sheer readableness. In fact, when Miss Jewsbury complained of the rubbish flooding the fiction market, her distinction between two categories of novels in this "rubbish heap" was based precisely on their readableness: while some were "readable and entertaining," others were "unwholesome and insipid" (July 3, 1869, p. 12).[2] It is evident that "amusing" and "readable" were epithets that carried considerable weight with the readers and greatly influenced them in their choice of novels.

Miss Jewsbury's reviews mirror no phenomenon of mid-Victorian England better than the stream of mediocre fiction in which the readers drowned, and not surprisingly she has plenty of negative comments to offer, ranging from "nonsense" and "rubbish" to her most derogatory epithet—"dull." Not unexpectedly, it is these negative reviews that best illustrate her wit and sense of humour, commented upon by her friends and contemporaries. The fun is achieved at the expense of the novelist criticised, though, and there are times when one wonders if *The 'Athenaeum' Exposed* was not justified in its attack on anonymity. Sweeping comments like "the title is decidedly the best part of the book" (July 29, 1854, p. 940) or "[*The Layman's Breviary*] sounds like a mild version of the treadmill" (March 7, 1868, p. 357) are scathing without being very informative. Forced to plod through thousands of pages of bad fiction every month, Miss Jewsbury naturally gave way to weariness: it is this resignation, this sense of frustration, that finds expression in her slashing comment that *Clouds and Sunshine* emanates "from that eminent and well-known firm Stuff & Nonsense" (Sept. 2, 1854, p. 1065). Numerous as such scornful remarks are, however, they constitute only a minute part of her criticism: the bulk of her reviews aim at fairness and maintain high professional standards.

---

[1] "Novels of the Day: Their Writers and Readers," *Fraser's Magazine,* 62 (1860), 210.

[2] See also Jewsbury's distinction in 1865 between two classes of bad novels—those which are dull, "over which the reader falls asleep" and those which are readable (April 29, 1865, p. 585).

George Eliot's thesis that the ministry of art "should be one of pleasure not of pain"[3] was only an indication of the widespread demand in contemporary criticism that art should, above all, be pleasing and not depressing. The use of novels as an escape from unpleasant reality and the notion that the novel should avoid unrelieved gloom perhaps stem from the Meliorist ideas of hopefulness and improvement through suffering and struggle which the Victorians cherished as their universe seemed to become more incoherent year by year. That Geraldine Jewsbury shared this mid-Victorian view of the escapist function of fiction is obvious. Reviewing a novel by Lady Georgiana Fullerton, she declares:

> In real life we meet with our own sorrows, and expect to meet with them; but in novels we look for a little poetical cheering up. We like to see an example set by the hero and heroine in the way of doing and suffering; but it is pleasant to have them endowed with a few palm-trees and a pleasant oasis, with a well of springing water, where they may settle down in the wilderness . . . (June 18, 1864, p. 834)

Writing about Mrs Gaskell's *A Dark Night's Work,* she objected that it was "as painfully depressing a book as we ever read" (May 30, 1863, p. 708). Just as George Eliot condemned Hawthorne's *The Blithedale Romance* in 1852 as "depressing and painful,"[4] Miss Jewsbury saw these two qualities as serious flaws in a novel: "Now, a book that depresses the spirits," she writes, "instead of bracing the energies and inspiring the reader with a brave cheerfulness, cannot be said to have a successful moral" (Aug. 15, 1863, p. 207 *Mary Lindsay*). We must remember that Miss Jewsbury's reflections mirror the tastes of the conventional, middlebrow reading public in the 1850s. And Miss Jewsbury's literary convictions did not change: in the 1860s she found herself firmly opposing new trends in fiction which she felt had a corrupting influence. For in her opinion, even if these new wicked novels could not be classified as downright immoral, they tended to inculcate "a false, perverted taste," since they reflected "the love of idle excitement" (June 1, 1867, p. 720). But Miss Jewsbury was fighting a losing battle in her attempt to uphold the moral earnestness which petered out in the fiction of the 1860s.

Miss Jewsbury often traced the false morality of a novel to the characters' inability to distinguish between right and wrong, their propensity "to do evil that good may come." That this moral problem was crucial to her can be seen from her own novel *Right or Wrong* (1859) which focuses on such issues. Although she found a true hero, in this respect, in George Eliot's Felix Holt, a man capable of discerning right from wrong and dedicating himself to a life

---

[3] Quoted by James D. Rust, "The Art of Fiction in George Eliot's Reviews," *Review of English Studies,* NS 7 (1956), 165.

[4] Rust, "The Art of Fiction in George Eliot's Reviews," p. 165.

of self-renunciation (June 23, 1866, p. 828), numerous novels, however, fell short of the mark. Mrs Annie Edwards' *The World's Verdict* is "unwholesome, morbid reading" with the "question of right and wrong" left "unsolved" (Jan. 26, 1861, p. 119).

As we have seen, mid-Victorian critics insisted on the close relation between real life and the morality of the novel and argued that young people's behaviour could be directly influenced by them. Consequently they attached great importance to poetical justice in fiction. The necessity of rewarding virtue and punishing vice sprang from their unchangeable principles of Christian morality and became even more important as the sensation novel of the 1860s depicted wicked heroines who held the public spellbound with their crimes. That adultery, bigamy, murder, elopement and attempted arson were tolerated at all by the middlebrow public must be ascribed to the fact that at the end of novels like *East Lynne* and *Lady Audley's Secret* vice was duly punished, a phenomenon on which the *Saturday Review* commented in 1867:

> To have the triumph of virtue almost invariably crowning the third volume may be said, in many cases, to be set off against, and a compensation for, the unnecessary vulgarities and atrocities of the first two. No half-educated men or women who are eaten up with a passion for novel-reading shut up their book with the conviction on their minds that moral obliquities pay. Drawing moral obliquity seems to pay well, but moral obliquity itself pays badly. The moral of all English literature of the day is that the humble curate is better off in the long run, than the ruffianly adventurer, or the cynical man of the world.[5]

A guardian of moral conventions, Miss Jewsbury naturally shared this demand for poetical justice. What is interesting, however, is that with her, this doctrine is connected with the escapist function of fiction. She admittedly prefers endings that savour of a happier world than this one, and she is convinced that novel readers do too: "men and women are still in some respects children," she writes, "who have not yet lost the primitive love of plum-cake and sugar-candy which distinguishes the golden age of humanity" (May 10, 1856, p. 584). She even suggests that the rewards which novels customarily bestow on deserving virtue not only satisfy the reader's sense of poetical justice, but actually constitute "the reason why such stories [mediocre ones] continue to be read by rational beings" (Nov. 17, 1855, p. 1335). Recognising and sharing the readers' wish to escape from stern reality into the land of poetical justice, she praises Trollope's *Can You Forgive Her?*, where "people reap the things they sow," and "the balance of poetical justice is held with unfaltering steadiness" (Sept. 2, 1865, p. 306). Poetical justice was thus a prerequisite serving as an affirmation of divine order for the mid-Victorians, who were

---

[5] "Novel-Reading," *Saturday Review,* Feb. 16, 1867, p. 197.

threatened by moral chaos as new scientific discoveries made their traditional concepts crumble.

Miss Jewsbury would have agreed with Mrs Oliphant's statement in 1867 that "English novels have for a long time . . . held a very high reputation in the world . . . for a certain sanity, wholesomeness, and cleanness unknown to other literature of the same class."[6] However, by the 1860s, as we have seen, the moral tone of fiction had changed radically: sensuality, crime and passion, cleverly drawn by Miss Braddon, Ouida and Rhoda Broughton, became the staple of English fiction. For Miss Jewsbury the baneful influence on readers of the moral transgressions and irregular unions in fiction was obvious. But shaped by the Victorian double standard, which set up different sets of moral values for men and women, she was particularly horrified "that the most questionable novels of the day should be written by women" (Feb. 17, 1866, p. 233). Quoting a scene in which a villain plans in detail to murder his mistress, she condemns Lady Bulwer Lytton's lack of reticence: "This would be shocking enough if it came from one of the coarser sex. From a woman, it is revolting" (April 15, 1854, p. 461).

Miss Jewsbury's reviews abound in remarks which reveal mid-Victorian attitudes to heroes and heroines. Having herself created a dark, ugly, strong and wicked hero of Sandian descent in her novel *Zoë* (1845), she accepts the "Byronic hero,—handsome, dark, and mysterious" (March 25, 1865, p. 420). What she, like so many of her fellow critics, could not tolerate was the kind of sensuality embodied in the "Don Juan of the Eugen Sue school." So, while implicit sensuality was condoned on certain conditions, explicit sensuality was obnoxious and harmful for women readers, trained to subdue the sexual side of their personality. One example of what Miss Jewsbury abhorred is illustrated by her quotation from the American novelist Ann Stephen's *Fashion and Famine:*

> 'The change of position loosened the heavy cord of silk with which a dressing gown, lined with crimson velvet, of a rich cashmere pattern, had been girded to his waist, thus exposing the majestic proportions of a person, strong, sinewy and full of flexible grace. His vest was off, and the play of his heart might have been counted through the fine and plaited linen that covered his bosom!!!' (Aug. 26, 1854, p. 1037)

Miss Jewsbury's escapist view of fiction was responsible for some of her prejudices about heroes. Writing about Jeaffreson's *Crewe Rise,* she explains that spectacles, which she herself was forced to wear, were as fatal to a hero as the loss of his two front teeth:

> We all of us are acquainted, in real life, with excellent men who have weak eyes and who wear spectacles without detracting from our regard,—but in a novel,

[6] [Margaret Oliphant], "Novels," *Blackwood's Magazine,* 102 (1867), 257.

where there is nothing but description to go upon, they are fatal to enthusiasm . . . Spectacles ought to be reserved as "poetical justice" for evil doers,
as these would effectually restrain them from making havoc with the hearts of
even the most susceptible young ladies. If Lara, the Corsair, and Don Juan had
been represented as wearing spectacles, it would have been an effectual antidote
to their immorality;—their adventures would not have induced so many em-
bargoes nor so much clandestine reading. (July 15, 1854, p. 874)

Miss Jewsbury's profuse comments about heroines illustrate some shortcomings of a minor fiction which today has deservedly fallen into oblivion. For instance, the "angel-heroine," a paragon of religion and high principle, was so
common and so out of touch with reality that Miss Jewsbury got the impression
from reading *The Heiress of Somerton* that "it is far easier to be an angel than
a good woman":

of all the angel heroines we have met with lately, the "Heiress of Somerton" is
the most amazing for precocious sagacity, amiability and works of supereroga-
tion . . . It is humiliating to see the quantity of virtues dashed off by ordinary
heroines with apparent ease, contrasted with the wear and tear of patience and
the self-control and good management required to steer through the difficulties
of a weekly washing-day with one stupid maid of all work! (March 11, 1854, p.
310)

Although Miss Jewsbury's stand on the woman question is best seen in her
reviews of books dealing with this issue,[7] many novels caused her to comment
on the changing role of women. With their growing awareness of their lack of
education, the shortage of outlets for their energies and the want of recognition
of their talents and intellects, heroines embodying these frustrations became
common. Hester and Ellinor, in the anonymous novel of the same name, repre-
sent this "daily increasing Class" who, Miss Jewsbury felt, "require sympathy
more" than those having to earn their living:

These are strong-minded, ardent women, endowed with talent and energy, with
a desire for adventurous outlying action, for which their position affords no ad-
equate outlet or employment. The pain and peril of large capabilities lying in a
ferment, with no recognized and appointed social functions to call them forth,
combined with the strong wayward temperament which of necessity accompanies
repressed activity,—offers a very complicated problem to a wise solution.
"Hester and Ellinor" is an attempt to work this perplexity clear . . . (Feb. 11,
1854, p. 180)

Though a poor novel in Miss Jewsbury's opinion, *Hester and Ellinor* is an example of minor fiction dealing with issues that more gifted writers were to give
voice to in later decades, and its heroines suggest a type of strong-minded

---

[7] See Monica Correa Fryckstedt, "New Sources on Geraldine Jewsbury and the Woman Question," *Research Studies*, 51 (1983), 51—63.

women such as we meet in Mrs Oliphant's Lucilla Marjoribanks in *Miss Marjoribanks* (1866) and Hardy's Bathsheba Everdene in *Far from the Madding Crowd* (1893).

Miss Jewsbury's anxious regard for the proprieties in her book reviewing may strike us as amusing in view of the heroine she had created in *Zoë* (1845). Although she was asked by Chapman and Hall to clothe Zoë with "a more liberal distribution of spotted muslin," the novel still shocked her contemporaries and was "put into a *dark cupboard* in the Manchester Library" since it was said to be harmful for the morals of young men.[8] In *Zoë,* the married heroine is rescued from a fire by the Catholic priest Everard; once safe in the family chapel, their passion breaks all bonds and he covers her face and neck with burning kisses. Less than ten years after *Zoë,* she protested against the lack of delicacy in the heroine of *The Young Husband,* who not only falls desperately in love but, what is worse, displays it "without the maidenly reserve which is an instinct even more than a principle" (Nov. 11, 1854, p. 1363). By then she had forgotten that her Zoë lacked the very principle she so strongly advocated. We must remember of course that what was permissible in novels in the 1840s might be a breach of the moral code of the 1850s when Victorian prudery reached its peak. So when Miss Jewsbury rejected fictional representation of questionable subjects in the 1850s, she was very much a spokesman of her time. Thus, when the heroine of Anthony Smith's *Martha* (1855) marries a man socially below her merely because of sexual attraction, Miss Jewsbury did not spare her invective: basing one's choice of partner on physical beauty "unaccompanied by intelligence, generosity, or any other desirable quality whatsoever," she wrote, "neither ennobles nor sanctifies this kind of attachment" (Sept. 1, 1855, pp. 1001—2).

Throughout her career, Geraldine Jewsbury was an implacable opponent of the fallen woman as a heroine of fiction, deploring in 1859 that "fallen angels are . . . the order of the day" (Aug. 20, 1859, p. 240). English novelists had, of course, for a long time included fallen women among their minor characters, but in the 1850s they began to place them at the centre of their novels. Undoubtedly, Miss Jewsbury would have shared Mrs Oliphant's condemnation of Mrs Gaskell for "choosing such a heroine at all" for her novel *Ruth*.[9] Apparently oblivious of the increased rescue work in the 1850s for saving fallen women, like Dickens' and Angela Burdett-Coutts' Urania Cottage, and the growing interest in the rehabilitation of such women, Miss Jewsbury remains the arch-moralist, constantly criticising novelists for focusing on a sinner. Her review of *Out of the Depths* (1859) is central since it fully accounts for the

---

[8] Tillotson, *Novels of the Eighteen-Forties,* pp. 60—61.
[9] [Margaret Oliphant], "Modern Novelists—Great and Small," *Blackwood's Magazine,* 77 (1855), 560.

reasons behind her repudiation and indicates perhaps the beginning of what must be regarded as her alienation from the tastes of the readers of the time:

> It is a strange and very questionable phase in the taste of the English reading public when the heroines of the novels pretend to be "unfortunate females," instead of those maiden fortresses of female virtue, which to have and to hold has been the ordinance from the beginning of time for the fair and fragile sex, and which to succeed in keeping against all assailants has, until now, been considered an indispensable crown of glory . . . "Out of the Depths" is another appeal to the sympathy which has set in for moral Blackamores, from the enterprising societies for washing them white from all the shades of sooty black down to the "innocent blackness." We protest against all attempts to bring any of them, however well converted or warranted, into books intended "to circulate in the bosom of families." Actual details of vice may be omitted . . . but the taint is in the subject itself. The cold, cruel shrinking and gathering up of skirts, lest they should touch "an unfortunate," which is the popular idea of what a virtuous woman does when in presence of the reverse, is more instinctive than moral; and though it is the fashion to urge women to be sympathetic and pitiful towards "fallen sisters," we recommend them to hold fast by their own instinct . . . Above all, we protest against these washed and perfumed Magdalens in story-books being given . . . as specimens of their class. (Aug. 20, 1859, p. 240)

Any attempt to lay the blame of the sin of seduction upon the man and to appeal against the unwritten laws that punished solely the woman, as in *Lizzie Wentworth* (1870), found no sympathiser in Miss Jewsbury. Curiously devoid of the Christian principles of charity and forgiveness, she sternly insisted that "if woman . . . stoops to folly, she must pay the penalty" (Aug. 6, 1870, p. 176). However, it is possible that her prudery appeared to be stronger than it actually was. Her official repudiation of sin and licentiousness perhaps emanated from her anxiety to conform to the standards of the conservative *Athenaeum* and she did desire to retain a stable society where middle-class women were innocent and pure and "fallen women" pariahs to be shunned by decent British matrons.

In the 1860s Miss Jewsbury became even less tolerant of outspokenness on sexual matters. In a sense, then, her taste evolved in an opposite direction from that of the reading public, which demanded spicier heroines and greater freedom in the presentation of sexual relationships. It is hardly an overstatement to say that Miss Braddon's *Lady Audley's Secret* (1862) was a watershed in English fiction when it comes to character presentation: it introduced a new type of heroine, the pretty, innocent looking, blond lady who was a bigamist and liar, guilty of arson and attempted murder. Lady Isabel Carlyle in Mrs Wood's *East Lynne* (1861), who eloped from husband and children only to repent it for the rest of her life, was also very important in setting a new pattern for heroines in the 1860s. With a tinge of nostalgia, the *Saturday* spoke of the "pre-Braddonian period," when "an angelic being with a weak spine, who, from the sofa, directed with mild wisdom the affairs of the family or the parish, was a favourite creation of our lady-novelists."[10]

Lady Audley had impressed her characteristics on English novels to such an extent that her golden hair set a fashion for other heroines. Reviewing *Miss Forrester* in 1865, Miss Jewsbury stated that

> Golden hair is become as plentiful in the modern female novel, as if some new gold-field had been discovered and thrown open; it is introduced on all occasions, and serves every purpose that the "soul looking from the eyes" used to do in former days. It moves to love; it averts wrath; . . . and the escape of a golden tress, with sunbeams in it, at some moment of supreme wickedness, is used as an extenuating circumstance . . . (Oct. 7, 1865, p. 466)

Blond hair had taken the place of beautiful eyes as a prerequisite for attractive, but sinful heroines, and when Miss Jewsbury described a heroine as "a Lady Audley sort of woman with yellow hair" and with "a dozen deadly secrets," she gave the readers a clearly recognisable clue of what they were to expect.

The reason for the success of these novels was by no means merely due to the reading public's love of sensational subject matter, but to the fact that they touched upon one of the hidden ills of Victorian society: the repressed and unfulfilled lives of women. Middle-class women, pent up in the Victorian home with few outlets for their energies and perhaps entrapped in loveless marriages, dreamed about passionate lovers, capable of arousing their slumbering emotions. Novels which depicted elopement, the only way to get out of the matrimonial straitjacket, were perilous literature for the Victorian woman regarded as a paragon anxious to inspire her children with noble and lofty ideals. Therefore, a novel like *Forbidden Fruit,* which made adultery attractive and thereby subverted the traditional moral code, was considered dangerous enough to earn Miss Jewsbury's anathema:

> We had begun to hope that English novels had ceased to offer an asylum to interesting heroines, endowed with virtues too exquisite for use; ladies, who finding it impossible to love their husbands, and equally impossible to respect the seventh commandment, break their marriage vows, because it is pleasanter to sin than not. We imagine that if the reports of proceedings in the Divorce Court had done nothing else, they had at least stripped the peculiar vice with which the Court has to deal of all romance and false sentiment, and shown the crime of adultery in its natural ugliness, as a breach of trust and a domestic treachery—a sin as mean and as base and as deteriorating to the individual, as its consequences are dangerous and inconvenient to society in general . . . The story of her [Lady Helen's] temptation and fall is told with a lack-a-daisical sweetness which confuses right and wrong . . . She is set before the reader as the most charming, excellent, high-principled of her sex . . . and all this to soften and beautify the fact

---

[10] "Novels, Past and Present," *Saturday Review,* April 14, 1866, pp. 438—39.

that she is faithless to her husband . . . Because Lady Helen is beautiful and fashionable her sin is touched very gently . . . More "ineffable" nonsense could scarcely be written than this story; there is no pretence of anything but perfect sympathy and admiration for men and women who yield to temptation, provided always that they are handsome, fashionable, and *well-dressed*. (July 25, 1863, pp. 110—11)

Provided it was treated as a deterrent, Miss Jewsbury did not oppose outright the fictional representation of elopement. But treatment was all. In *The Red-Brick House* "the picture of the desolate home, after the guilty flight of the wife and mother" had a "quiet power that makes it very effective" (Dec. 22, 1855, p. 1497). Similarly, she accepted a heroine who deserts her home only to spend the rest of her life duly repenting her "sinful" deed: "The moral is," Miss Jewsbury stated, "that those who will not endure a little which comes to them in the way of their appointed duty, will have to endure a great deal in the effort to escape and walk in their own ways—an excellent moral, and a good purpose to illustrate" (Sept. 10, 1864, p. 337). Inability to bear an uncongenial husband and home could only be condoned if the husband was a cheat or a gambler. The heroine of *Falkner Lyle* (1866), who brings to mind Helen Huntingdon in Anne Brontë's *The Tenant of Wildfell Hall*, the first English heroine to run away from her husband and that on good Christian grounds, reveals on what conditions Miss Jewsbury was willing to condone elopement: "her conduct secures the reader's sympathy, and the severest stickler for wifely duty will find no fault with her when she separates herself from her husband, taking away the child, when home becomes an unfit residence" (March 10, 1866, p. 329). What was shocking to Anne Brontë's readers of 1848, evidently seemed quite acceptable in 1866, even to a reviewer concerned with preserving the sanctity of marriage.

It was not only to the direct presentation of physical love scenes between hero and heroine that Miss Jewsbury objected. In her view, to depict "the love of a man of mature years for a very young girl" could hardly be anything but disagreeable in a novel (Feb. 5, 1859, p. 185) and to make uncle and nephew "rivals for the love of a young girl," "shocks the reader and infringes all the laws of romance" (May 28, 1859, p. 710). Nor could she, any more than Mrs Craik in her *Macmillan's* review, accept Maggie Tulliver's love for Stephen Guest in *The Mill on the Floss:* for "the love described is not of a high nature," she contends, "it is mere personal attraction, a passionate inclination, which swallows up honour, duty, humanity, ties of kindred and friendship; it is the essence of selfishness" (April 7, 1860, p. 468). Love presented in fiction must be unselfish, honourable and noble lest it shake the foundations of the Victorian family; it must be the ideal kind of love guiding the lives of the characters in Miss Yonge's *The Heir of Redclyffe* and Mrs Craik's *John Halifax, Gentleman.*

The high claims made for the novel as an art form were frequently challenged by mid-Victorian reviewers who attacked the mass-production of fiction.

Trollope's statement that many continue producing novels "till their work has become simply a trade with them,"[11] reflects a general concern with the status of the novel. Was it simply a commodity catering for a market constantly demanding fresh wares, or could it rival poetry and drama as an art form? The fact that in one decade, the 1850s, Mrs Catherine Gore and James Grant each published over twenty novels, that from 1848 to 1869 Miss Anne Manning had no fewer than forty-one novels available at Mudie's Select Library, proves that mass-produced novels were a characteristic of the genre. Weary of reading such "stuff," Miss Jewsbury protested against the "mechanical dexterity" and "manufactured air" (May 5, 1855, p. 520) which degraded fiction to a commodity; indeed, according to her, authorship had "become a knack—a pursuit to be learnt like fancy work, or illuminating, or any elegant occupation—and taken up to beguile time" (June 20, 1863, p. 810).

With the exception of a few writers like G.P.R. James, James Fenimore Cooper and Frederick Marryat, it was usually women novelists who were guilty of churning out innumerable novels at the rate of one or two a year. Miss Jewsbury regrets that Miss Sewell gave herself "too little pause between her works" (June 9, 1855, p. 672) and asks Miss Manning in a review "*why* not pause a little, and give to one novel the time now divided over two?" (April 16, 1859, p. 515). She forgets, however, that many women were hard pressed by financial needs, supporting an invalid parent or children on their incomes as in the case of Mrs Oliphant and Ouida. With them novel-writing had decidedly become a trade, the only one which could earn them a decent living. But while some of the popular women novelists wrote good novels, the great majority of them are found on a level far lower than that occupied by Ouida and Miss Manning.

[11] Trollope, *An Autobiography,* p. 209.

Chapter Four
Realism, Plot, Characterisation and Subject Matter

The most crucial issue of mid-Victorian literary criticism was the demand for realism in fiction. That a novel should strive to give a true representation of life became a doctrine to which the best-known novelists and critics adhered. For Trollope "truthful" and "natural" were favourite words of praise, and for George Eliot, then reviewing fiction in the *Westminster* and the *Leader,* "simple veracity" was the yardstick by which she condemned numerous inferior novels.[1] The novel should hold up a "looking-glass" to society and frequently succumbed to a kind of "detailism," as a contemporary critic put it, whose technique was often likened to that of photography.[2] In nearly all of her reviews written in the 1850s, Miss Jewsbury emerges as a strong advocate of the kind of realism which Lewes mockingly called "coat and waistcoat realism." There was nothing quite like a well-drawn picture of English domestic life for bringing out the reviewer's admiration, and time after time she praised novels for possessing "the minuteness of fine old Dutch painting" (March 17, 1849, p. 271), for setting forth a story with a "reality that looks like a daguerreotype from facts" (July 15, 1854, p. 874) and for providing sketches that "look like what they are—photographs from the life" (April 3, 1858, p. 433).

Miss Jewsbury's belief in realism can also be seen in her reaction to titles. As a rule she conformed to the current taste for long titles, containing an explanatory sub-title, and for titles constructed around the name of the heroine or the hero. But as a realist, she strongly objected to fiction wrongly bearing the sub-title "a story of real life." Her weariness with the many unrealistic stories that flooded the market is obvious in her review of *Anna Clayton: A Tale of Real Life:*

---

[1] Graham, *English Criticism of the Novel,* p. 20.
[2] B[uchanan], "Society's Looking-Glass," *Temple Bar,* 6 (1862), 130—32.

From an extensive experience in novel reading, we can assert that the great majority of stories professing to be of 'real life' might be more truly called tales of Bedlam. We have seldom read 'a story of real life' without feeling thankful that both the scenes and the people were safely shut up between two boards . . . (July 28, 1855, p. 873)

Misleading titles aroused both Miss Jewsbury's venom and vein of satire. For her, *The Wife's Temptation: A Tale of Belgravia* "might just as appropriately have been called a tale of Bedlam as a tale of Belgravia" (June 18, 1859, p. 808) and a "Story of Neutral Tint" brings out her sense of ridicule: "Neutral tint! Why, if dealing in battle, and suicide, and sudden death, bigamy, broken hearts, delirium tremens, shipwreck . . . can be called writing a story in neutral tint, we would like to know what is meant by vivid colouring" (July 7, 1860, p. 15).

If the mid-Victorians demanded that fiction should present the truth and nothing but the truth, they did by no means want the whole truth. Both Lewes and George Eliot believed in a modified realism that avoided the sordid sides of life, which they held were unsuitable for artistic treatment, and George Meredith resented what he called "gross realism."[3] For Miss Jewsbury too, the idea that art should be morally edifying was incompatible in many cases with a presentation of the naked truth. On these grounds, she criticised Charles Reade's *The Cloister and the Hearth* (1861) for introducing details, "far more coarse than was necessary" and "all the horrors of the dirt and close confinement of an over-crowded lodging" (Nov. 2, 1861, p. 577). Obviously, this demand for a modified realism originated in the escapist function of fiction: the novel should serve as an escape from the squalid sides of life to the tranquillity of the Victorian family circle. Her comments on James Grant's *Phillip Rollo* further support this idea, for, to her, the charm of this book came from "the skill with which the *look of reality* is kept and all needlessly revolting details of war and carnage are avoided" (April 22, 1854, p. 485 [italics added]). Evidently, it was not a presentation of the reality of war that the *Athenaeum* reviewer looked for, but "the look of reality."

Although a staunch supporter of domestic realism, Miss Jewsbury was not averse to romance provided it was readable and interesting. It is noteworthy that she judged adventure stories by their own standards, standards based on popularity rather than on critics' esteem. Like the average reader, she overlooked the "inherent impossibilities" in James Grant's fiction and accepted what she was told without asking any inconvenient questions, without applying her critical judgment. "Mr. Grant is like Alexander Dumas in his facility of narration and the boldness of his incidents. Both belong to a

[3] E. Arthur Robinson, "Meredith's Literary Theory and Science: Realism Versus the Comic Spirit," *PMLA*, 53 (1938), 857.

theatrical school of fiction," she observed, "but both will find more readers than critics, so long as it pleases them to continue to write" (Nov. 21, 1857, p. 1453). Miss Jewsbury's willingness to be absorbed by what she herself called "entirely impossible novels," may seem contradictory in view of her perceptive appreciation of major works like *Adam Bede,* but again it is one of the paradoxes of Victorian times that one and the same reader could enjoy serious art and yet be fascinated by romantic adventure novels. Nevertheless, like others in her day, she placed domestic novels and romances in completely separate compartments. For the boundaries between reality and romance were essential to the mid-Victorians; without them, the moral, rational universe began to crumble. Fantasy was inextricably separated from reality and Miss Jewsbury showed great consternation at a novel that professed to be "a romance of real life."

In the sometimes confusing discussion of realism versus idealism, the novels of minor novelists were described as a "looking-glass" as distinguished from the "magic mirror" that major novelists succeeded in creating. What the intellectual elite of mid-Victorian England, represented by Bagehot, Masson, Lewes, George Eliot and Meredith, demanded was "idealism," by which they meant realism with an idealising tincture. It was rare, however, that Miss Jewsbury looked for, as Lewes did, a "vision of realities in their highest and most affecting forms."[4] But the conventional bastion of domestic realism was not entirely proof against the stirring demands for "idealism" which grew around her. As early as 1854 she complained that a novel "suggests nothing more than what it tells" (April 29, 1854, p. 522 *Nannette*) and that the anonymous Mrs Oliphant had failed in *Matthew Paxton* since "in the attempt to be *real,* he [sic] has become simply *literal,* and lost all insight into the life that inhabits and gives shape to details in themselves most insipid and prosaic" (Sept. 23, 1854, p. 1138). The yearnings for a new kind of realism that went beyond the "daguerreotype" depiction of reality were thus strong among all categories of critics.

The interest of such mid-Victorian critics as Lewes and George Eliot in the structure of the novel was mainly expressed in their concern for unity of plot. Miss Jewsbury shared their demand for cohesion and constantly complained of poorly constructed works whose parts were disconnected: one unusually confusing plot is compared to "a country dance in confusion—hands across and back again—down the middle and up again—with everybody in the wrong place" (Aug. 4, 1855, p. 900) and in another novel the incidents have "no other cohesion . . . than the stitching that holds the pages together." Never averse

---

[4] Lewes, *The Principles of Success in Literature,* (1865: rpt. Farnborough, Hants., Gregg International Publishers Ltd., 1969), p. 40.

to subplots which furthered the elucidation of the main story, she praised Wilkie Collins precisely for his ability to attain unity in his complex plot structure.

Whereas Miss Jewsbury emerges as a conservative reviewer of conventional taste on the issue of realism, her views on character drawing resemble those of George Eliot, George Henry Lewes and George Meredith, who insisted on psychological characterisation or "dramatic ventriloquism" as Lewes called it.[5] The representation of character was seen by them as the highest department of art: to give reality to a work of fiction the author had to make the reader feel, as Lewes argued, "that not only did such events occur, but that there was an inherent necessity in the characters and situations which brought out the events precisely in this order."[6] Throughout her career Miss Jewsbury places the art of creating characters above the ability to invent a good plot. The characters must be life-like and give the reader "insight into the workings of human nature" (Aug. 21, 1858, p. 231). As in real life, the incidents should be subservient to character, being rather "the consequence of the acts and motions of the human beings concerned in them than the causes of weal or woe" (July 23, 1859, p. 113).

Miss Jewsbury's criticism of lifeless characters is generally conveyed in the critical metaphors of the time: characters are drawn in "black and white," like "marionettes," "effaced slides in a magic lantern" or "creatures made out of canvas and cardboard" and "wax or sugar" and seem like "masks in a Christmas pantomine." However, when Miss Jewsbury referred to characters as "unpleasant" it was meant to deter the British matron from taking a novel from Mudie's, because, in her opinion, there was such a thing as being too realistic, verging on the naturalistic, in portraying characters. Although William Gilbert's *De Profundis,* full of "low characters," displays both talent and cleverness, it is "not a pleasant book" and depicts a world uncongenial to the feelings of genteel readers who "will be apt to feel that the strain of fraternity and equality with unwashed and uneducated associates is carried too long without any intermission or change of scene or people" (Jan. 28, 1865, p. 124).

While favouring characters drawn "from within, not from without" (March 17, 1849, p. 271), Miss Jewsbury, like George Eliot, was averse to excessive character analysis leading to a morbid dissection of minds and feelings; the psychological probings into a character's motives and emotions, to be mastered later by Henry James, Conrad, Woolf and Joyce, were far beyond the pale of this *Athenaeum* reviewer. Neither Dickens, Thackeray nor Bulwer-Lytton penetrated into the interior, secret life that every man leads in seclusion from

---

[5] Quoted in Alice R. Kaminsky, "George Eliot, George Henry Lewes and the Novel," *PMLA,* 70 (1955), 1003.

[6] Quoted in Morris Greenhut, "George Henry Lewes as a Critic of the Novel," *Studies in Philology,* 45 (1948), 495.

his fellow men. But in the 1860s, the sensation novelists began to exploit the irrational elements of the human psyche in their aim to account for the erratic behaviour of murderers and bigamists. However, Miss Jewsbury could not understand this new tendency to introspection. It is obvious that her sympathies had stagnated at a point where even the otherwise so conventional Mrs Craik revealed too much of the characters' inner life in order to win the *Athenaeum* reviewer's approval: interestingly conceived in the form of two private journals, Mrs Craik's *A Life for a Life* (1859) displayed "too much melancholy self-analysis . . . to be pleasant to the natural selfishness of third persons" (Aug. 6, 1859, p. 174). Mrs Penny's *The Romance of a Dull Life* (1861), in which the heroine suffers from unrequited love, was for Miss Jewsbury, "like being present at a demonstration of vivisection":

> The intense passionate affection, buried beneath the silent timid manner, is very well given; . . . the little gleams of hope and their gradual fading away . . . are painted with wonderful skill and minuteness; but they make of the story a mere anatomical diagram, showing how the nerves quiver and the heart beats under this kind of torture . . . (Nov. 9, 1861, p. 615)

To show young girls with beating hearts and nerves quivering from unrequited love was too disconcerting for an age whose prudery and hypocrisy served as a gag repressing subversive ideas. Young girls should be gentle, meek and submissive and novels depicting their hidden emotions were undoubtedly a threat to the very moral fabric of society.

Although critics in the 1850s were increasingly concerned with such issues as point of view, the relation between the narrator and his subject matter, the disappearance of the author from his narrative and dramatic presentation of scene, Miss Jewsbury's reviews contain relatively few comments on narrative technique. Addressing primarily middlebrow readers of the upper middle classes, she left technical matters to the more intellectual critics, concentrating instead on questions of readability, immorality, endings and the nature of heroines. Nevertheless, like Meredith, who often complained that " 'scenes are narrated . . . not presented,' "[7] Miss Jewsbury endorsed the widespread demand for dramatic presentation of scene. She criticised Harriet Parr's *Maude Talbot* for incidents which "are all narrated, not transacted upon the scene" (March 4, 1854, p. 271). But her negative reactions to innovations in narrative technique further illustrate her basically traditional outlook on fiction, an attitude no doubt shared by the average Mudie customer. One novel she considered "inartistically put together, the end being placed at the beginning" (Dec. 30, p. 1865, p. 920), and although she recommended Meredith's "charming" *Emilia in England,* she was unable to appreciate his brilliant mastery of

---

[7] Quoted in Stang, *The Theory of the Novel,* p. 106.

structure: "It would be a great improvement," she wrote, "if the author could conceal his art, and write more simply" (April 30, 1864, p. 610).

Miss Jewsbury's *Athenaeum* reviews frequently touch upon the typical form of the Victorian novel, which was almost always published in three volumes. This convention, a straitjacket sacred to the financial interests of publishers and circulating libraries alike, was frequently condemned: "the necessity of writing three volumes," she complained, "has lain heavily on the author" (Nov. 5, 1864, p. 598). The fatal necessity of filling three volumes weakened stories and became a pitfall to many novelists. Indeed, the dragging of the third volume was so common that when Miss Jewsbury found the last volume the best one, she felt the need to point out this exception: "It is written in the *in*verse ratio to most novels:—the first volume being somewhat heavy, in the second the story moves more briskly, and the third volume is extremely interesting" (May 24, 1856, p. 648). Her censure emanates from her concern with the artistic unity of a work of fiction: to condense a novel too much or to drag it out to suit the Procrustean bed prescribed by publishers and Mr Mudie was equally harmful for a novel's proportions.

Paying little attention to narrative technique in the fiction she reviewed, Miss Jewsbury was, however, keenly concerned with its subject matter. At a time when novels were meant for family reading, there was a lively discussion of what could and what could not be treated in fiction. By the 1850s, when the silver-fork school, which had occupied such a prominent place during the two preceding decades, was slowly ebbing out, novelists began to explore new areas, to venture into the unknown spheres of back streets and fishing villages peopled by craftsmen and artisans. In 1851 Miss Jewsbury pointed to this change in taste and topic areas, exemplified in Mrs Oliphant's anonymously published *John Drayton:*

> Novels faithfully represent the prevailing tendency of public taste. Some years ago they condescended to deal with nothing less transcendent than the sumptuous boudoirs of beautiful countesses . . . they have now taken up an entirely different line: They seek for their heroes and heroines in the streets and gutters—paint life in factories,—and discuss their . . . daily struggles and privations with the minuteness and zeal bestowed on the 'gilded saloons' . . . This vein has not yet been worked out. It is an unknown land,—a new world of which we are still anxious to obtain tidings . . . (Sept. 6, 1851, p. 984)

Reflecting the taste of the ordinary reader, for whom Mudie's Select Library was catering, Miss Jewsbury's attitude acquires great importance as an indication of the confines within which a novelist who aspired to success had to stay. She pronounced strong, at times bigoted, opinions on what did not fall within the pale of fiction, and one of her severest phrases of reprobation was that a subject was "unfit for the ordinary reader." While in the 1850s her opinions pretty well reflected middlebrow tastes in reading matter, she developed, as Rosenmayer observes, "a conservative's resistance to the revolution in subject matter taking place in the 1860's and 70's."[8] In fact, she seems at times to deplore the rift that had arisen between her own taste and that of the public, as for instance in 1863 when she commented that "in these days, readers require some broader subject of interest than the love affairs of young men and maidens" (Aug. 22, 1863, p. 240) and that "in the present day, readers are, we *fear* grown too hard-hearted to be interested through three volumes by the fluctuations of the hopes and fear of two young ladies and two young gentlemen" (Sept. 19, 1863, p. 366 [italics added]).

When judging episodes describing sexual attraction and seduction, Geraldine Jewsbury was, as we have seen, little open to compromise. But a number of other topics also made a novel unfit for the ordinary reader and thus reduced its chances of being included on Mudie's lists. Bodily functions and physical violence were constantly rejected. Confinements described in detail were just as unpalatable as the incidents of the dissecting-room and the operating-theatre which made *Ernest Graham* "not a pleasant book, nor one adapted for ordinary readers" (June 30, 1866, p. 861). Miss Jeewsbury's horror was fully brought out by *Clara Vaughan,* describing a party of students preparing to dissect a live cat (April 30, 1864, p. 610) and by *Black Moss,* in which an undertaker poisons the streams of fresh water by allowing deadly liquids from the graves to infiltrate them. Such a novel was, in Miss Jewsbury's opinion, "a perverse exercise of talent on disagreeable subjects" (Aug. 20, 1864, p. 240). What particularly aroused her disgust was the fictional representation of Satan. Neither the *Athenaeum* nor Mudie's readers could stomach such a breach of the proprieties:

> We are all of us accustomed to the soothing belief in a 'guardian angel' . . . but readers are not prepared to receive into a novel the great, fallen archangel himself introduced bodily, with 'moth-shaped' wings and 'sooty pennons,' proper to work harm and evil to the hero, with a good archangel, as bright as the other is black, to counteract all his machinations . . . (Aug. 20, 1859, p. 241)

Discussing "novels of disease" in 1855, Mrs Oliphant argued that it was "a great error to make any affliction, like that of hereditary insanity, the main subject of a story."[9] Her remarks were occasioned by two novels, one of which was Miss Jewsbury's *Constance Herbert* which portrays the sufferings of the heroine, who renounces marriage on account of insanity running in the family. Both Mrs Oliphant and George Eliot, in the *Westminster,* rejected the novel, the latter considering it so didactic that she could only review it as a moral tract.[10] But for Miss Jewsbury, hereditary insanity had its fascination. Unlike

[8] Rosenmayer, "Geraldine Jewsbury: Novelist and Publisher's Reader," p. 370.

[9] [Margaret Oliphant], "Modern Novelists—Great and Small," *Blackwood's Magazine,* 77 (1855), 561.

[10] James D. Rust, "The Art of Fiction in George Eliot's Reviews," *Review of English Studies,* NS 7 (1956), 168.

Mrs Oliphant, she praised *The House of Raby,* since it "seeks to hold up to view the terrible risk incurred by all who marry when they are conscious of inheriting any taint of insanity" (Dec. 16, 1854, p. 1524) and recommended *Gilbert Massenger,* published the same year as her own *Constance Herbert,* for focusing "upon a subject that just now seems to possess a peculiar fascination for authors,—hereditary insanity" (Nov. 24, 1855, p. 1366). Obviously it was not the physical manifestations of insanity that attracted her, but "the moral duty it entails of self-sacrifice" (Nov. 24, 1855, p. 1366), a subject which might involve human tragedy likely to spellbind readers.

Chapter Five

Some Major Novelists: Trollope, George Eliot, Collins and Meredith

Anthony Trollope

"If Mudie were asked who is the greatest of living men," E.S. Dallas wrote in 1859, "he would without one moment's hesitation say—Mr. Anthony Trollope."[1] If *we* were to select one novelist as representative of mid-Victorian fiction, we might do worse than endorse the choice of the *North British Review* in 1864 of Trollope as "the novelist *par excellence* of the moment."[2] Never placed in the high rank occupied by Eliot's and Thackeray's masterpieces, his novels were, nevertheless, widely acclaimed by readers and critics alike for giving pleasure and amusement: in fact, it is difficult to find a single critique in the Critical Heritage volume on Trollope which is not basically positive towards this author, who successfully entertained the great public of the circulating libraries for nearly three decades. This widespread appreciation, I would suggest, originates in the very qualities which were embedded in the middlebrow mid-Victorian audience.

Setting before the public the petty intrigues of society, household feuds and human frailty, Trollope captured the surface world with a minuteness of detail that lent an air of reality to his novels. The *North British Review* perceptively sums up precisely what the mid-Victorians admired in him: "It is not merely that the incidents are such as occur, and the characters such as may be met with every day. The atmosphere also is that of real life."[3] A lifelike picture of the surface world, injected with a healthy morality, became the formula then for

[1] E.S. Dallas, *The Times*, 23 May 1859, p. 12. Quoted in *Trollope: The Critical Heritage,* ed. Donald Smalley (London: Routledge & Kegan Paul, 1969), p. 103.
[2] "Mr. Trollope's Novels," *North British Review,* 40 (1864), 370.
[3] "Mr. Trollope's Novels," p. 371.

what middlebrow readers expected from a "pleasant" novel and found in Trollope.

Reviewing nine of Trollope's novels from *The Warden,* his first great success in 1855, to *The Last Chronicle of Barset* in 1867, Miss Jewsbury emerges as the *Athenaeum* reviewer *par excellence* when it comes to his early novels. All of her reviews are considered significant enough to be reprinted in the Critical Heritage volume, one of them tentatively ascribed to H.F. Chorley and the others headed "Unsigned notice." Like most of her colleagues, Miss Jewsbury emphasised the entertainment to be derived from Trollope's novels: his "life-like characters" who "stand upright on their feet, as real men and women would," his ability to write "with a plain, photograph-like reality" and his sense of fun placed his writings well above the general run of novels. The key words "real," "reality," "life-like" and "photograph-like" indicate that Miss Jewsbury's enthusiasm was based on Trollope's talent for verisimilitude. Commenting on *The Last Chronicle of Barset,* she further clarifies her standpoint:

> It is not given to every one to create characters out of the work-a-day world—neither better nor worse than persons whom we all meet every day—and yet to be able so to lay bare their hearts and stories that the reader accepts them as friends and acquaintances . . . The series of Barsetshire Chronicles have all been singularly real in their interest, and veraciously like Nature in the living characters introduced . . . if the reader does not believe in Barsetshire and all who live therein . . . the fault is not in Mr. Trollope, but in himself. (Aug. 3, 1867, p. 141)

While admiring his art, most critics agreed about his defects: his tendency to write too fast and too much, his lack of inventive faculty which made the plot, as Miss Jewsbury pointed out, "merely the support over which the vine is trained" (March 26, 1859, p. 420) and his proneness to serve a dish of disjointed sketches under the guise of a novel. On one point, however, Miss Jewsbury emerges as more moralistic than most other critics. With the exception of the *Eclectic Review,* the *Athenaeum* was alone in expressing indignation at *The Warden,* which, in spite of being a "clever" and "amusing" novel, was found guilty of a serious flaw: "If the turning aside of a public charity from its original and palpable intention be *wrong,* no smartness of writing or levity of speech can make it *right;* and it is the grave fault in this lively, pleasantly written book, that the right and wrong of the subject are melted down into a matter of perfect indifference" (Jan. 27, 1855, p. 107).

The word "real" expresses only one side of contemporary admiration for Trollope; the word "pleasant" is equally important. For what mid-Victorians liked to see portrayed in their fiction was precisely "pleasant reality." Becoming increasingly positive towards Trollope's novels in the 1860s, Miss Jewsbury acclaimed the same qualities in *Can You Forgive Her?, The Claverings* and *The Last Chronicle of Barset* as in his first successful novels. Although fiction had become more introspective and psychological, "subjective" as Miss Jewsbury somewhat contemptuously called it, she clung to her old-fashioned ideals of lifelike characters and real incidents. Thus in *The Claverings* she strikingly observed, "there was room . . . for deeper studies in human nature: but the book in that case might not have been so pleasant to read" (June 15, 1867, p. 783). In other words, the "pleasant reality" so delightfully depicted in Trollope's novels seemed to Miss Jewsbury infinitely preferable to any probings of minds which might result in unpleasantness, an unpleasantness which might threaten the stability of the Victorian world.

George Eliot

It is little known that the *Athenaeum* reviewer judging George Eliot's five novels from *Adam Bede,* her first great success in 1859, to *Felix Holt* in 1866, and whose opinions on *Romola* are quoted in the Critical Heritage volume, was Geraldine Jewsbury.[4] This body of criticism proves that she responded fully to the challenge presented by George Eliot's novels. Nevertheless, she judged them by the same standards she always applied to fiction, namely whether it presented a true picture of reality or not and whether its effect on the reader was pernicious or beneficial.

For a novel *Adam Bede* was exceptionally widely noticed and, generally, with approval and even admiration. Like the *Saturday Review,* which recommended "persons who only read one novel a year . . . to make their selection, and read Adam Bede,"[5] Miss Jewsbury instantly discerned the novel to be a work of genius:

> The works of true genius seem the most natural things in the world,—so right, that one cannot imagine them different,—so exactly what is needed, that they come as matters of course like daily bread or sunshine . . . In fine, the more true genius there is in a man's work, of whatsoever kind it be, the less it has of startling, unequal or spasmodic; it partakes of the mysterious quietness of Nature. (Feb. 26, 1859, p. 284)

Its verisimilitude made Miss Jewsbury judge it as a recording of reality rather than invention: "the story is not a story," she claimed, "but a true account of a place and people who have really lived." The "quiet power" and the absence of exaggeration and straining for effect resulted in the reader's total acceptance of Eliot's Loamshire.

---

[4] David Carroll, editor of *George Eliot: The Critical Heritage* only refers to Miss Jewsbury's review as "Unsigned review." (London: Routledge & Kegan Paul, 1971), p. 196.

[5] Unsigned Review, *Saturday Review,* 26 Feb. 1859, pp. 250—51. Quoted in *George Eliot: The Critical Heritage,* p. 73.

By selecting the author's description of her peasant artisan hero for an extract, Miss Jewsbury indicated her admiration for Eliot's ability to cross the class barrier and depict the lives of "painstaking honest" men like Adam and Seth Bede, lives which were of concern, she argued, to the population at large:

> There is, too, the secret of the substantial worth of England, the secret of her strength; it is not the number of men and women with brilliant reputation and lyrically recognized name and fame, that makes the enduring prosperity of a nation, but it lies in the amount of worth that is *un*recognized, that remains dumb and unconscious of itself, not clever, but with a certain honest stupidity that understands nothing but doing its best and doing its work without shirking any portion of it. (Feb. 26, 1859, p. 284)

What Geraldine Jewsbury forgot, however, was that George Eliot was not alone in attempting to give voice to the unrecognised worth of an unknown layer of society. Though never attaining Eliot's intellectual level or refined craftsmanship, Mrs Gaskell had tried in 1848, as she says in the "Preface" to *Mary Barton,* "to give some utterance to the agony which, from time to time convulses this dumb preople," i.e. Manchester workers. Besides, Dinah Maria Mulock Craik's *John Halifax* (1856), which opens among tanners at a reeking tannery, had also introduced the public to the relatively unknown world of farmers, craftsmen and labourers. That *Adam Bede* was generally perceived as a novelty can perhaps be explained by the fact that it was the first time the pen of genius attempted to give voice to what seemed a hitherto dumb section of society.

Geraldine Jewsbury was right in predicting that *The Mill on the Floss* (1860) would "not . . . obtain the same acceptance as 'Adam Bede' " (April 7, 1860, p. 467). The conflicts of passion and conscience, depicted in the third volume, aroused the most indignant criticism George Eliot encountered in her entire career.[6] Characteristic of the contemporary reaction to *The Mill on the Floss* was Mrs Craik's review in *Macmillan's*. She voiced the stern morality of a large segment of the reading public when she denounced the perilous doctrine preached in the novel. She asked whether it would "lighten any burdened heart, help any perplexed spirit, comfort the sorrowful, succour the tempted, or bring back the erring into the way of peace."[7] Surprisingly enough, Geraldine Jewsbury did not join in the chorus of negative criticism on moral grounds. She recognised the author's powerful delineation of the heroine's inner conflicts, the internal struggle between temptation and duty. "The struggle is not the less fierce in Maggie," she writes, "because it is ignoble, nor is the temptation less because it is base." Perhaps the power of genius made her more broad-minded and forget her otherwise rather narrow yardstick by which she ordinarily

---

[6] David Carroll, "Introduction" to *George Eliot: The Critical Heritage,* p. 13.
[7] [D.M. Craik], "To Novelists and a Novelist," *Macmillan's Magazine,* 3 (1861), 444.

measured novels on moral grounds. Her reservations, however, are implied by such qualifiers as "ignoble" and "base."

Placing *Silas Marner* (1861) on the same level as *Adam Bede,* reviewers unanimously paid it the highest tribute: for the *Saturday Review,* George Eliot was without a rival in portraying the lower middle class, "this unknown, and to most people unknowable section of society" and her works were "a new revelation of what society in quiet English parishes really is and has been" (April 13, 1861, p. 369). Less interesting and sensitive than her previous Eliot critiques, Miss Jewsbury's review is largely devoted to re-telling the plot. With relief she noticed that Eliot had returned to the orthodoxy of *Adam Bede,* avoiding scenes which are "in the least morbid or questionable" as, it is implied, she had done in *The Mill on the Floss* (April 6, 1861, p. 65). Like the famous E.S. Dallas, who praised the novel's realism in *The Times,* Miss Jewsbury expressed her admiration for the homely realism of *Silas Marner,* "a Dutch picture," whose hero "takes a hold on the reader's sympathy, by the truth with which the inward workings of his life is laid bare" (April 6, 1861, p. 465). Her ability to see the novel as a means of widening the reader's sympathy would have won George Eliot's full approval. The *Athenaeum* review ends on a note that indicates Miss Jewsbury's perception of what was perhaps the author's most important intention:

> Readers who desire only to meet with high society and good company in their novels, and who consider it impossible to feel an interest in the fortunes of weavers and farmers, may leave 'Silas Marner' alone, for they will meet with nothing higher than the Squire;—those who can feel sympathy with human nature, however humbly embodied it may be, will find 'Silas Marner' comfortable reading. (April 6, 1861, p. 465)

Romola (1863) was a turning-point in George Eliot's career in the sense that it divided the reading public into those who perceptively hailed the latest development of her genius and those who gave vent to their nostalgia for the bucolic charm of her early novels. While often belonging to the first group, critics were nonetheless aware that they were writing primarily for the second. They admitted invariably that *Romola* was less popular than its predecessors, but like the *Westminster Review* and the *Spectator,* the *Athenaeum* was not slow to recognise its merits. Writing for middlebrow readers, Miss Jewsbury honestly declared that the novel was neither entertaining, nor as successful as the author's English novels. However, not distracted in her judgment by the much admired intimate realism of the early novels, Miss Jewsbury fully grasped the depth of George Eliot's mind and responded to her stern morality:

> There are noble things to be found in 'Romola,' which will make the reader's heart burn within him. It will be scarcely possible to rise from the perusal without being penetrated by the 'joy of elevated thoughts,' without feeling a desire to cease from

a life of self-pleasing, and to embody in action that sense of obligation, of obedience to duty, which is, indeed, the crowning distinction that has been bestowed on man, the high gift in which all others culminate. (July 1, 1863, p. 46)

With the publication of *Felix Holt, the Radical* in 1866 the readers returned to the familiar haunts of Loamshire. The contemporary reception of the novel was mixed, partly due to its labyrinthine plot and lack of stature of Felix Holt. Seen against the spectrum of opinions, sampled in the Critical Heritage volume on George Eliot, Miss Jewsbury's *Athenaeum* review emerges as highly positive. Like the *Westminster* and the *North American Review,* she drew attention to the dramatic quality of the novel, comparing the scene between Mrs Transome and her former lover to "a scene of a tragedy acted by Rachel" (June 23, 1866, p. 828) and just as she admired the noble portrait of Savonarola drawn in *Romola,* she focused her interest on the character of Felix Holt. A noble idealist, Holt "is dedicated to a life of self-renunciation for the good of his fellow-men in this life, and not the aim of his own mere personal salvation in another world" (June 23, 1866, p. 828). When the *Athenaeum* reviewer claims that "the wise and noble thoughts make the beauty and the worth of 'Felix Holt' " (June 23, 1866, p. 828), it is an indication that she shared George Eliot's code of self-renunciation and fulfilment of duty. One of the reasons why Miss Jewsbury allowed this author greater freedom in subject matter and treatment was, no doubt, that she always sensed the great moral seriousness that was the foundation of Eliot's art.

Both in the case of Trollope and of George Eliot the number of Miss Jewsbury's reviews enables us to assess her approach to these novelists and to see her as the *Athenaeum* spokesman on important phases of their careers. Other important mid-nineteenth century novelists, however, such as Wilkie Collins and George Meredith, occur so sporadically among her reviews as to give us but a fragmented, though at times interesting, picture of her views on their achievement.

Wilkie Collins

Chiefly remembered for *The Woman in White* (1860), which initiated the craze for the novel of sensation, and *The Moonstone* (1868), Collins was one of the most widely read novelists of his day and succeeded, like Dickens, in appealing to a highly diversified public, ranging, in Norman Page's words, from " 'porters and boys' " to "intellectuals and public figures such as Matthew Arnold . . . Lord Macaulay and Mr. Gladstone" and his novels were to be found "in every drawing-room in the country, as well as in every back-kitchen."[8]

---

[8] Norman Page, "Introduction" to *Wilkie Collins: The Critical Heritage* (London: Routledge & Kegan Paul, 1974), p. 19.

Miss Jewsbury reviewed three of his books for the *Athenaeum,* two of which, the reviews of *Hide and Seek* (1854) and *The Moonstone* (1868) are reprinted in the Critical Heritage volume on Collins with the reviewer's name given.

On its publication in 1854, *Hide and Seek* met with general praise and was considered by the *Spectator* and *Bentley's Miscellany* as a great improvement on his previous novels *Antonina* and *Basil.* Miss Jewsbury also lavished praise on *Hide and Seek,* noticing with relief that Collins had left the "close, stifling, unwholesome" atmosphere of his early novels and that he had "ceased walking the moral hospital," presenting human nature like a "demonstration in morbid anatomy" (June 24, 1854, p. 775). Acknowledged, even by his depreciators, as a master of skilfully contrived plots, Collins fascinated Miss Jewsbury with his dexterity: "there is not a single scene, or character, or incident, however trivial, that does not in some way tend to carry on the story and to bring on the *dénoument*" (June 24, 1854, p. 775). That Miss Jewsbury judged Collins by his own standards rather than look for qualities which were not part of his aim becomes clear when we compare her reception of *After Dark,* a collection of short stories published in 1856, with George Eliot's review in the *Westminster.* Whereas Eliot, though admitting Collins's "effective presentation of a mystery," saw "the neglect of character" and his inability "to interest us in his personages" as the chief defect of *After Dark,*[9] Miss Jewsbury, not looking for character drawing, emphasised the author's careful workmanship and his capacity for holding the reader spellbound by using a technique reminiscent of Poe's.

The reception of *The Moonstone* varies greatly from journal to journal. Highbrow critics, grudgingly admitting that "among the makers of conundrum-novels" Collins was "the only one whose writing was endurable by cultivated taste,"[10] saw *The Moonstone* as unworthy of his reputation as a novelist. Forgetting her usual insistence on moral lessons, noble sentiments and truthfulness to human nature, Miss Jewsbury was simply overwhelmed by the novel's readability: her reaction was not unlike that of the masses of middle-brow readers who had been eagerly awaiting the next instalment of *The Moonstone* when it was serialised in *All the Year Round.* She was in good company, for both *The Times* and Harper's *New Monthly Magazine* strongly recommended the novel. When evaluating writers as different as George Eliot and Wilkie Collins, Miss Jewsbury seems to be applying different sets of critical standards. In the case of Collins, her standards are less stringent, she is willing to be simply entertained, yielding to her taste for adventure and escapism.

[9] [George Eliot], "Art and Belles Lettres," *Westminster Review,* 65 (1856), 640.
[10] Unsigned review, *Spectator,* 25 July, 1868, pp. 881—82. Rpt. in *Collins: The Critical Heritage,* p. 172.

George Meredith

The early novels by George Meredith which Geraldine Jewsbury reviewed for the *Athenaeum—The Ordeal of Richard Feverel* (1859), *Emilia in England* (1864) (later re-named *Sandra Belloni*) and *Vittoria* (1867)—failed to make an impact on the public at large. It is interesting to see how Miss Jewsbury responded to what Michael Wolff, surveying the literature of 1859, has called "the most modern and the least conventional" novel published that year—*The Ordeal of Richard Feverel*.[11] Mudie's Select Library bought three hundred copies of the novel, but when the reviewer for the *Spectator* accused it of having "a low ethical tone"[12] and when Miss Jewsbury declared that it was "about as painful a book as any reader ever felt himself inexorably compelled to read through" (July 9, 1859, p. 48), Mudie apparently read the novel himself and decided not to circulate it. Even ten years after its publication, in 1869, when six of Meredith's novels were available in Mudie's Catalogue, *Richard Feverel* was still considered unsuitable for family reading and could not be borrowed from the leading circulating library.

While giving proof of originality and promise, *Richard Feverel* was, according to Miss Jewsbury, unacceptable on account of its unpleasant subject. Although her censure was shared by the *Leader,* the *Critic* and the *Saturday,* her condemnation of the novel's painfulness appears narrow-minded compared with the perceptive analysis found in the *Saturday Review.* Miss Jewsbury disapproved of *Richard Feverel* for another reason: it did not measure up to her demands for photograph-like realism: "it is *not* true to real life or human nature; only true to an abstract and entirely arbitrary idea." With an ironical twist she added that, to her, the "only comfort the reader can find on closing the book is—that it is not true" (July 9, 1859, p. 48). With her limited literary ideals of pleasant everyday realism, Miss Jewsbury could make nothing of Meredith's characters who were, in the words of Samuel Lucas of *The Times,* "more entirely symbols and shadows of his thought than ordinary everyday denizens of the world about him." Indeed, it would be "unfair," Lucas argued, "to try him by the standard relations of novels to life."[13] Since those were precisely the norms by which Miss Jewsbury judged fiction, it is not surprising that she expressed a hope that Meredith would "use his great ability to produce something pleasanter next time" (July 9, 1859, p. 48).

---

[11] Michael Wolff, "Victorian Reviewers and Cultural Responsibility," in *1859,* p. 281. Quoting from Miss Jewsbury's *Athenaeum* review of *The Ordeal,* Wolff does not identify the reviewer and refers to her as "he" (p. 281).

[12] *Spectator,* quoted in Stang, p. 207.

[13] Samuel Lucas, *The Times,* 14 Oct. 1859, rpt. in *Meredith: The Critical Heritage,* ed. Ioan Williams (London: Routledge & Kegan Paul, 1971), p. 78.

With *Emilia in England* (1864), Meredith did produce "something pleasanter." This novel was, in Miss Jewsbury's view, "a charming story" which she eagerly recommended to the readers of the *Athenaeum*. What she objected to, however, was Meredith's shortcomings as a storyteller, which resulted in novels which were not half as readable as the products of, for instance, Wilkie Collins, who, lacking Meredith's genius, possessed the necessary ability to spellbind his readers with a good story. On this point, then, Miss Jewsbury was akin in her criticism to the critic and historian Justin M'Carthy who criticised *Emilia in England* in the *Westminster:*

> The reader is never carried away by the story; he never loses sight of the narrator; he never for a moment feels as if he were moving among the people of the novel, sharing their trials and their joys. Mr Meredith falls into the common error of intellectual men who go about to construct a story upon purely intellectual principles.[14]

Set during the Italian rising of 1848, *Vittoria* (1867) was planned to make a popular appeal by its vigorous external action and narrative interest. To Meredith's disappointment, however, it met with a mixed reaction among contemporary reviewers, who were baffled to find so much ability combined with such serious defects. Miss Jewsbury, for instance, protested against the complexity of the plot and wondered: "How are human beings with limited faculties to understand all the distracting threads of this unmerciful novel?" (Feb. 23, 1867, p. 248) The fact that the bulk of her review is devoted to a retelling of the plot may of course be an indication that she was uncertain how to judge it. Although Miss Jewsbury sensed Meredith's gift as a writer in the early novels she reviewed, she could not appreciate a certain intellectual quality in them: they did not offer the kind of pleasant entertainment which she liked to recommend to her readers.

---

[14] Justin M'Carthy, "Novels with a Purpose," *Westminster Review,* 26 (July 1864), rpt. in *Meredith: The Critical Heritage,* p. 133.

Chapter Six
The Domestic Fifties

In the second half of the 1850s Geraldine Jewsbury experienced a particularly active period as a reviewer: dozens of novels were entrusted to her and she was frequently responsible for the "New Novels" section of the *Athenaeum*. Most of these novels belonged to a genre of fiction which proved particularly congenial to Miss Jewsbury's taste—the domestic novel. Enjoying its heyday in the 1850s, the genre remained alive, however, well into the 1860s, for many novelists who helped set the pattern carried on in the same vein even after the sensation novel had become the favourite reading of the Victorian middle-classes. Though written in three different decades, Mrs Dinah Mulock Craik's novels *The Ogilvies* (1849), *John Halifax* (1856), and *A Noble Life* (1865) all embody the spirit of what we might term the domestic fifties.

It is difficult perhaps to find a better description of a domestic novel than the one offered by Mrs Craik herself in *Christian's Mistake:* her novel was, she said, a "simple record of six months' household history, such as might have happened in any life . . . it includes no extraordinary events; and is the history of mere ordinary people . . ."[1] Women novelists naturally dominated the genre. On account of their experience of running the narrow but intricate domain that a Victorian household constituted, they became experts at rendering the everyday incidents which were the staple of domestic fiction. However, their leading position was also ascribed to another cause: they were generally believed to be "moral" writers in a sense that their male counterparts were not. Women novelists "set to work," as the *Christian Remembrancer* explained, "to prove a point—starting with this point, and framing the story to set it off."[2] In fact, fiction provided them with a forum, akin to the clergyman's pulpit, in which to spread their moral message. Reviewing Mrs Craik's *A Life for a Life,* the

---

[1] [D.M. Craik], *Christian's Mistake* (Leipzig: Tauchnitz, 1865), p. 303.
[2] "Our Female Novelists," *Christian Remembrancer,* 38 (1859), 306.

Saturday Review clearly sums up the influential position of the domestic novelist:

> On the whole, she [the novel-writer] is far more powerful, more popular, and more unfettered than the preacher. Nor do we much regret her influence. If better sermons get to the public in the new than in the old-fashioned way, why should we object? We may, indeed, be glad that the inequality of the sexes is remedied. The rules of the Christian church prevent women from taking part in the public service; but now they have found a way, perfectly decorous and feminine, of giving us sermons . . . (Dec. 10, 1859, p. 709)

That such moral "household histories," written mainly *by* women and *for* women, should have been given in very large numbers to Geraldine Jewsbury to review is hardly surprising, since she was the leading woman reviewer on the staff of the *Athenaeum* during the 1850s and as such particularly apt to judge the fiction intended for her sex. Although the majority of her reviews deal with novelists who were little known even in the 1850s, a fair number are devoted to the domestic novelists whom the mid-Victorians ranked as the most prominent exponents of the genre. Miss Jewsbury reviewed 6 novels and 4 children's books by Mrs Craik, 5 + 2 by Miss Georgiana Craik, 7 by Mrs J. Hubback, 6 by Miss Julia Kavanagh, 5 by Miss Henrietta Keddie (pseud. Sarah Tytler), 7 + 2 by Miss Anne Manning, 7 by Mrs Anne Marsh, 13 by Mrs Margaret Oliphant, 9 by Miss Harriet Parr (pseud. Holme Lee), 4 + 1 by Emma Worboise and 5 + 3 by Charlotte Yonge.

Novelists such as Holme Lee or Miss Keddie are hardly known today even among students of the Victorian novel, yet their domestic novels were avidly read by the mid-Victorians. The best indicators of what novels were popular are no doubt the Catalogues of Mudie's Select Library, since only fiction sufficiently in demand would be stocked. This largely neglected source of information opens up new perspectives on prevailing literary tastes and helps us see the great and lasting vogue of the domestic novelists whom Miss Jewsbury reviewed in the *Athenaeum*. A check at, roughly, ten years intervals proves that many of the domestic novels of the 1850s were in fact read not only well into the 1860s, but figured on Mudie's lists even after World War I:[3]

---

[3] Sara Keith, "Mudie's Select Library: Principal Works of Fiction in Circulation in 1848, 1859, 1869." Typescript. Ann Arbor. Michigan, 1955 has proved very helpful for my study.

Numbers of novels in the Catalogues of Mudie's Select Library

	1888	1900	1908	1918	1928
D.M. Craik	28	30	30	31	7
Georgiana Craik	22	27	10	10	4
Lady Fullerton	8	9	6	6	3
Mrs J. Hubback	2	0	0	0	0
Julia Kavanagh	10	14	0	0	0
Henrietta Keddie	31	53	73	75	12
Anne Manning	26	28	0	0	0
Anne Marsh	4	0	0	0	0
Margaret Oliphant	53	100	75	76	52
Harriet Parr	22	25	18	18	3
Emma Worboise	43	43	44	44	6
Charlotte Yonge	41	71	74	74	19

Quite expectedly, the writers best known today, Mrs Oliphant and Miss Yonge, come out as the champions of the genre, surviving after the First World War. A mediocre novelist like Mrs Hubback, however, representative of a host of minor women writers, was apparently very much a product of her time, and the morally elevating Julia Kavanagh and Anne Manning seemed to have had little to offer a generation facing the chaos and confusion of the war. What is surprising, though, is that forgotten novels like Anne Manning's *Clarinda Singlehart* (1855) and Julia Kavanagh's *Rachel Gray* were both included in Mudie's Catalogue for 1900 and that Holme Lee had 18 of her novels listed in Mudie's Catalogue for 1918. This suggests that even when Miss Braddon, Rhoda Broughton, Ouida, George Gissing, George Moore and Joseph Conrad held the reading public in a firm grip, the quiet stream of domestic fiction was a strong undercurrent which appealed to a sizeable part of the reading public. Evidently Holme Lee's, Miss Kavanagh's and Miss Manning's novels inculcated values and set standards that were still viable at the turn of the century because they formed the backbone of Victorian society.

What strikes a modern reader when comparing Geraldine Jewsbury's reviews of domestic fiction with the actual novels themselves is that the *Athenaeum* reviewer did not always comment on what, to us, seems particularly characteristic of the genre. This can only be explained by the fact that, like other mid-Victorians, she took the religious message so completely for granted that she left it without comment. Innumerable domestic novels were built around the Biblical saying, "Thy will be done." Submission to God's will, resignation and endurance were qualities prescribed for mankind in general, but it was particularly important for women readers to embrace such moral precepts in order to conform to the womanly ideal. The examples of this are manifold. On discovering a ten-year-old letter, which, had it been posted in time, would have prevented her lifelong spinsterhood, Miss Manning's Clarinda Singlehart meekly submits: " 'O God, thy will be done,' thought she, 'on earth as it is in heaven!' "[4] The constant insistence on endurance and on the necessity of bearing one's burdens, seldom mentioned in Miss Jewsbury's reviews, no doubt reflects the hard lot of innumerable Victorian women dependent on a father, a brother or a husband for a home and unable to influence the family finances or decide about their children's education: Miss Yonge's heroine Violet slowly learns "to see in little trials the daily cross."[5]

If "Thy will be done," "Do unto others" and "Bear thy burdens" strike a modern reader as the predominant themes of the domestic novels which Miss Jewsbury reviewed, "Do thy duty" is also an all-pervasive concept. For Captain Hepburn in Mrs Hubback's *The Old Vicarage* "the grand object of life" is not professional honour, but "to do my duty in the state of life to which it has pleased God to call me."[6] In the struggle between duty and love, duty is always presented as the right course of action. Mrs Craik's John Halifax speaks on behalf of the whole genre when he states that "one right alone I hold superior to the right of love,—duty."[7] When Holme Lee's Gilbert Massenger refrains from marriage so as not to impart hereditary insanity to his progeny, his self-denial and fulfilment of duty bring "peace within."[8] These moral lessons, which frequently appear mawkish and meek in the extreme to us, were thus so much part of the spirit of the domestic novels of the 1850s that they were usually not commented on by reviewers like Miss Jewsbury.

By placing home and wifehood at the centre of the submissive heroine's life, novelists of course reflected prevailing social conditions in their books, but, they also provided fictional patterns with which their women readers could identify themselves. Many of the domestic novels Miss Jewsbury reviewed read like pleasantly laid out lessons for young wives about to shoulder the responsibilities of running a Victorian household. At a time when girls married young, sometimes at the age of sixteen, it was paramount to instil in their impressionable minds the ideals and duties connected with matrimony in order to safeguard the stability of the Victorian home. A wife should be, as the novelist Holme Lee phrased it, "the glory and crown of a household; the stay of the old, the joy of the young, the very pride and happiness of her husband's life" (*Gilbert Massenger,* pp. 317—18). A young heroine's matronhood begins when she suffers the hero to call her "by the holy name of 'wife.' "[9] Not until the wedding ceremony is she able, with divine approval, to give a free expression to her love.

[4] [Anne Manning], *Some Account of Mrs. Clarinda Singlehart* (London: Hall, Virtue & Co., 1855), p. 94.

[5] Charlotte Yonge, *Heartsease* (Leipzig: Tauchnitz, 1855), I, 222.

[6] Mrs. J. Hubback, *The Old Vicarage* (London: Skeet, 1856), II, 309.

[7] [D.M. Craik], *John Halifax, Gentleman* (1856; rpt. London: Dent, 1969), p. 383.

[8] Holme Lee, *Gilbert Massenger* (London: Smith, Elder & Co., 1855), p. 250.

[9] [Anne Marsh], *Margaret and Her Bridesmaids* (London: Hurst and Blackett, 1856), III, 95.

Mrs Marsh's heroine Margaret behaves according to this pattern: her "sensitive maiden heart opened to let the wife's devotion enter, and Harold knew that the grave alone could extinguish the love expressed in that glance."[10] Although Miss Jewsbury remained a spinster all her life, she did not discuss this glorification of the British matron. Like other mid-Victorians, she perhaps subscribed to the idea that wifehood was both honourable and enviable. Lilian, in *The Wife's Trials,* at last re-united with her reformed husband, may serve as an example of this idolatry:

> She was going to govern a little kingdom of her own—to order, conduct, beautify, and replenish the said little kingdom to the best of her ability; she was going to organize a home to ensure her husband's happiness, and to take her place among the matrons of the land, to occupy that position in society which befitted the wife of Mr. Basil Hope, the heir of beautiful, ancient, time-honoured Hopelands![11]

Just as Miss Jewsbury did not express her views on the glorification of matrimony, she left other characteristics of domestic fiction without comment. Her silence on what to us is only too blatant indicates that certain traits were an inherent part of the genre, indeed, inseparable from it in the eyes of the mid-Victorians. The purifying influence of the heroine's love of the profligate hero is only one example. When Charlotte Yonge's Arthur Martindale in *Heartsease* wonders "what would become of the world if wives were not better than their husbands," (II, 186), he voices a tacit assumption generally shared by readers and writers of domestic fiction. Explicitly didactic, Miss Craik's *Mildred* (1868) points to the ennobling effect of Mildred's love on her gambling husband. She came to him "as angels come to lost souls"[12] and asked "Has no man ever yet been raised by a woman?" (p. 240). Here, a wife's love is a boon from heaven and only "through faith in her love" can her husband find his way back to God. But for domestic novelists no earthly love could replace divine love. We need only recall Jane Eyre's "dangerous" propensity to make Rochester her God to appreciate the conflict. Emma Worboise's Lilian, whose "chief joy" was in "earthly hopes" is punished, for those "who take for their strongest support a reed of mortality" are bound to suffer[13] and the only consolation Julia Kavanagh can give her heroine Rachel Gray, who failed to win her father's love, is "Complain not, murmur not, Rachel, if thou has not thy father upon earth, remember that thou hast thy Father in Heaven!"[14]

In this throng of known and, mostly, unknown novelists, Miss Jewsbury placed three above the rest: Margaret Oliphant, Dinah Mulock Craik and

---

[10] [Marsh], *Margaret and Her Bridesmaids,* I, 44.
[11] [Emma Worboise], *The Wife's Trials* (London: Thickbroom Brothers, 1858), p. 55.
[12] Georgiana M. Craik, *Mildred,* (Leipzig: Tauchnitz, 1868), p. 187.
[13] [Worboise], *The Wife's Trials,* p. 35.
[14] Julia Kavanagh, *Rachel Gray* (Leipzig: Tauchnitz, 1856), p. 306.

Charlotte Yonge, a ranking that coincides with the judgment of posterity. Mrs Oliphant was probably, with some 125 books, as her biographers claim, "the most prolific writer of the nineteenth century."[15] Hearing that her first novel, *Passages in the Life of Mrs. Margaret Maitland* (1849) had made such a success as to be taken by Mudie, she admitted that his patronage was nothing less than "a sort of recognition from heaven."[16] Although her first novel contains some clever delineations of Scottish character and custom, the group of novels called "The Chronicles of Carlingford" attain social comedy which places this under-rated novelist on the level of Trollope and Mrs Gaskell.

The relish for Scottish novels was strong in the 1850s and Jeaffreson argued that "the best living writer of them is, beyond doubt, Mrs Oliphant."[17] Reviewing thirteen of her novels, Miss Jewsbury also preferred those set in Scotland. Thus she praises *Magdalen Hepburn* (1854) for being a "carefully-executed picture of the society and state of manners in Scotland at the dawn of the Reformation" (July 15, 1854, p. 874), while regretting that in *Orphans* (1857) Mrs Oliphant "quits Scottish ground" and consequently "loses her power" (Jan. 30, 1858, p. 144). By 1860, however, the reviewers had forgiven her for leaving Scottish ground and the *Spectator* even prophesied that *Lucy Crofton* would win the admiration of Thackeray. What Miss Jewsbury found admirable in this novel was Mrs Oliphant's insight into female psychology, her delineation of Clara Crofton's long drawn-out sorrow after losing her only child; "the inner hidden life of the wife, and the sorrow of her bereaved motherhood, into which her husband . . . cannot enter is touched with a skill and delicacy that attests its truth, whilst it keeps clear of becoming wearisome or morbid" (Jan. 21, 1860, p. 93). But again a great change of taste has taken place since the mid-nineteenth century. For what Miss Jewsbury did not find "wearisome and morbid," a modern reader is likely to reject as sentimental in the extreme. Clara Crofton's stereotyped way of overcoming her bereavement is only one case in point: ". . . is not this the explanation of those words that are writ in tears, 'Whom he loveth, he chasteneth?' Whoso bears his sorrow bravely, tenderly, whose rising up, goes on from it with an undiscouraged heart, is victor over all life and all its trials . . ."[18]

Unfortunately Miss Jewsbury was never given any of the Carlingford novels to review. It would have been interesting to see her reaction to *Miss Marjoribanks* (1866), for instance, which is free from the overt preaching found

[15] Colby, *The Equivocal Virtue*, p. xiv.

[16] Quoted in Amy Cruse, *The Victorians and Their Books* (London: Allen & Unwin, 1935), p. 315.

[17] Jeaffreson, *Novels and Novelists*, II, 383.

[18] [Margaret Oliphant], *Lucy Crofton* (1859; rpt. London: Hurst and Blackett, 1860), p. 39.

in *Lucy Crofton* and shows Mrs Oliphant moving towards a more humorous manner, bolder and seasoned with a note of protest.

In the 1850s, before Mrs Oliphant had begun her Carlingford novels, contemporary critics generally rated Mrs Dinah Mulock Craik above her. What her novels excelled in was, as the *Gentleman's Magazine* phrased it, in being "not merely pure, but purifying."[19] Clearly, Miss Jewsbury and other mid-Victorian readers felt enormously attracted by the quiet resignation and the unshaken faith in God expressed in Mrs Craik's novels, and in the 1860s, when Miss Braddon and Mrs Henry Wood invaded the literary marketplace, her "healthy" novels came to epitomise the moral stability conservative critics yearned for. In 1866 the *British Quarterly Review* gave a plausible explanation of Mrs Craik's success:

> Mrs. Craik's great charm is a repose of manner, a quiet dignity of style, which, while it impresses all the readers by its calm purity, appeals more especially to the cultivated and refined. *Restful* is, perhaps, the term that can best be applied to her writings. She does not look deep down into the inner conflicts, the great moral struggles of our nature from which George Eliot draws back the veil . . . she says, "see, men and women have lived and suffered here. Be patient and steadfast, you who live and suffer; endure as they endured, and you will also find rest and peace. Do right, do your duty, and be patient: all must be well, for God is over all."[20]

John Halifax, Gentleman (1856), the story of a good selfmade man of unflinching integrity, courage and industry, took the public by storm and by the end of the century 250,000 copies had been sold, 80,000 of which were the sixpenny edition.[21] Its tone of unsullied purity and goodness was generally praised by the literary weeklies. While acclaiming the domestic setting of *John Halifax* "as beautifully painted," Miss Jewsbury differed rather strongly from other critics in not accepting the portraiture of the pure hero wholesale: John Halifax was "too much idealized," she argued. Anxious to make her hero perfect, Miss Jewsbury protested, the author had "thrown a fictitious rose-coloured tint over a character that could have dispensed with any such aid" (April 26, 1856, p. 520).

Though best known for *John Halifax,* Mrs Craik herself ranked *A Life for a Life* (1859) highest. Here she breaks new ground both as to plot and the manner in which the story is told. The novel consists of the journals of the hero and heroine, "his story" and "her story" in alternate chapters, and illustrates two issues—punishment of crime and courtship. Dr Urquhart has slain a man in his youth by mistake and spends the rest of his life doing penance for the

[19] "The Lady Novelists of Great Britain," *Gentleman's Magazine,* 40 (1853), 21.
[20] "The Author of 'John Halifax,' " *British Quarterly Review,* 44 (July 1866), 33.
[21] Mrs. Parr, "Dinah Mulock (Mrs. Craik)" in Mrs Oliphant et al., *Women Novelists of Queen Victoria's Reign* (London: Hurst & Blackett, 1897), p. 248.

John Halifax, Gentleman

THE STORY OF HIS YOUTH

BY

DINAH MARIA CRAIK

EDITION FOR SWEDISH SCHOOLS WITH

EXPLANATORY NOTES

BY

R. E. ZACHRISSON

LEKTOR

ANDRA UPPLAGAN

18 77

STOCKHOLM

A. V. CARLSONS BOKFÖRLAGS-AKTIEBOLAG.

Title page of *John Halifax, Gentleman*, edited and annotated for Swedish secondary schools. 2nd ed. Stockholm, 1918.

secret deed. His victim turns out to be, not unexpectedly in the world of sentimental fiction, his fiancée Theodora's brother. Whereas the *Christian Remembrancer* criticised Mrs Craik for her advanced view that repentance was sufficient for total remission from punishment, Miss Jewsbury thinks the author should have put in "more criminal element in the accident." For to her Dr Urquhart's "sickly remorse for an unintentional act" is nothing but "morbid ultra-heroism" (Aug. 6, 1859, p. 173). What she reacts to, then, is nothing less than the "false" psychology of sentimental fiction.

Curiously enough, Miss Jewsbury failed to perceive what other critics termed the "dangerous" bent of *A Life for a Life.* In her portrayal of Theodora's love for Dr Urquhart, Mrs Craik insists on the individual's right to trust to her/his feelings, her/his right to contract a sacred bond that cannot be violated by parental interference. In view of Miss Jewsbury's strict insistence on filial duty, it is strange that she did not take exception to a novel which aimed at changing the readers' opinion on courtship. The *Christian Remembrancer,* however, perceived the implications of Mrs Craik's argument:

> What she evidently aims at is the greater equality of woman with man in the marriage relation . . . Mind should rather meet mind on equal terms . . . the attraction in each must be mutual and simultaneous . . . when a certain amount of deep pure affection is generated it becomes a divine power . . . Passive obedience is of course out of place in this system, and a love . . . thus spoken between two thoughtful . . . congenial souls, becomes an indissoluble tie, before that ceremonial tie is formed . . .[22]

That a domestic novel with such revolutionary undertones failed to draw a strong reaction from Miss Jewsbury may be due to the fact that she was at times a careless reviewer, drowning in a constant flood of mediocre fiction which she sometimes perused too quickly to discern its full implications.

Few writers wrote novels with a loftier motive than Charlotte Yonge. This well-educated High Church novelist aimed at inculcating Christian virtues in young impressionable minds, and her *The Heir of Redclyffe* (1853) established a pattern of endurance and self-sacrifice that made it one of the most influential novels of the time. In fact, Miss Yonge's hero, Sir Guy Morville, belonged, according to *Fraser's,* to "those Heaven-commissioned messengers who seem to be sent to show us what our Lord meant when he said of the little children that were brought to him, 'of such is the Kingdom of Heaven' . . ."[23] Equally influential on readers and on other novelists was no doubt the patient Griselda type of heroine Miss Yonge drew in Amy of *The Heir of Redclyffe* and Violet in *Heartsease*—gentle, yielding women who possess a strong sense of duty, faith and endurance.

Miss Jewsbury contributed to the general accolade that followed on the appearance of Miss Yonge's *Heartsease* (1854). Just as *Fraser's* considered Violet one of the "most attractive creations that ever sprang to life at the poet's bidding,"[24] Miss Jewsbury greatly admired Miss Yonge's heroine: Violet "is not endowed with any talent . . . with nothing but the simple idea that she must do her own duty; and her gentle straightforward simplicity works like a charm

[22] "Our Female Novelists," *Christian Remembrancer,* 38 (1859), 308.
[23] "Heartsease: or, The Brother's Wife," *Fraser's Magazine,* 50 (1854), 503.
[24] "Heartsease," *Fraser's Magazine,* 50 (1854), 503.

upon the whole family'' (Nov. 18, 1854, p. 1396). But to her mind, the novel's strength lay in the author's "daguerrotype" reproduction of domestic life: the "minute etching of incident and character" (Nov. 18, 1854, p. 1396).

Many domestic novelists, less known than Mrs Oliphant, Mrs Craik and Miss Yonge, were also great favourites with Miss Jewsbury. Their novels are, in a sense, more representative of the great mass of domestic fiction than minor "classics" like *John Halifax* or *The Heir of Redclyffe*. Hence, in their mediocrity lies their typicality. Few may have heard of, much less read, Mrs Hubback, Holme Lee, Julia Kavanagh and Henrietta Keddie, yet their fiction still appealed to numerous readers at the turn of the century, since Mudie then still stocked 92 of their novels.

The mid-Victorians' view of the contemporary literary scene was based on a different hierarchy from the one we have come to accept when we look at the fiction of the last century. Less than a month after reviewing *John Halifax,* Miss Jewsbury encountered a novelist whom she considered a worthy competitor to Mrs Craik. For in her opinion Mrs Hubback's morally impeccable *The Old Vicarage* "may hold up its head amongst the best" in the "harvest of good novels" of the season (May 10, 1856, p. 584). Similarly, by placing the review of Holme Lee's *Thorney Hall* before Mrs Gaskell's *North and South* in the "New Novels" section on April 7, 1855, devoted to these two novels alone, the *Athenaeum* indicates the high regard Holme Lee enjoyed among contemporary readers.

The Anglo-Irish novelist Julia Kavanagh's novels teach their readers to feel sympathy with the sorrow and suffering of ordinary people. Compared with Mrs Craik's novels, her *Rachel Gray* (1855) strikes a graver note: it was "far too lugubrious" according to the *Saturday Review* (Dec. 22, 1855, p. 143). However, George Eliot was not slow to appreciate that *Rachel Gray* explored new areas. In spite of the author's "failure" in treating her subject, she willingly admitted that *Rachel Gray* was "commendable" for occupying "ground which is very far from being exhausted."[25] Miss Jewsbury, on the other hand, held up *Rachel Gray* as an exemplar of a nearly perfect domestic novel, "wrought from the humblest and simplest of materials" (Jan. 12, 1856, p. 40). Set in "low" London surroundings among sempstresses and shopkeepers, the novel won her admiration for its strong moral pathos. For this is the kind of novel which, as she phrased it, "no one can read . . . and not feel a good influence from it" (Jan. 12, 1856, p. 40).

The vogue for Scottish novels, initiated by Scott and Galt and continued by Mrs Oliphant and Mrs Craik, was so strong as to make the appearance of Henrietta Keddie's *Phemie Millar* (1854) "pall a little from repetition" as the

---

[25] [George Eliot], *"Rachel Gray,"* Leader, Jan. 5, 1856, p. 19.

Spectator observed, since "the public has latterly had too many delineations of humble or middle Scottish life" (p. 438). But Miss Jewsbury had evidently not tired of Scottish novels, for Miss Keddie's *Phemie Millar, Nut-Brown Maids* (1859) and *My Heart's in the Highlands* (1861) were all reviewed favourably in the *Athenaeum*.

Like *Rachel Gray, Phemie Millar* is one of the few novels that won Geraldine Jewsbury's unreserved admiration. Set in the small Scottish fishing town of Craiginch, it centres on family incidents like courtship, trousseau sewing, watching at fever beds, shopping expeditions to Edinburgh and family discussions around the hearth, intermingled with the local colour provided by the "herring harvest," visits to farm-houses, lost boats and Greenland vessels, told to a large extent in Scottish dialect. But although the incidents are far too slight to hold a modern reader's attention throughout three volumes, *Phemie Millar* presents an interesting heroine and consequently proves that mediocre fiction may well have redeeming qualities. Six years before George Eliot brought Maggie Tulliver before the public, Henrietta Keddie broke the traditional pattern for heroines of domestic fiction. "Neglected, undervalued, ridiculed, despised," Phemie Millar was little suited to her surroundings. Had she been a boy, her father "would have bred her to the bar, and she might have been a judge," but being a girl, her fate was "to pour out tea and order dinners."[26] Miss Jewsbury instantly spotted Phemie as a creation far above the general run of meek and submissive girls:

> Phemie Millar, with her crude, ardent, intellectual aspirations, in the midst of a commonplace, uncongenial domestic employment,—with her oddness, her short-comings—her earnest simple-minded desires to do better—her artistic instincts that have a touch of genius—the temptations, and hopes, and disappointments of her young girlish life, which ripens and developes into a rich and noble womanhood—make her as charming and unpretending a heroine as we have met with for many a day. (April 22, 1854, p. 490)

For once Miss Jewsbury was able to see beyond the convention of the saintlike heroine and appreciate Phemie Millar, suffering from inner conflicts and weakness. "The bairn is 'ower wise' " was the general opinion in Craiginch and her "disposition was in as great confusion as her drawers" (I, 15). Consciously or unconsciously, George Eliot probably drew on reminiscences of Miss Keddie's heroine when she created her Maggie Tulliver in *The Mill on the Floss* (1860).

Few novelists perhaps illustrate better the predominant taste for domestic fiction among the educated classes than Mrs Marsh(-Caldwell). Her *Emilia Wyndham* (1846) was regarded as a trend-setter, in which the heroine combined "pa-

---

[26] [Henrietta Keddie], *Phemie Millar* (London: Hurst and Blackett, 1854), I, 306.

tience, perseverance, endurance, gentleness, and disinterestedness." These qualities constituted, the *New Monthly Magazine* contended in 1852, "the heroism of our day."[27] In fact, Mrs Marsh's novels appeared as a barometer, capable of gauging the moral climate of the nation: their popularity was seen by the *Dublin University Magazine* as a proof that their society was still a sound one:

> The eminent success of the works now before us . . . we regard as a very favourable attestation to the soundness of our public opinion. The author is indisputably a writer of true genius and of great power, but it is also one who dedicates high endowments to the service of Him who has given them. The popularity of such a writer must necessarily exert a beneficial influence over a people prepared to prize them.[28]

Miss Jewsbury's admiration for Mrs Marsh's *Margaret and Her Bridesmaids* (1856) contrasts sharply with the severe judgment of the *Saturday* which deplored this "rubbish." Admittedly mediocre from our point of view, the novel nevertheless presents a heroine who possesses remarkable freshness. Of great moral integrity, the straightforward Lotty (wrongly called Lotte in the *Athenaeum*) caught Miss Jewsbury's eye and she praised "the little, wilful, wild, brave, fascinating Lotte" as "the gem of the book" (April 12, 1856, p. 458). But it is the novel's moral excellence that appeals most to the *Athenaeum* reviewer. Again, what barely holds a modern reader's attention through three volumes, appears a "fascinating" novel to Miss Jewsbury on account of the "comfort" and "profit" the readers will derive from it.

Among the various genres of fiction, Miss Jewsbury ranked the domestic novel highest. Sharing the period's rage for homely, "household histories," she expressed her admiration for Miss Yonge's and Miss Kavanagh's "minute etching" and, above all, for the sound moral message embodied in their novels: Rachel Gray and Violet Martindale both set important patterns of Christian faith and endurance for Victorian women readers. If it is to Miss Jewsbury's credit as a reviewer, however, that, in this throng of paragons of virtue, she singled out unconventional heroines like Phemie Millar and little Lotty for her praise, her sound reaction against sentimental exaggerations is even more noteworthy. Mrs Craik's "idealized" portrait of John Halifax and her overstressing of Dr Urquhart's crime, the pivot on which the plot of *A Life for a Life* hinges, were more than this admirer of moral novels could accommodate.

[27] "Female Novelists. Mrs Marsh Caldwell," *New Monthly Magazine*, 96 (1852), 316.
[28] "Mrs. Marsh Caldwell," *Dublin University Magazine*, 34 (1849), 575.

Chapter Seven
The Wicked Sixties

A reader tired of the wholesome domestic novels of Charlotte Yonge, Mrs Oliphant and Mrs Craik, which had enjoyed their greatest vogue in the 1850s, only had to order a novel by Miss Braddon or Mrs Wood to be removed from conventional realism and mid-Victorian stodginess into a world of crime and vice. In the early 1860s a state of mind known as "sensation mania" seized the nation: alarmed at the undeniable popularity of the sensation novel, Victorian reviewers looked back with nostalgia to the 1850s as the golden age of domestic realism when the English novel was known for its sanity and wholesomeness. While producing a hitherto unseen publishing bonanza, sensation novels fostered a love of excitement that in the eyes of many had a harmful effect on the moral stamina of the public. In 1867 Geraldine Jewsbury indignantly protested against the morally undermining qualities of such literature:

> Now, a taste for foolish, easy entertainment, that requires no effort of mind, deteriorates the moral strength and vigour which ought to underlie even the amusements of responsible and rational creatures. Without any positive immorality, the modern class of novels is pervaded by a vague, relaxing element, in which no brave or strong principle of virtue can exist. (June 1, 1867, p. 720)

What distinguished sensation fiction in its heyday during the 1860s was the mingling of realism and romance, the two contradictory modes of literary perception prevalent in the 1850s. This disregard of what had been seen as two mutually exclusive categories of art provoked grave objections from literary critics: when a sensation novel was attacked for "artistic fault," it was precisely this mixture that was being challenged. Cherishing the validity of both fantasy and fact, sensation novelists took pains to make their "fantastic" novels "real" to the minutest detail. But absolute truth could not appeal to the spirit of Victorian realism, which drew a line between fiction and real life. As Mrs Oliphant wrote about an incident in *Hard Cash,* "such a thing might happen in fact; but fiction is bound as fact is not . . . and must consider *vraisemblance* as well as absolute truth."[1]

---

[1] [Margaret Oliphant], "Charles Reade's Novels," *Blackwood's Edinburgh Magazine,* 106 (1869), 510. Quoted in Hughes, *The Maniac in the Cellar,* p. 51.

Whereas the domestic realism of the 1850s stressed the portrayal of character and slighted plot, the sensation novel of the 1860s harked back to melodrama for its focus on plot: characters do not create plot, but are plunged into action, action that focuses on violent crime, preferably murder, robbery, fraud, bigamy, mistaken identity and the return of the dead alive. The focal point of the typical sensation novel is always a woman. Heroines like the bigamist Aurora Floyd, who married her father's groom, or Lady Audley, guilty of pushing her first husband down a well and of attempted arson, and tainted with insanity, undermined the most cherished values of the mid-Victorians and even seemed to threaten the sanctity of the home. When the "angel of the hearth" was no longer the innocent and pure lady she seemed, the implications of this were devastating: social and moral chaos now infected the domesticity of the novel.

Mid-Victorian reviewers' objections to sensation novels also arose from the nearness of the events they narrate. It was no longer medieval Italian castles with trap-doors and secret passages, characteristic of early nineteenth-century Gothic novels, which were presented to the readers, but contemporary English country houses where respectability concealed depths of unknown crime. Sensationalism was thus dangerous, the *Saturday Review* observed, "in proportion as the murderers and forgers and bigamists and adulterers are pople like ourselves, such as we might meet any day in ordinary society . . . the nearer the sinners approach to men of our own time and our own class, the more likely are their sins to do us harm."[2]

Whereas the sensation novel was anachronistic in its use of stage melodrama and popular romance, it was also prophetic, moving toward an absurdist perspective. The exploration of crime festering beneath a respectable, "normal" surface created a sense of doubt among readers: things were no longer what they seemed. When the arbitrary, the uncontrollable and the nightmarish gain the upper hand, both the universe and human conduct appear irrational. The unmistakable tendency of the sensation novel to undermine the Victorian perception of reality where "truth" and "human nature" appeared predictable and unchangeable was totally alien to the realist perspective from which both Mrs Oliphant and Miss Jewsbury judged fiction. One example is Mrs Linnaeus Bank's *Stung to the Quick* in which, Miss Jewsbury writes, "in the midst of sober, discreet provincial society there is let loose a heroine who is worthy to be the sister of Manfroni the One-handed Monk" (Jan. 11, 1868, p. 55). Similarly, in *Miss Jane Larpent,* Miss Jewsbury's criticism of the heroine, on trial for a couple of murders, centres on the disconcerting contrast between appearance and reality: a " 'crown of yellow hair . . . like the dim amber locks that clothe a saint's head pictured on Minster windows,' " a " 'fair, meek face,

[2] "Novels and Life," *Saturday Review,* Feb. 13, 1864, p. 189.

so timid and yet so strangely frank in its trusting openness,' " all in the Lady Audley fashion, conceals a murderess (June 1, 1867, p. 720).

Though conservative in literary taste, the *Athenaeum* was by no means averse to sensation novels and lavishly praised both Mrs Wood's *East Lynne* and Miss Braddon's *Lady Audley's Secret*. Miss Jewsbury's attitude to the feverish productions of the sixties, however, constitutes a good measuring-rod gauging the widening rift between her own conservative taste and the readers' steadily growing demand for sensational subject matter. As early as 1859 she wearily complained that "if there is a wedding it is ten to one but it is a bigamy" (Oct. 15, 1859, p. 497) and she protested against the "murders . . . lawsuits, disinherited heirs, faithless wives . . . people reputed dead and authentically buried returning to life" (May 28, 1859, p. 710). In 1860 when Miss Jewsbury commented on the trick of bringing back the supposedly dead first wife, she stated that this was "a questionable expedient" since already at that time, "it has been so often used that one doubts whether it *can* carry an author safely much longer" (Feb. 25, 1860, p. 268). This suggests that the lurid incidents cleverly explored by Miss Braddon and Mrs Wood in the 1860s had already been used, though with much less craftsmanship, by minor writers. So when Mrs Wood made the supposedly dead Lady Isabel Carlyle in *East Lynne* return disfigured to her husband's home and, working as the governess of her own children, watch his new wife's happiness, the novelty is not Lady Isabel's return *per se,* but the novelist's persuasive depiction of the heroine's inner torment, repentence and death. Again, a recognised writer drew on the store of incidents found in the current minor fiction that has now, and deservedly so, fallen into oblivion.

Miss Jewsbury's attitude to sensation novels is ambivalent, depending on whether fiction was to be judged as commodity or art. Like so many others, she was irresistibly thrilled by the excitement provided by the circumstantial-evidence novels and readily admitted that "secret chambers and winding passages have a charm, after their kind, much stronger than sensible people will own" (June 21, 1862, p. 818). Reviewing J.C. Jeaffreson's *Live It Down,* a novel which "turns on the traditional 'skeleton' said to haunt everybody's closet," she willingly granted that "an authentic history of somebody else's 'skeleton' has an attraction for every reader" (March 28, 1863, p. 419). On the other hand, she objected to the inferior quality of "machine-made articles . . . manufactured by the score" (Jan. 11, 1868, p. 54).

The success of Mrs Henry Wood's *East Lynne* (1861) is the story of how a moderately clever novel, marketed in the proper way, took the mid-Victorian reading public by storm. Rejected by Chapman and Hall's reader George Meredith, it was spotted by Geraldine Jewsbury as a potential hit in spite of its poor English and, at her recommendation, published by Bentley in 1861. Like Wilkie Collins, Dickens and Miss Braddon, Mrs Wood appealed to a wide spectrum of readers, from the scullery maid at the bottom of the social ladder to the lady of the manor, with interesting tales that cleverly combined domesticity and sensationalism. In her novels the traditional values of purity and domestic bliss are upheld and wickedness and virtue meet with their due reward. At the close of the century, Adeline Sergeant explained the secret of Mrs Wood's popularity in the following way:

> Mrs. Wood's stories, although sensational in plot, are purely domestic. They are concerned chiefly with the great middle-class of England, and she describes lower middle-class life with a zest and a conviction and a sincerity which we do not find in many modern writers, who are apt to sneer at the *bourgeois* habits and modes of thought found in so many English households . . . Mrs. Henry Wood never satirises, she only records. It is her fidelity to truth, to the smallest domestic detail, which has charmed and will continue to charm, a large circle of readers, who are inclined perhaps to glory in the name of 'Philistine.'[3]

Mrs Wood began her career in her mid-forties with *Danesbury House* (1860), a prize tale for the Scottish Temperance League which earned her £ 100. Reviewing eight of Mrs Wood's novels for the *Athenaeum,* Miss Jewsbury immediately recognised the talent displayed in *Danesbury House:* though generally averse to temperance tales, she praised the "spirited delineations of life and character" (March 24, 1860, p. 407) which seemed very promising. *The Shadow of Ashlydyat* (1863) is one of the rare instances in which Miss Jewsbury both read a book in manuscript (she recommended Bentley to publish it) and reviewed it for the *Athenaeum.* When she judged it to be the best book Mrs Wood had written, she was in good company, for the *Spectator* also ranked it as "probably her cleverest work" (Dec. 5, 1863, p. 2828). Miss Jewsbury's review is interesting since it focuses on Mrs Wood's ability to suggest the contrast between outer and inner life, between appearance and reality:

> The power to draw minutely and carefully each character, with characteristic individuality in word and action, is Mrs Wood's especial gift; this endows her pages with a vitality which carries the reader to the end, and leaves him with the feeling, that the veil which in real life separates man from man has been raised, and that he has, for once, seen and known certain people as intimately as if he had been their guardian angel. This is a great fascination; (Jan. 23, 1864, p. 119)

But Miss Jewsbury was soon to perceive the unevenness of Mrs Wood's novels, produced too quickly to do justice to her talent. While *Oswald Cray* (1864) seemed "dull and long drawn out" (Dec. 24, 1864, p. 859), others, in spite of their deficiencies, possessed a redeeming quality which would ensure them popularity among the wide public—readableness:

> in different degrees they possess a quality that covers a multitude of sins. Their *readableness* is recognized by those who are most alive to their faults; and to the undiscerning and not fastidious people who form the majority of novel-readers they are sources of keen excitement. (July 1, 1865, p. 12)

[3] Adeline Sergeant, "Mrs. Crowe, Mrs. Archer Clive, Mrs. Henry Wood" in Mrs. Oliphant et al., *Women Novelists,* pp. 187—88.

Weary of inventing new stories at such a pace, Mrs Wood turned out inferior, slipshod work which failed to please even Miss Jewsbury, who was willing to overlook many flaws provided a novel was readable. In *Elster's Folly,* she declared, the author "seems too much fatigued to move the wires of his [sic] puppets" (July 21, 1866, p. 76) and similarly *Lady Adelaide's Oath,* though a story full of "incident, suspense and mystery," displays "commonplace workmanship" (March 23, 1867, p. 383). Endowed with considerable power to invent good plots and dramatic situations, Mrs Wood was no doubt a case of misused talent. Perhaps she would have attained a higher place among English novelists had she avoided mere sensationalism and confined herself to the faithful rendering of English middle-class life in which *East Lynne* abounds.

If Mrs Wood's novels emerge as products of an observant and unsettled age, fusing domesticity and sensationalism, so do Miss Mary Elizabeth Braddon's. In some respects the two novelists had similar careers: together with Wilkie Collins they were responsible for initiating the craze for sensationalism; they both became famous overnight with early novels, *East Lynne* and *Lady Audley's Secret*; they were both extremely prolific, Mrs Wood producing over fifty novels and Miss Braddon over eighty, and both of them created heroines whose abandon and unrestraint, in defiance of Victorian propriety and decorum, constituted their fascination. But whereas Mrs Wood is moralising in her portrayal of the heroine dying of sin and remorse, Miss Braddon is tough and cynical, deliberately undermining traditional moral values and working on the subconscious anxieties of the age. In fact, some contemporary critics rightly saw Miss Braddon as the more dangerous, the more subversive of the two.

The well-educated daughter of a solicitor of a good family, Miss Braddon was supporting herself in London around 1860 by turning out lurid serials anonymously for the *Halfpenny Journal* and *Reynolds' Miscellany* when she met John Maxwell, a young magazine publisher. Her domestic life with Maxwell, with whom she had five illegitimate children, was her well-kept secret.[4] She is a rare example of a novelist who managed to cross the boundary between the newly literate audience, demanding murder and violence rendered in easily accessible language in the penny dreadfuls, and the general reading public subscribing to Mudie's Select Library at a guinea per annum.

Miss Jewsbury reviewed four of Miss Braddon's early novels for the *Athenaeum—Eleanor's Victory* (1863), *Sir Jasper's Tenant* (1865), *The Lady's Mile* (1866) and *Charlotte's Inheritance* (1868)—and recommended Bentley to take on *Aurora Floyd,* which she at once spotted as an embryonic best-seller when it was serialised in Maxwell's *Temple Bar* in the summer of 1862. However, when Maxwell asked £ 600 for it, her business sense let her down and she

---

[4] Hughes, *The Maniac in the Cellar,* p. 120.

urged Bentley not to go beyond £ 300.[5] This financially unsound advice added *Aurora Floyd* to Tinsley's list, a list which was to include *Lady Audley's Secret,* the hit of the season in the autumn of 1862. That Miss Jewsbury, like Henry James, admired *Aurora Floyd* is hardly surprising. Besides fulfilling all the requirements of an exciting plot contingent on a secret, a strong air of suspense sustained to the end and wicked characters, it also presented two contrasting female figures who would have caught Miss Jewsbury's interest. Herself very unfeminine, independent, smoking and making men offers, she must have been delighted with Miss Braddon's satire on the Amelia Sedley type of heroine, so cleverly drawn in Lucy Floyd, Aurora's cousin:

> Talbot Bulstrode's ideal of woman was some gentle and feminine creature crowned with an aureole of pale auburn hair; some timid soul with downcast eyes, fringed with golden tinted lashes; some shrinking being, as pale and prim as the mediaeval saints in his pre-Raphaelite engravings, spotless as her own white robes, excelling in all womanly graces and accomplishments, but only exhibiting them in the narrow circle of a home.[6]

It is noteworthy that the woman ideal held up for emulation by Miss Yonge and others in the early 1850s had altered in the 1860s, when "fast" young women became so common as to enable Miss Braddon to mock at the meek Lucy Floyd.

Though an admirer of *Aurora Floyd,* Miss Jewsbury was disappointed in *Eleanor's Victory,* the first Braddon novel she reviewed for the *Athenaeum.* To her it seemed "inferior in force and interest both to 'Lady Audley's Secret' and 'Aurora Floyd' . . . since there is less substance in the plot, and far less interest in the working out" (Sept. 19, 1863, p. 362). The review is, however, devoted to a discussion of Miss Braddon's talent and to a plot summary of *Eleanor's Victory* and does not really pinpoint her objections to the novel.

Sir Jasper's Tenant, Miss Braddon's eighth three-volume novel, hardly rises above the level of mechanical ingenuity, and not unexpectedly Miss Jewsbury comments on "the general resemblance in the structure of her plots" (Oct. 21, 1865, p. 537). Contrary to the *Spectator's* and the *Saturday's* wholesale denunciation of what they saw as a defective and weak novel, Miss Jewsbury adopts a surprisingly lenient attitude in the *Athenaeum.* She was simply carried away by its readableness, praising not only Miss Braddon's remarkable power of observation and her ability to reproduce conversation but, more specifically, her excellence at what she called "scene-painting" which turned her stories into plays.

The tremendous success of *Lady Audley's Secret* proved Miss Braddon's for-

---

[5] Gettman, *A Victorian Publisher,* pp. 201—02.
[6] Mary Elizabeth Braddon, *Aurora Floyd,* (Leipzig: Tauchnitz, 1863), I, 51.

tune as well as her literary fate. To continue as a bestseller writer meant satisfying the public's demand and attempts to deviate from the self-imposed pattern might risk her earning capacity. In 1866, however, Miss Braddon abandoned murder and mystery and wrote her first social novel, *The Lady's Mile,* which contains, as her biographer argues, "in embryo many elements of her 'new manner.' "[7] This interesting novel challenges the cherished mid-Victorian myths of respectability and the feminine ideal and exposes the marriage market and the hollowness of matrimony. The Lady's Mile, the famous carriage path in Hyde Park which gives the novel its name, is made to symbolise the confines of a respectable woman's actions. Having crossed "the barrier" by living with Maxwell, Miss Braddon was no doubt aware of the ostracism that awaited women like herself, once the secret was revealed. Mr Smythe, in the novel, explains women's dilemma at the opening of *The Lady's Mile* thus:

> The lives of the women of the present day are like this drive which they call the Lady's Mile. They go as far as they can, and then they go back again . . . If they went any farther, I suppose they would be lost in some impenetrable forest depth in Kensington Gardens . . . the barrier that divides the path from the gardens is a palpable iron railing . . . But on the highway of life the boundary-line is not so clearly defined. There are women who lose themselves in some unknown region beyond the Lady's Mile, and whom we never hear of more . . . On this side, the barrier they pass seems so slight a one . . . but when the desperate wanderer pauses for a moment on the other side to look backward, behold! the thorny hedgerow is transformed into a wall of brass that rises to the very skies, and shuts out earth and heaven.[8]

The *Athenaeum* review of *The Lady's Mile* reveals some of Miss Jewsbury's limitations as a critic. When Miss Braddon resigned "her sceptre over the realm of the sensation novel" and chose to depict manners and morals, the result of this change was, according to Miss Jewsbury, dull. Her failure to discern Miss Braddon's undeniable talent for social satire can only be explained by the fact that she had expected to find another mystery story. One even suspects that she might have resorted to skimming and skipping, consequently not seeing the real merits of the novel, merits that one would expect Miss Jewsbury to be the first to detect.

Whereas Miss Jewsbury's judgment of *The Lady's Mile* can be summed up in the word "dull," the *Saturday,* more perceptively, dwelt on Miss Braddon's severe criticism of the marriage system. Focusing on two heroines, Florence Crawford, a mercenary girl who admittedly "sells" herself "for diamonds, and carriages, and horses, and servants" (II, 137), to a rough Manchester millionaire, and Lady Cecil, who marries without love a true-hearted and

[7] Wolff, *Sensational Victorian,* p. 178.
[8] Mary Elizabeth Braddon, *The Lady's Mile* (Leipzig: Tauchnitz, 1866), I, 17—18.

generous barrister, Laurence O'Boyneville, who neglects her for his work, *The Lady's Mile* was, according to the *Saturday,* "uncomfortable" reading for all married men. Miss Braddon's picture of conjugal unhappiness was not only disturbing, it was disconcerting to the mid-Victorian ideal of womanly purity that "the comely and agreeable matron at the other side of the hearth is at any given moment meditating flight with a suitor of bygone days" (May 12, 1866, p. 565).

The plot of *The Lady's Mile* did not violate the moral code of the time: both heroines avoid crossing the barrier that divides the path from the gardens. Whereas Florence turns down the proposal from the lord she has been flirting with, Lady Cecil narrowly escapes eloping with her old suitor and only love, Hector Gordon. But what neither Miss Jewsbury nor the *Saturday* perceived was that this, now little known, novel not only presents a grave criticism of matrimony, but even argues for woman's freedom from male dominance. Had they done justice to this aspect of the novel, they would have judged it just as perilous for young women readers as Rhoda Broughton's "wicked" novels. Just because there were no scenes conflicting with the Victorian sense of prudery, nothing violating the sexual code, the novel was supposed to be harmless. But, anticipating the attack on the institution of marriage in, for instance, Gissing's *The Odd Women,* Hardy's *Jude the Obscure* and Ibsen's *A Doll's House, The Lady's Mile* exposes the sufferings of women who have submitted to the bondage of a marriage without love and implicitly argues for women's freedom. Mrs Champernowne, a thirty-year-old widow is, no doubt, Miss Braddon's mouthpiece in the novel. Having been married off to a stranger on leaving her convent, she recalled how she "had the best and kindest of masters . . . but it was bondage, and I thirsted for liberty" (II, 161). Contrasted with the two "bondslaves" Florence and Lady Cecil, Mrs Champernowne becomes Miss Braddon's herald of a new age, an age when women would no longer have to sell themselves to get a home:

> This was the woman who had enslaved many men, but for whom independence was too dear a treasure to be bartered lightly. She had been the slave of an old man's caprices, and had endured her slavery with all womanly patience and gentleness; but having won her freedom, she was not inclined to accept any new bondage. (II, 286)

Blind to Miss Braddon's attempt to give a psychologically convincing picture of a woman hovering on the brink of adultery while fighting against the temptation of leaving her home "for the fatal protection of a lover" and ignoring Miss Braddon's implicit message that woman's happiness lay in love and independence, rather than in family and duty, Miss Jewsbury was in this instance curiously imperceptive, merely associating the author's name with the staple of *Lady Audley.*

Miss Jewsbury accepted the sensation novels of Mrs Wood and Miss Braddon, but the "unhealthy" products of Ouida and Rhoda Broughton, the two other very popular women novelists of the 1860s, called down her reprobation. When Tauchnitz included Ouida's dashing romances of fashionable life among Disraeli, Kingsley, Eliot and Dickens in his "Collection of British Authors" series, her fame spread all over Europe and to America. Her name became synonymous with "romantic absurdity, sentimental extravagance, and exaggerated inaccuracy,"[9] but, above all, with "wicked."[10] Everyone read Ouida, although, as Dobrée points out, "her books were not allowed to lie about on drawing-room tables,"[11] and the craze for her novels was compared by the *Contemporary Review* to "a sort of mental dram-drinking."[12] The sharp social divisions of Victorian society may explain her tremendous appeal: middle-class people were eager to find out how fashionable society lived and how emancipated it was and Ouida's depictions of high life fulfilled their expectations.[13]

Miss Jewsbury urged Bentley not to publish Ouida's novels. *Under Two Flags* was, she reported, so "trashy & meretricious" that, although it would no doubt prove profitable, it would *"lower the character of yr house."*[14] Applying the same criteria by which she judged domestic novels, she contended that this novel was *"not* a story that will do any man or woman or child any good to read."[15] Yet Geraldine Jewsbury's reviews of five of Ouida's early novels, *Strathmore* (1865), *Chandos* (1866), *Idalia* (1867), *Under Two Flags* (1867) and *Tricotrin* (1868) prove that even a staunch advocate of domestic realism slowly gave way to "mental dram-drinking" and let herself reluctantly be swept into Ouida's exuberant world of imagination. Her attitude was ambivalent, however. Although she found *Strathmore* "interesting," it was "as fantastic and unwholesome as the smoke which curls up from the perfumed pipe of the smoker of haschish" (July 29, 1865, p. 142). Susceptible to the narcotic effect of Ouida's novels, she began to apply solely the criterion of readability when judging *Chandos.* Here the novelist turns "her kaleidoscope so briskly," she stated, "that the reader is never allowed to stop to expose or protest against the nonsense in which he is involved" (June 16, 1866, p. 797).

[9] Malcolm Elwin, *Victorian Wallflowers: Studies in Nineteenth Century English Literature* (London: Jonathan Cape, 1934), p. 282.

[10] Alan F. Walbank, ed., *Queens of the Circulating Library: Selections from Victorian Novelists 1850—1900* (London: Evans Brothers Ltd., 1950), p. 155.

[11] Edith C. Batho and Bonamy Dobrée, *The Victorians and After, 1830—1914* (London: Cresset Press, 1938), p. 319.

[12] Vincent E.H. Murray, "Ouida's Novels," *Contemporary Review,* 22 (1873), 921.

[13] Elwin, *Victorian Wallflowers,* p. 299 and Eileen Bigland, *Ouida,* pp. 34—35.

[14] Letter from GEJ to Bentley quoted by Rosenmayer in "Geraldine Jewsbury: Novelist and Publisher's Reader," p. 567.

[15] Letter from GEJ to Bentley quoted by Gettman in *A Victorian Publisher,* p. 196.

Accustomed to Ouida's "torrents of words" which she thought "utter nonsense," Miss Jewsbury nevertheless admits that *Idalia* is "both easy and entertaining to read" (March 2, 1867, p. 283): in fact, she even confesses that "it is decidedly pleasant to be taken so completely out of the region of realities" (March 2, 1867, p. 283). But it would not do for an *Athenaeum* reviewer to devour *Idalia* like an anodyne. To appease her conscience, she pointed to the unwholesome bent of the novel: reading it is, she admitted, like "inhaling the perfumed smoke of incense; it is a novel that produces a sense of dissipation in the reader." Thrilled by the adventures of Sir Fulke Erceldoune, so fantastic that "the Three Musketeers rolled into one would have . . . failed under the tasks," Miss Jewsbury obviously disapproved of the novel's sensuality which might "turn the heads of susceptible youths" and "exercise a perilous influence over the gentler sex" (March 2, 1867, p. 283). Idalia was much more "wicked" than Aurora Floyd or Lady Isabel Carlyle, for she could inspire love in a man, which, as Ouida tells us, "sweeps away his memory, his honour, his reason, his ambitions, his very nature."[16] Idalia's and Erceldoune's passionate love indeed breaks the bonds of mid-Victorian conventions and consequently was considered harmful by Miss Jewsbury. When the hero held Idalia in his arms "with the loosened trail of her hair floating over his chest and his ceaseless kisses on her lips" (II, 158), "when his heart throbbed against hers . . . she had known that she had loved him with the love she had deemed . . . impossible to her nature" (II, 36). It is curious, however, that Miss Jewsbury chose not to comment on a more unusual side of Idalia. A woman of rare courage, integrity and enterprise, she "knew that she had in her what would have found power to rule an empire" (II, 32). Faced with imprisonment and torture, she refuses to yield to her enemy and thus betray her friends. Her courage makes the villain Villaflor exclaim: " 'Mother of God! What a man you would have been!—you would have ruled the world!' " (II, 32) Although Miss Jewsbury did not comment on Idalia's "masculine" qualities, it was no doubt precisely the combination of passion and power in Ouida's heroine that appealed to mid-Victorian women who looked to fiction as an escape from the boredom of their daily lives.

Under Two Flags enjoyed a more lasting fame than any of Ouida's previous novels and introduced her most famous hero and heroine, Bertie Cecil, "Beauty" of the Guards, and Cigarette. Numbed perhaps by what the *Spectator* called the "epicene" tone of the book (Feb. 1, 1868, p. 138), Miss Jewsbury objected only mildly to Ouida's heroes, who seemed to her an "immortal" kind of "well-made marionettes." But the *Saturday* was more severe in its criticism. It hoped that it had "seen the last of curaçao-drinking, velvet-clad, idiotic young noblemen, with muscles developed in direct proportion to their vices,

[16] Ouida, *Idalia. A Romance* (Leipzig: Tauchnitz, 1867), II, 30.

Cover of Swedish edition of the second part of Ouida's *Under Two Flags*. Stockholm, 1923.

and in inverse proportion to their brains" (Jan. 25, 1868, p. 121). All three weeklies reflect contemporary critics' ambivalence to Ouida's feverish romances: they all use such words as "interesting," "absurd," "impossible," "unwholesome," "talent" and "merit." Perhaps their attitude illustrates their inability to fit the eccentric Ouida into any of the existing standard compartments of romance, sensationalism and domestic realism.

Whereas Mrs Wood and Miss Braddon had respectively nineteen and ten books listed in the Catalogue of Mudie's Select Library for 1869, there was one writer who was too "wicked" to find favour with Mudie in the sixties—Rhoda Broughton. Creating a scandal with her first two novels *Not Wisely, But Too Well* (1867) and *Cometh Up as a Flower* (1867), she gained wide popularity and was favourably received at the publication of *Red As a Rose Is She* (1870) and *Good-bye Sweetheart!* (1872). However, Miss Jewsbury's connection with Miss Broughton is confined to her first two novels, which she read in manuscript for Bentley. Since she only reviewed *Cometh Up* for the *Athenaeum,* her attitude to Miss Broughton must be inferred both from her reaction to this novel and to *Not Wisely* as revealed in her reader's report. Apparently Rhoda Broughton believed that Miss Jewsbury alone was responsible for the reviewing of her novels in the *Athenaeum,* for after the publication of *Red As a Rose Is She,* she wrote to Bentley, her publisher, that she was "surprised at the mildness of *Athenaeum's* abuse. I am sure I dont recognise old Jewsbury's pen dipped in vinegar and gall."[17] Highly sensitive to the pain negative reviews inflicted on her, Miss Broughton revealed her anguish in a letter to Bentley:

> I positively *dread* the *Saturday.* I cannot get used to the coarse and indiscriminate abuse with which I am belaboured. To my dying day it will make me wince. It is so bitter not to be able to answer: to sit under their gross unfairness—their flagrant misrepresentations.[18]

But in 1894, fourteen years after Miss Jewsbury's death, Rhoda Broughton did answer: in the ruthless portrait of Miss Grimstone in *A Beginner,* she caricatured this *Athenaeum* reviewer, whose criticism of *Cometh Up* had been devastating.[19] Having failed with her own novel, the awe-inspiring Miss Grimstone "tomahawks" novels for the *Porch,* slaying them with her "vindictive pen."[20] *A Beginner* denounces the absurd power of anonymous critics and ridicules readers' willingness to let themselves be manipulated. The heroine, Emma Jocelyn, is told by her publisher that "it needs only a distinct expression of approval from one or two of the organs, to which the sheeplike race of

---

[17] Letter quoted in Michael Sadleir, *Things Past,* (London: Constable, 1944), p. 104.
[18] Letter of Nov. 28, 1873 to Bentley quoted in Sadleir, *Things Past,* p. 106.
[19] Elaine Showalter, *A Literature of Their Own,* p. 177.
[20] Rhoda Broughton, *A Beginner* (London: Bentley and Son, 1894), pp. 142 and 144.

circulating-library readers look to make up their minds for them, in order to blossom into a distinct success" (pp. 131—32).

Why then were over ten thousand copies sold of *Cometh Up As a Flower* within seven years,[21] and why was it not available in 1869, two years after its publication, at Mudie's Select Library? Of course, one might argue that since Mudie could not satisfy the readers' demand, they bought their own copies,[22] but the question of the popularity of *Cometh Up* and *Not Wisely* remains to be answered. The *Spectator* was not far off the mark when it pronounced Miss Broughton a "novelist of revolt" (Oct. 19, 1867, p. 1173). With unparallelled frankness, her first two novels describe the strong feelings of young girls falling in love and hint at their frustration and sexual needs in a male-dominated society. What stamped Rhoda Broughton as a dangerous new voice and made her a rebel in the eyes of her contemporaries was her rejection of the reticence and prudery which novelists of the time, from Trollope to Mrs Oliphant, had tacitly observed. It is precisely this revolt that merits our attention. In her "determination not to be mawkish and missish," Trollope says in his *Autobiography,* "she has made her ladies do and say things which ladies would not do and say"[23]: their actions and feelings revealed a repressed sexuality in women that the mid-Victorians preferred to ignore.

Not Wisely, But Too Well, on which Miss Jewsbury wrote a very negative report to Bentley,[24] tells the story of the "soft," "round," "fully-developed" Kate Chester, a passionate girl who "would flirt with the undertaker who came to measure her for her coffin,"[25] and the self-indulgent Colonel Dare Stamer, who had "not done one atom of good to any human being" and to whom "women were fair game" (I, 50). In this young girl, brought up in a middle-class

---

[21] Walbank, *Queens of the Circulating Library,* p. 193.

[22] Bentley's printings of *Cometh Up as a Flower* were as follows:

March 2, 1867	500 copies at 21 sh.
July, 1867	250 copies at 21 sh.
Sept. 1867	250 copies at 21 sh.
Nov. 21, 1867	1,500 copies at 6 sh.
1868	2,250 copies at 6 sh.
1870	1,000 copies at 6 sh.
1871	1,000 copies at 6 sh.
1872	1,000 copies
1873	1,250 copies
1874	1,500 copies
1876	1,500 copies
1878	2,500 copies

A List of the Principal Publications Issued from New Burlington Street, 1829—1898 (London: Richard Bentley and Son, 1893—1920).

[23] Trollope, *Autobiography,* p. 235.

[24] Rosenmayer, "Geraldine Jewsbury," p. 649.

[25] [Rhoda Broughton], *Not Wisely, But Too Well* (Leipzig: Tauchnitz, 1867), I, 260.

English home, "there were wells of undeveloped passion . . . whose depths his [Col. Stamer's] plumb-line could not fathom" (I, 52). Contemplating Col. Stamer, she experienced feelings which were highly unbecoming to a mid-Victorian maiden:

> . . . every minute, there was revealed to her, within her soul, a bottomless depth, a wild, mad, reckless fervour of passion, which bid fair to blast all the life that lay before her . . . withering up all her little innocent joys with the furnace-breath of its fiery flame, taking the sap out of her girl's pleasures. (I, 47—48)

Hovering on the brink of elopement and adultery, Kate resists temptation and remains virtuous. But the moral foundation of the novel is only apparent, for its dominating theme is the sensuality and secret yearnings of a young girl, a theme which was, as contemporary observers feared, bound to stir up perilous feelings in women readers who recognised a part of themselves never spoken about openly.

In her private life a passionate woman without maidenly reserve, Geraldine Jewsbury, the reader and the reviewer, identified herself with the official code of prudery and reticence and denounced *Not Wisely* in her Bentley report, as "the most thoroughly sensual tale I have read in English for a long time—artless imitation & exaggeration of Guy Livingstone only *without* the talent."[26]

Miss Jewsbury did her utmost to stop Bentley from publishing Rhoda Broughton's early novels. Ruled by her sense of propriety, she failed to appreciate Miss Broughton's unrestrained rendering of women's emotions. The *Spectator,* on the other hand, greeted *Not Wisely* as a prose paean to love: the author had represented "a delirium of passion, a love fever, such as hitherto only poets have ventured to depict" (Oct. 19, 1867, p. 1173) and Kate Chester was compared in this review to Francesca of Rimini. However, it is probably only because adultery was depicted as a degradation and because the novel was a powerful lesson of how temptations should be met, that the *Spectator* could praise it.

Miss Jewsbury's *Athenaeum* review of *Cometh Up As A Flower* was devastating: in horror, she suggested that it was the work of a man, "destitute of refinement of thought or feeling, and ignorant of all that women either are or ought to be" (April 20, 1867, p. 514). The "mixture of slang and sensuality," the "sensual sentimentality" and the "self-indulgent emotion" permeating the novel were what Miss Jewsbury objected to. Strongly averse to the direct representation of love scenes, she found the account of Nelly Lestrange (the heroine) "coarse and flippant even as the confidential narrative of a fast young man of the order of 'jolly dogs' to a kindred companion" (April 20, 1867, p.

---

[26] Report to Bentley of July 2, 1866 quoted in Rosenmayer, p. 562.

514). Miss Jewsbury attacked the supposedly male author for misrepresenting women's feelings: "the only two phases of existence which the author ... seems to think women recognize, are the delight of being kissed by a man they like, and the misery of being kissed by one they don't like. These two points seem to fill up his idea of the whole duty of women" (April 20, 1867, pp. 514—15). Had she but known that the anonymous novelist was a woman, her censure would have been still graver. In offering undesirable patterns of female behaviour and in revealing the hidden emotions of mid-Victorian women, Rhoda Broughton transgressed the tacit moral code which denied women sexuality and lifted the veil from a territory whose existence the prudish Miss Jewsbury, in her official role, preferred to ignore.

The reasons for Miss Jewsbury's strong reaction against *Cometh Up* can only be appreciated by a brief look at the novel itself. By strolling alone in a church-yard late in the evening, Nelly Lestrange, with "red hair and a wide mouth," sets the tone of unladylike behaviour at the opening of the novel, an impression that is re-inforced by her clandestine meetings with Major Richard (Dick) M'Gregor, "a tall, broad-shouldered man," with "a beautiful bronzed face, with the scar of a sabre running down the cheek." Nelly experiences dangerous feelings, implying her latent sexuality, feelings which Dick brings to the surface: "the dark gray eyes looked full into mine, with an expression I had never seen in mortal eyes before; an expression that sealed my lips, and sent a sort of odd shiver—a shiver that had nothing to say to cold, through my frame."[27] Driven to marry the wealthy Sir Hugh, partly to save her aged father from debts, the unhappy Nelly meets her beloved, bound for India with his regiment, one last time. Only his sense of honour saves her from eloping. In substance this scene does not differ much from Lady Cecil's planned elopment with her old lover from her loveless home and uncongenial husband in Miss Braddon's *The Lady's Mile,* but what distinguishes Miss Braddon from Miss Broughton is that whereas the former implicitly suggests feelings, avoiding uncontrolled out-bursts of passion, the latter lets her heroine act and talk with an abandon that was as startling as it was unacceptable in a novel intended for family reading:

> "If you go," I said in my insanity, throwing myself into his arms, "I'll go too. Oh! for God's sake take me with you!"
> He strained me to his desolate heart, and we kissed each other wildly, vehemently . . .
> "Oh, take me, take me with you!"
> My hair fell in its splendid ruddy billows over his great shoulder, and my arms were flung about the stately pillar of his throat . . .
> "For God's sake stop tempting me! I'd sooner cut your throat than take you! Do you think it would be loving you to bring you down to a level with the scum of the earth?" (pp. 343—44)

[27] [Rhoda Broughton], *Cometh Up as a Flower. An Autobiography* (Leipzig: Tauchnitz, 1867), p. 34.

Though a warning against illicit love in line with the official morality code, such a scene illustrated the passion that turned a moral scene into an immoral one and contributed to making Miss Broughton unacceptable to Miss Jewsbury, and to Mr Mudie until well into the 1870s when the moral climate had altered.

In her review, Geraldine Jewsbury quoted Nelly Lestrange's mercenary attitude to her marriage to Sir Hugh as an example of the novel's coarseness. But what the *Athenaeum* reviewer, so shocked by the novel as a whole, overlooked was that Nelly's flippant tone concealed the suffering of a women who had sacrificed herself to save her beloved father threatened by constant financial worries: Miss Jewsbury was not perceptive enough to hear the despair of many Victorian women in Nelly's ponderings on her wedding morning:

> I felt no tremor, no shyness; only a huge loathing, an infinite despair! One forgets to be coy and maidenly, when one's every pulse and nerve is thrilling with a mighty horror; when, loving one man frenziedly, one is about to be delivered over, bound to the tender mercies of another. (p. 309)

Asking for money from her fiancé, Sir Hugh, Nelly comments on the bartering aspect of her future marriage with a flippancy that reveals more than it conceals: " 'If I take money from you I must marry you,' I said calmly, 'I could not do it else.' It seemed to me the most matter-of-fact piece of barter in the world; so much young flesh and blood for so much current coin of the realm" (p. 291). The physical repulsion Nelly feels for her husband was a dangerous confession to make, dangerous because it went against the grain of the picture of the ideal family even to hint at physical incompatibility between man and wife. Sir Hugh's "property," she must tacitly abide his caresses while her "buyer's arm—that arm which seems to be burning into my flesh like a brand" (p. 304) lay around her waist. The fact that Miss Broughton refused to paint the conventional picture of the meek wifely paragon and in its stead confronted her readers with a young wife who felt like a branded bondslave was reason enough for conservative critics like Miss Jewsbury to reject her.

With regard to Rhoda Broughton, Geraldine Jewsbury's taste differed widely from that of the reading public. For a less negative opinion we must go to the *Spectator's* courteous review which suggested that "Rhoda's studies of female sensuality are part of a wiser apprehension of women's roles in the climate of mid-Victorian social change" (Oct. 19, 1867, p. 1173). In other words, eyeing the "wicked" sixties with a nostalgia for the respectable, domestic fifties, Miss Jewsbury was willing to accept crime but not sex: whereas Mrs Wood and Miss Braddon both found favour with her, the "wicked" Ouida and Rhoda Broughton were beyond the pale.

Appendix
Checklist of Geraldine Jewsbury's *Athenaeum* Reviews

Below is a chronological list of Miss Jewsbury's reviews in the *Athenaeum*. For the sake of space, long titles have been shortened whenever it does not affect the identification of the book and publishers' names have been omitted. Original spelling and capitalisation have been retained. Reviews which open a weekly number of the *Athenaeum* are preceded by "(opens issue)" and reviews which are found in separate sections are marked "NN" = "New Novels," "NW" = "Novels of the Week" and "OLT" = Our Library Table." A few novels were considered important enough to be reviewed separatedly, outside any of these sections.

The attribution of anonymous books and of the numerous books published under "By the Author of . . ." is a major problem. Whenever I have been able to trace the author's name, it is given within square brackets. In my search for authors, I have relied on William Abbatt, comp., *The Colloquial Who's Who: An Attempt to Identify the Many Authors, Writers and Contributors Who Have Used Pen-Names, Initials, etc. (1600—1924). Also a List of Sobriquets, Nicknames, Epigrams, Oddities, War Phrases etc.* 2 vols. (New York: Argonaut Press Ltd., 1966); *The British Museum Catalogue of Printed Books*; William Cushing, *Anonyms: A Dictionary of Revealed Authorship* (London: Sampson Low, Marston, Searle & Rivington, 1890) and James Kennedy et al. eds., *Dictionary of Anonymous and Pseudonymous English Literature* 6 vols. By Samuel Halkett and John Laing. (Edinburgh: Oliver and Boyd, 1926).

1849

March 17
Margaret. A Tale of the Real and the Ideal. [Sylvester Judd] pp. 270—72.

1850

Oct. 19
Anschar: a Tale of the North. By R.J. King-Parker. pp. 1087—88.

1851

April 19
Yeast. A Problem. [Charles Kingsley] p. 428.

Sept. 6
John Drayton, the Liverpool Engineer. [Margaret Oliphant] p. 948.

Sept. 13
Lady Selina Clifford. Edited by Lady Dormer. 2 vols. pp. 968—69.

Sept. 20
Life and Its Lessons. By Mrs. Hubback. 3 vols. pp. 992—93.

Sept. 27
OLT *Jasper Lyle: a Tale of Kafirland.* By Mrs. [Harriet] Warde. p. 1020.

Oct. 4
The Lily and the Bee. By Samuel Warren, F.R.S. pp. 1041—43.
OLT *Musgrove: a Story of Grisland Spa, and other Tales.* By Mrs. Gordon. 2 vols. p. 1045.

Oct. 11
Lady Avice. A Tale of the Day, pp. 1063—64.

Nov. 1
Deck and Port; or, Incidents of a Cruise to California. By the Rev. Walter Colton. p. 1140.

Nov. 29
The Fair Carew; or Husbands and Wives. pp. 1247—48.

Dec. 6
Daughter Deborah. By the Author of 'The Miser's Secret.' 3 vols. p. 1277.

1854

Feb. 11
OLT *Hester and Ellinor: A Tale.* p. 180
OLT *The Evil Star: A Novel.* By E. Colburn, Esq. 3 vols. p. 180.
OLT *The Phrenologist's Daughter: A Tale.* p. 181.
OLT *Revelations of School Life.* By Cantab. [George Simpson] 2 vols. p. 181.

Feb. 18
OLT *The Star-Chamber: an Historical Romance.* By W. Harrison Ainsworth. 2 vols. p. 211.
OLT *Lady Lee's Widowhood.* By Edward Bruce Hamley, Capt. R.A. 2 vols. p. 212.
OLT *Clinton: a Book for Boys.* By William Simonds. p. 212.

March 4
Maude Talbot. By Holme Lee. [Harriet Parr] 3 vols. pp. 270—71.
OLT *Agnes Valmar: a Novel.* 3 vols. p. 277.
OLT *Lessons and Trials of Life.* By the Author of 'Bertha's Journal.' [Jane Marcet] p. 277.
OLT *The Broken Sword; or, a Soldier's Honour.* By Adelaide O'Keeffe. p. 277.

March 11
OLT *Progress and Prejudice.* By Mrs. Gore. 3 vols. p. 310.
OLT *Walter Hurst; or, Early Struggles at the Bar.* By Herbert Greville Pelham. 3 vols. p. 310.
OLT *The Heiress of Somerton.* 3 vols. [Mrs. (or Miss) D. Spencer Thomson] p. 310.
OLT *World-Worship.* By Eleanor Griffiths. p. 310.

March 25
OLT BOOKS FOR CHILDREN pp. 373—74.
Memoirs of a Doll. Adapted from the French by Mrs. Besset.
The Lost Child: a Tale of London Streets. By Mrs. Besset.
A Home-Book for Children of all Ages.
Stuyvesant: a Franconia Story. —

Caroline:a Franconia Story.— Agnes: a Franconia Story. By Jacob Abbott.

April 1

Emmanuel Appadocca. By Maxwell Phillip. 2 vols. pp. 398—99.

OLT *Janet Mowbray.* By Caroline Grautoff. 3 vols. p. 404.

April 8

OLT *The Heir of Vallis.* By William Mathews. 3 vols. pp. 435—36.

April 15

Behind the Scenes; a Novel. By Lady Bulwer Lytton. 3 vols. pp. 460—61.

OLT *Atherton, and other Tales.* By Mary Russell Mitford. 3. vols. p. 463.

April 22

Philip Rollo. By James Grant. 2 vols. pp. 485—86.

OLT *Phemie Millar.* By the Author of 'The Kinnears.' [Henrietta Keddie] 3 vols. p. 490.

April 29

OLT *Nannette and her Lovers.* By Talbot Gwynne. p. 522.

OLT *The Lamplighter.* [Maria Susanna Cummins] p. 522.

May 6

OLT *The Great Highway.* By S.W. Fullom. 3 vols. p. 554.

OLT *Flora Lyndsay.* By Mrs. [Susannah] Moodie. 2 vols. pp. 554—55.

May 13

Angelo: a Romance of Modern Rome. 2 vols. p. 585.

May 20

The Iron Cousin. By Mary Cowden Clarke. 2 vols. pp. 612—13.

June 3

OLT *Vara; or the Child of Adoption.* p. 683.

June 10

Bokinga: a Novel. By Moreton Rae. p. 710.

June 17

OLT *The Pirate's Fort.* By Louisa Mac Nally. p. 749.

June 24

NN (whole section) *Hide and Seek.* By Wilkie Collins. 3 vols. p. 775.

NN *Edward Willoughby.* By the Author of 'The Discipline of Life,' & c. [Lady Emily Ponsonby] 2 vols. pp. 775—76.

NN *The English Envoy at the Court of Nicholas I.* By Miss Julia Corner. p. 776.

July 1

NN (whole section) *Dona Blanca of Navarre.* By Don Francisco Navarro Villoslada. 3 vols. pp. 811—12.

NN *Katherine Ashton.* By the Author of 'Amy Herbert,' & c. [Elizabeth Sewell] 2 vols. p. 812.

July 8

OLT *Sir Gervase Grey.* By Mrs. Gordon. 3 vols. p. 846.

July 15

NN (whole section) *Magdalen Hepburn.* By the Author of 'Passages in the Life of Mrs. Margaret Maitland.' [Margaret Oliphant] 3 vols. p. 874.

NN *Crewe Rise: a Novel.* By John Cordy Jeaffreson. 3 vols. p. 874.

OLT *Clara Morison: a Tale of South Australia during the Gold Fever.* 2 vols. [Catherine Ellen Spence] p. 879.

July 22

NN (whole section) *Jerningham: a Story.* 2 vols. p. 907.

Transmutations; or, the Lord and the Lout. By N. or M. p. 907.

July 29

OLT *The Lost Treasures; or, Scenes from the Drama of Life: a Tale.* p. 940.

OLT *Matrimonial Shipwrecks.* By Annette Marie Maillard. 2 vols. p. 940.

Aug. 5

OLT *The Life and Adventures of a Clever Woman.* By Mrs. Trollope. 3 vols. p. 969.

OLT *The Cabin by the Wayside: a Tale for the Young.* By Lady Campbell. p. 969.

Aug. 12
OLT *Lewell Pastures*. By the Author of 'Sir Fredrich Derwent,' & c. [Mary Rose Stuart Kettle] 2 vols. p. 992.
Vivia: a Journal. By Mrs. Elphinstone Dalrymple. 2 vols. p. 992.

Aug. 26
(open issue) *The Private Journal and Literary Remains of John Byrom*. Edited by Richard Parkinson. Vol. I., Part I. pp. 1033—35.
Fashion and Famine. By Mrs. Ann S. Stephens. pp. 1036—37.
OLT *Gold: a Tale for the Times*. p. 1042.
OLT *The Brief Career; or, the Jews's Daughter: a Novel*. By Capt. Horrocks. 3 vols. p. 1042.

Sept. 2
OLT *Clouds and Sunshine*. By Mary Alicia Taylor. p. 1065.
OLT *Man and Money; or, the Two Rivals*. From the French of Emile Souvestre. p. 1065.
OLT *The Vision of a Midsummer Morning Dream*. By F. Starr. p. 1065.

Sept. 23
Hungarian Sketches in Peace and War. From the Hungarian of Moritz Jökai. p. 1135.
OLT *Matthew Paxton*. Edited by the Author of 'John Drayton,' &c. [Margaret Oliphant] 3 vols. p. 1138.
OLT *Crystal Palace Guide*. By Samuel Phillips. p. 1138.
OLT *Ida May*. By Mary Langdon. Edited by an English Clergyman p. 1138.
OLT *Sabina: a Sicilian Tale of the Thirteenth Century*. By John Brampton Philpot. p. 1138.

Sept. 30
The Pride of Life: a Novel. By Lady Scott. 2 vols. p. 1167.
OLT *The Happy Colony*. By Robert Pemberton. p. 1169.

Oct. 7
OLT *The Convent and the Manse*. By Hyla [Jane Dunbar Chaplin]. p. 1198.

Oct. 14
OLT *Millie Howard*. By Mrs. Henry Lynch. p. 1232.

Oct. 21
NN (whole section) *Idaline: a Story of the Egyptian Bondage*. By Mrs. J. B. Webb. [Mrs. Annie Webb-Peploe] p. 1263.
NN *A Physician's Story*. By Heberden Milford. 3 vols. p. 1263.
NN *Life's Lesson: a Tale*. p. 1263.
OLT *Charles Dallaway; or, the Restless Man*. p. 1265.

Oct. 28
OLT *Sunbeams in the Cottage*. By Margaret Maria Brewster. p. 1302.
OLT *Sunshine and Gloom: a Tale of Modern Life, founded on Fact*. By William Gould. p. 1302.

Nov. 4
Zana; or, The Heiress of Clare Hall. By Mrs. Ann S. Stephen. pp. 1330—31.

Nov. 11
The Young Husband. By Mrs [Elizabeth Caroline] Grey. 3 vols. pp. 1363—64.
OLT *The Virginia Comedians; or, the Old Days in the Old Dominion*. 2 vols. p. 1366.
OLT *The Bride of the Wilderness*. By Emerson Bennett. p. 1366.
OLT *The School for Politics: a Dramatic Novel*. By Charles Gayarré. p. 1366.

Nov. 18
Heartsease; or, the Brother's Wife. By the Author of 'The Heir of Redclyffe.' [Charlotte Yonge] 2 vols. pp. 1396—97.
OLT *The Curate of Overton*. [Marion Harland] 3 vols. p. 1397.
OLT *Alone* p. 1397.

Dec. 2
NN (whole section) *May and December: a Tale of Wedded Life*. By Mrs. Hubback. 3 vols. pp. 1458—59.
NN *Arvon*. By C. Mitchell Charles. 2 vols. p. 1459.
OLT *The Last Earl of Desmond: a Historical Romance*. 2 vols. p. 1462.
OLT *Hope Campbell; or, Know Thyself*. By Colusin Kate. p. 1462.

OLT *Matrimonial Speculation.* By Mrs. Moodie. p. 1462.

Dec. 16
The House of Raby. [Jane Margaret Hooper] 3 vols. p. 1524.
OLT *The Old Chelsea Bun-House.* By the Author of 'Mary Powell.' [Anne Manning] p. 1525.
OLT *Anne Boleyn; or, the Suppression of the Religious Houses.* p. 1525.

Dec. 23
BOOKS FOR BOYS AND CHILDREN
A Boy's Adventures in the Wilds of Australia. By William Howitt.
The Castle Builders. By the Author of 'Heartsease.' [Charlotte Yonge]
Pippins and Pies. By J. Sterling Coyne.
The Blue Ribbons. By Anna Harriett Drury.
Faggots for the Fireside. By Peter Parley.
Emily Vernon; or, Filial Piety exemplified. By Mrs. Drummond.
Historical Chapters relating to many Lands. Adapted for Children.
The Young Child's Lesson Book; or, What shall I Learn First? By Mr. W. Cort.
Amusing Tales adapted to the Capacities of Children. By Miss Corner.
Esperanza; or, the Home of the Wanderers. By Anne Bowman. pp. 1556—57.
OLT *The Quiet Heart.* By the Author of 'Katie Stewart.' [Margaret Oliphant] p. 1557.
OLT *Women as they Are.* By the Author of 'Margaret; or, Prejudice at Home.' 2 vols. p. 1557.
OLT *Dashwood Priory.* By E. J. May. p. 1557.
OLT *Afraja: a Norwegian and Lapland Tale.* Translated by Edward Joy Morris. p. 1557.

1855
Jan. 6
OLT *Phillip Lancaster.* By Maria Norris. 3 vols. p. 15.
OLT *March Winds and April Showers.* By 'Acheta.' [L. M. Budgen] pp. 15—16.

OLT *Alice Nugent; or, Seed for Coming Days.* p. 16.
OLT *Charles Random; or, Lunatics at Large.* By Thomas White. 3 vols. p. 16.
OLT *Oakley Mascott: a Novel.* By L. Howe. 2 vols. p. 16.
OLT *Mary Ellis; or, Life and its Mistakes.* By A. Probirer. 3 vols. p. 16.

Jan. 13
OLT *Students Abroad.* By R.B. Kimball. p. 48.

Jan. 20
OLT *The Step-Son: a Domestic Romance of the Present Day.* By F. N. Dyer, Esq. 2 vols. p. 80.
OLT *Later Years.* By the Author of 'The Old House by the River.' [William Cowper Prime] p. 80.
OLT *A Dozen Pair of Wedding Gloves.* pp. 80—81.
OLT *My Brother; or, the Man of Many Friends.* By an Old Author. [Mrs Sarah Ellis] p. 81.

Jan. 27
The Warden. By Anthony Trollope. pp. 107—08.

Feb. 24
Mammon. By Mrs. Gore. 3 vols. p. 229.

March 3
OLT *The Cousins: a Tale.* With a Preface by the Author of 'Naomi.' [Annie Webb-Peploe] p. 263.
OLT *Past Meridian.* By Mrs. L. H. Sigourney. p. 263.
OLT *The Californian Crusoe.* p. 263.

March 10
OLT *The Family Feud.* By Adam Hornbook. p. 291.
OLT *The Riches of Poverty: a Tale.* By Mrs. Eccles. p. 291.

March 17
NN *The Secret History of a Household.* By the Author of 'Alice Wentworth.' [Noell Radecliffe] 3 vols. p. 314.
OLT *Quicksands of Fashion.* By Mrs. Martin Lucas. 3 vols. p. 319.

OLT *Married Women: a Novel*. By the Author of 'Broomhill; or, Country Beauties.' 3 vols. p. 319.

March 31
NN *Westward Ho!* By Charles Kinglsey. 3 vols. p. 376.

April 7
Sisters of Charity. By Mrs. Jameson. pp. 399—400.
NN *Thorney Hall*. By Holme Lee. [Harriet Parr] p. 403.
OLT *My Life; or, the Autobiography of a Village Curate*. By Eliza R. Rowe. p. 405.
OLT *Leaves from a Family Journal*. From the French of Émile de Souvestre. p. 405.

April 14
OLT *The Moslem and the Christian*. By Sadyk Pasha. 3 vols. p. 432.

April 28
The Life of the Rev. Robert Newton, D.D. By Thomas Jackson. p. 483.
OLT *The Wife's Trials: a Novel*. [Emma Worboise] p. 487.
OLT *A Romance of the Bush*. By E. P. R. p. 487.

May 5
OLT *Willy Reilly*. By William Carleton. 3 vols. p. 519.
A Long Look Ahead. By A. S. Roe. p. 519.
Some Account of Mrs. Clarinda Singlehart. By the Author of 'Mary Powell.' [Anne Manning] p. 520.

May 19
OLT *The Mormon's Own Book*. By T. W. P. Taylder. pp. 583—84.

May 26
The Monarchs of the Main. By George W. Thornbury. 3 vols. pp. 610—11.
OLT *The Exile: a Tale of the Sixteenth Century*. By Phillip Phosphoros. p. 618.
OLT *The Pride of the Mess*. By the Author of 'Cavendish.' [William Johnson Neale] p. 618.

May 26
OLT *My Brother's Keeper*. [Anna B. Warner] p. 618.
OLT *Sisters of Charity*. p. 619.

June 2
OLT *The Career of a Rising Man: a Novel*. By M. Viener. 3 vols. p. 643.
OLT *Love* versus *Law; or, Marriage with a deceased Wife's Sister: a Novel*. By Joseph Middleton. 3 vols. p. 643.
OLT *May Flowers*. By 'Acheta.' [Miss. L. M. Budgen] p. 644.

June 9
OLT *Cleve Hall*. By the Author of 'Amy Herbert.' & c. [Elizabeth Sewell] 2 vols. pp. 672—73.

June 16
OLT *Frank Hilton*. By James Grant. p. 704.
OLT *The Honeymoon*. By Alfred W. Cole. p. 704.
OLT *Stanhope Burleigh; or, the Jesuit in our Homes: a Novel*. By Helen Dhu. p. 704.

June 23
OLT *Lights and Shadows of English Life*. By the Authoress of 'Clara Cameron.' 3 vols. p. 731.
OLT *Inez: a Tale of the Alama*. p. 731.

June 30
OLT *Catherine Irving: a Novel*. By the Author of 'Ada Gresham.' [Mary Anne Needell] 3 vols. p. 760.

July 7
OLT *The Jealous Wife*. By Miss Pardoe. 3 vols. p. 789.
OLT *The Rival Roses*. By the Author of 'Royalists and Roundheads.' [Elizabeth M. Stewart] 3 vols. p. 789.
OLT *A Glance behind the Grilles of Religious Houses in France*. [Mrs. William Pitt Byrne, née Julia Clara Busk] p.790.

July 14
A Letter to the Queen on Lord Chancellor Cranworth's Bill. By the Hon. Mrs. Norton.

Woman in the Nineteenth Century. By Margaret Fuller Ossoli. Edited by B. Fuller. pp. 811—12.
OLT *The Hearts of Steel.* By James M'Henry, M. D. pp. 812—13.

July 21
OLT *Constantine; or, the Last Days of an Empire.* By Capt. Spencer. 2 vols. p. 841.
OLT *The World in Light and Shade.* By Alfred W. Cole. p. 841.
OLT *Olympia in the Crimea; or, the Cave of Inkermann.* p. 841.
OLT *The Search for a Publisher; or, Counsels for a Young Author.* p. 841.
OLT *Turn around my Dining-Room.* By W. Carr p. 841.

July 28
The Private Journal and Literary Remains of John Byrom. Edited by Richard Parkinson, D. D. Vol. I, Part II. pp. 871—72.
OLT *Anna Clayton; or the Mother's Trial. A Tale of Real Life.* [F. M. Dimmick] p. 873.
OLT *The Next-Door Neighbours.* By the Author of 'Temptation; or, a Wife's Perils.' [Caroline Leigh Gascoigne] 3 vols. p. 873.
OLT *Sunbeams—[Les Rayons du Soleil].* pp. 873—74.
OLT *Amy and her Mother: a Picture of Life.* By Edward Whitfield p. 874.

Aug. 4
OLT *Evelyn Lascelles: an Autobiography.* Edited by Julia Addison. 3 vols. p. 900.

Aug. 11
OLT *My Travels.* By Capt. Chamier. 3 vols. p. 925.
OLT *The Brothers Basset.* By Julia Corner. p. 925.
OLT *Motley.* By Cuthbert Bede, B. A. p. 925.
OLT *Le Curé Manqué; or, Social and Religious Customs in France.* By Eugène de Courcillon. p. 925.

Aug. 18
OLT *Paul Ferroll: a Tale.* By the Author of 'IX Poems by V.' [Caroline Clive] pp. 947—48.
OLT *My Brother's Wife: a Life History.* By Amelia B. Edwards. p. 948.
OLT *Narmo and Aimata: a Tale of the Jesuits in Tahiti.* p. 948.

Aug. 25
A Lost Love. By Ashford Owen. pp. 968—69.

Sept. 1
OLT *Martha. A Sketch from Life.* By Anthony Smith pp. 1001—02.
OLT *Love* versus *Money. A Novel.* 2 vols. p. 1002.
OLT *The Country Magistrate. A Novel.* By Lord B******* [Frederick Richard Chichester, Earl of Belfast] 3 vols. p. 1002.

Sept. 29
OLT *Little Millie, and her Four Places.* By Maria Brewster. p. 1115.
OLT *Adrien.* By Annette Marie Maillard. p. 1115.
OLT *Aristobulus.* By M. Kavanagh. 3 vols. p. 1115.
OLT *Selfishness; or, Seed Time and Harvest.* By Mrs. Toogood. p. 1115.

Oct. 6
The Prophets; or, Mormonism Unveiled. [Orvilla S. Belisle]
Female Life among the Mormons. By the Wife of a Mormon Elder Recently from Utah. [Maria Ward] pp. 1147—48.
OLT *My First Season.* By Beatrice Reynolds. Edited by the Author of 'Charles Auchester,' &c. [Elizabeth Sarah Sheppard] pp. 1150—51.
OLT *The Cabman's Holiday: a Tale.* By Catherine Sinclair. p. 1151.

Oct. 13
OLT *Tales.* By Annie C. Saunders. p. 1186.
OLT *Blenham.* By E. Elliott. p. 1186.

Nov. 17

NN *Kitty Lamere; or, a Dark Page of London Life: a Tale.* By Augustus Mayhew. p. 1335.

NN *Catherine the Egyptian Slave in 1852.* By the Rev. W. J. Beaumont, M. A. p. 1335.

NN *Cross Purposes; or, the Way of the World.* By Margaret Casson. p. 1335.

NN *The Last of the Czars.* By W. R. Brame. p. 1335.

NN *Tales for the Marines.* By the Author of 'Los Gringos.' [Henry Augustus Wise] p. 1335.

NN *The Watchman: a Tale.* By J. A. Maitland. p. 1335.

NN *Twice Married: a Story of Connecticut Life.* p. 1335.

NN *Ellie; or, the Duncan Comedy.* By John Esten Cooke. p. 1335.

NN *The Hidden Path.* By Marion Harland. p. 1335.

Nov. 24

OLT *Cross Purposes: a Novel.* By Catherine Sinclair. 3 vols. p. 1366.

OLT *The Lances of Lynwood.* By the Author of 'The Little Duke,' 'Heartsease,' & c. [Charlotte Yonge] p. 1366.

OLT *Charles Worthington.* By Harry Singleside. p. 1366.

OLT *Gilbert Massenger.* By Holme Lee. [Harriet Parr] p. 1366.

OLT *Everley: a Tale.* [Miss Cornish] p. 1366.

Dec. 1

OLT *Doctor Antonio: a Tale.* By the Author of 'Lorenzo Benoni.' [Giovanni Ruffini] pp. 1400—01.

OLT *Simplicity and Fascination.* By Anne Beale. 3 vols. p. 1401.

OLT *The Faces in the Fire.* By James Frederick Pardon. p. 1401.

OLT *Adventures of my Cousin Smooth.* By Timothy Simpleton p. 1401.

Dec. 8

OLT *Lilliesleaf.* [Margaret Oliphant] 3 vols. p. 1432.

OLT *The House of Elmore: a Family History.* [Frederick William Robinson] 3 vols. pp. 1432—33.

Dec. 15

OLT *The Adventures of the Caliph Haroun al Raschid.* Recounted by the Author of 'Mary Powell.' [Anne Manning]. p. 1464.

OLT *Alfred Leslie: a Story of Glasgow Life.* [Frederick Arnold] p. 1464.

OLT *Sir Thomas; or, the Adventures of a Cornish Baronet in North-Western Africa.* By Mrs. R. Lee. p. 1464.

OLT *Parish and other Pencillings.* By the Author of 'Kirwan's Letters' p. 1464.

My MS.: a Tale of Olden Islington. By the Author of 'Anne Boleyn.' p. 1464.

Dec. 22

OLT *The Red-Brick House.* By Hester Lynch. p. 1497.

OLT *Malvern; or, the Three Marriages.* By Mrs. Hubback. 3 vols. p. 1497.

OLT *The Yellow Frigate; or, the Three Sisters.* By James Grant. p. 1497.

OLT *The Battle on the Bosphorus.* By F. C. Armstrong, Esq. 3 vols. p. 1497.

OLT *Nonpareil House; or, the Fortunes of Julian Mountjoy.* By Henry Curling. 3 vols. p. 1497.

Dec. 29

OLT *The Birth-day Council; or, How to be Useful.* By Mrs. Alaric A. Watts. p. 1531.

OLT *Unconscious Influence.* By Catherine D. Bell. p. 1531.

OLT *Mia and Charlie; or, a Week's Holiday at Rydal Rectory.* p. 1531.

OLT *Dunellan Manse; or, Times and Trials of the Disruption.* By Sarah Elizabeth B. Patterson. p. 1531.

OLT *Blanche and her Betrothed.* Told by Herself. 3 vols. p. 1531.

1856

Jan. 5

NN *The White Chief: a Legend of Northern Mexico.* By Capt. Mayne Reid. 3 vols. p. 12.

NN *Christian Melville*. By the Author of 'Mathew[sic] Paxton.' [Margaret Oliphant] pp. 12—13.

NN *Zaidee: a Romance*. By Margaret Oliphant. 3 vols. p. 13.

Jan. 12

AMERICAN NOVELS

Helen Leeson. p. 40.

Lily. by the Author of 'Busy Moments of an Idle Woman.' p. 40.

Caste: a Story of Republican Equality, by S. A. Storey, jun. p. 40.

OLT *Rachel Gray: a Tale, founded on Fact*. By Julia Kavanagh. pp. 40—41-

Jan. 19

OLT *The Spirit of the Holly*. By Mrs. Owen, p. 73.

OLT *Jeanne de Vaudreuil; or, Humiliation*. p. 73.

OLT *Mary Mathieson; or, Duties and Difficulties*. [Mrs. Scott] p. 73.

OLT *Oeland: a Thread of Life*. By Alice Somerton. p. 73.

Jan. 26

NN (whole section) *The Lady of Fashion*. By the Author of 'The History of a Flirt.' 3 vols. p. 104.

NN *Princess Ilse: a Legend*. Translated from the German by Lady Maxwell Wallace. p. 104.

NN *Family Interests: a Story Taken from Life*. p. 104.

NN *A Book about Naughty Boys*. By Champfleure. p. 104.

NN *The Owlet of Owlstone Edge*. By the Author of 'S. Amolius,' & c. p. 104.

NN *Dorothy: a Tale*. [Margaret Agnes Colville] p. 104.

NN *Laura Gay: a Novel*. 2 vols. p. 104.

Feb. 9

OLT *The Bush-Boys; or, the History and Adventures of a Cape*. By Capt. Mayne Reid. p. 169.

OLT *Farmer and his Family in the Wild Karoos of Southern Africa*. By Capt. Mayne Reid. p. 169.

Feb. 16

OLT *Amberhill*. By A. J. Barrowcliffe. 2 vols. p. 199.

OLT *Man and his Money: its Use and Abuse*. By the Rev. W. K. Tweedie, D. D. p. 199.

OLT *Wings and Stings: a Tale for the Young*. By A.L.O.E. [Charlotta Tucker] p. 200.

Feb. 23

OLT *The Monctons: a Novel*. By Susannah Moodie. 2 vols. p. 231.

OLT *Claude de Vesci: a Tale*. 2 vols. p. 231.

March 1

After Dark. By Wilkie Collins. 2 vols. p. 260.

March 22

OLT *Our Own Story; or, The History of Magdalene and Basil St. Pierre*. By Selina Bunbury. 3 vols. p. 360.

March 29

OLT *Life's Chances: a Novel*. 3 vols. p. 393.

April 5

OLT *Madeline Clare; or, the Important Secret*. By Colburn Mayne, Esq. 3 vols. pp. 425—26.

April 12

NN *Margaret and her Bridesmaids*. By the Author of 'Woman's Devotion.' [Anne Marsh] 3 vols. p. 458.

April 26

THE WAR *Eastern Hospitals and English Nurses*. By a Lady Volunteer. 2 vols. pp. 484—85.

NN (whole section) *The Ring and the Veil: a Novel*. By James Augustus St. John. 3 vols. p. 520.

NN *Beyminstre*. By the Author of 'Lena,' & c. [Ellen Wallace] 3 vols. p. 520.

NN *John Halifax, Gentleman*. By the Author of 'The Head of the Family,' & c. [Dinah Mulock Craik] 3 vols. p. 520.

OLT *The Two Homes: a Tale.* By the Author of 'Amy Grant.' [Miss Hopton] p. 521.

May 10
NN *The Old Vicarge: a Novel.* By Mrs. Hubback. 3 vols. p. 584.
NN *Diamonds and Dust.* [Henry Noel Humphreys] 3 vols. p. 584.
NN *Chateau Lescure; or, the Last Marquis: a Story of Britanny and La Vendée.* p. 584.
OLT *The Emigrant's Home.* By W. H. G. Kingston, Esq. p. 584.
NN *Coldstreams and the Musqueteers: a Novel.* By Thomas Litchfield, Esq. 3 vols. p. 584.
OLT *The Wilderness of the World: a Novel.* By Eustace Mitford. 3 vols. p. 584.

May 24
Perversion; or, the Causes and Consequences of Infidelity: a Tale for the Times. [William John Conybeare] 3 vols. pp. 642—43.
NN (whole section) *The Heirs of Blackridge Manor.* By Diana Butler. 3 vols. p. 648.
NN *The Old Grey Church.* By the Author of 'Trevelyan.' 3 vols. [Lady Lucy Caroline Scott] p. 648.
NN *Leonora.* By the Hon. Mrs. Maberly. 3 vols. p. 648.
NN *Elsie Seymour; or, the Contrast.* By A. Wygorn. 3 vols. p. 648.
NN *Glenmorven; or, Nedley Rectory: a Tale.* By H. T. Mülissy. p. 648.
NN *Jerville: a Tale.* By the Rev. H. S. M. Hubert, M. A. pp. 648—49.
NN *The Way Home.* [Mrs. Margaret F. Barvour] p. 649.
NN *Sibert's Wold: a Tale.* By the Author of 'A Trap to Catch a Sunbeam,' & c. [Matilda Anne Mackarness] p. 649.
NN *Shoepac Recollections: a Wayside Glimpse of American Life.* By Walter March. p. 649.

June 7
AMERICAN TALES.
The Planter's Victim; or, Incidents in American Slavery. pp. 712—13.
Winny and I. p. 713.
The Widow Bedott Papers. With an Introduction. By Alice B. Neale. p. 713.
Rose Clark. By Fanny Fern. p. 713.
Nellie of Truro: a Tale from Life. [Mrs. Hornblower, née Jane Elizabeth Roscoe] p. 713.
Modern Pilgrims. p. 713.
Meister Karl's Sketch-Book. By Charles G. Leland. p. 713.

June 14
Hertha. By Fredrika Bremer. Translated by Mary Howitt. p. 739.

June 21
OLT *Veiled Hearts. A Novel.* By the Author of 'The Wife's Trials.' [Emma Jane Worboise] 3 vols. p. 778.
OLT *Randal Vaughan.* By C. Warren Adams, Esq. 2 vols. p. 778.

June 28
NN (whole section) *Evelyn Marston.* By the Author of 'Emilia Wyndham,' & c. [Anne Marsh-Caldwell] 3 vols. p. 808.
NN *The Linesman; or, Service in the Guards.* By Col. Elers Napier. 3 vols. pp. 808—09.
NN *Henry Lyle; or, Life and Existence.* By Emilia Marryat. 2 vols. p. 809.
NN *The Crown Ward.* By Archibald Boyd. 3 vols. p. 809.
NN *Clara Howard.* p. 809.
OLT *Ismeer; or, Smyrna and its British Hospital in 1855.* By a Lady. [Martha Nicol] p. 809.

July 5
OLT *The Beleaguered Hearth: a Novel.* p. 838.

July 19
NN (whole section) *The Man of the World; or, Vanities of the Day.* By W. S. Fullom. 3 vols. p. 896.
NN *Compensation, a Story of Real Life.*

[Lady Henrietta Georgiana Marcia Lascelles Chatterton]. 2 vols. p. 896.

NN *De Cressy: a Tale.* By the Author of 'Dorothy.' [Mrs. Margaret Agnes Paul] p. 896.

NN *Ellesmere; or, Contrasts of Character.* By L. S. Lavenu. 2 vols. pp. 896—97.

NN *Gloucester Cathedral.* By John Randal Clarke. p. 897.

NN *Sunshine and Shadow. A Novel.* By the Author of 'Mabel.' [Maria Susanna Cummins] p. 897.

NN *The Hugenot Exiles.* p. 897.

NN *Diana Wynyard.* By the Author of 'Alice Wentworth,' & c. [Noell Radecliffe] 3 vols. 897.

Aug. 2

NN *Claude Wilford: a Romance.* By T. One. pp. 959—60.

NN *Harry Ogilvie; or, the Black Dragoons.* By James Grant. p. 960.

NN *The Engima: a Leaf from the Archives of the Wolchorley House.* By an Old Chronicler. p. 960.

NN *The Green Hand: being the Adventures of a Naval Lieutenant.* By George Cupples. p. 960.

NN *Jessie Melville.* [David Pae] p. 960.

Aug. 9

AMERICAN BOOKS

Zoe; or, the Quadroon's Triumph. By Mrs. Elizabeth D. Liviemore. p. 991.

The Good Time Coming. By T. S. Arthur. pp. 991—92.

The Old Homestead. By Mrs. Anne Steevens. p. 992.

Wolfsden. By J. B. p. 992.

Wau-Bun; or, Early Days in the North-West. By Mrs. John H. Kinzie, of Chicago. p. 992.

Aug. 16

OLT *The Quadroon.* By Capt. Mayne Reid. 3 vols. p. 1019.

Aug. 23

NN (whole section) *Eveleen.* By E. L. A. Berwick. 3 vols. pp. 1050—51.

OLT *Ben Sylvester's Word.* By the Author of 'The Heir of Redclyffe,' & c. [Charlotte Yonge] p. 1051.

OLT *Helen Lincoln: a Tale.* By Carrie Capron. p. 1051.

Aug. 30

(opens issue) *Dred: a Tale of the Great Dismal Swamp.* By Harriet Beecher Stowe. pp. 1079—80.

Sept. 6

OLT *Zuriel's Grandchild: a Novel.* By R. V. M. Sparling. 3. vols. p. 1116.

OLT *A Boy's Voyage round the World.* p. 1116.

OLT *Sketches and Tales of the Shetland isles.* By Eliza Edmonston. p. 1116.

OLT *Characters and Incidents; or, Journeyings through England and Wales.* By J. W. King. p. 1116.

Sept. 13

NN (whole section) *Arthur Brandon: a Novel.* [Mrs. Mary Isabella Brotherton] 2 vols. p. 1140.

NN *Young Singleton.* By Talbot Gwynne. 2 vols. p. 1140.

OLT *The Merchant Vessel.* By the Author of 'Man-of-War Life.' p. 1141.

OLT *After the Wedding.* By the Author of 'Home Truths for Home Peace.' p. 1141.

OLT *The Happy Cottage.* By the Author of 'Kate Vernon,' &c. p. 1141.

Sept. 20

The Hills of the Shatemuc. By the Author of 'The Wide, Wide World.' [Elizabeth Wetherell] pp. 1163—64.

OLT *Memorials of Agmondesham and Chesham Leycester: in two Martyr Stories.* p. 1164.

OLT *The Sparrowgrass Papers; or, Living in the Country.* By Frederic S. Cozens. pp. 1164—65.

OLT *The French Pastor at the Seat of War.* By Emilien Frossard, Translated from the French. p. 1165.

OLT *The Blind Girl of Wittenberg.* Translated from the German, by John G. Morris. p. 1165.

Sept. 27
The Private Journal and Literary Remains of John Byrom. Edited by Richard Parkinson, D.D.F.S.A. Vol. II, Part I. pp. 1187—88.
OLT *Elmwood; or, Helen and Emma.* By Cora Mayfield. pp. 1188—89.

Oct. 11
OLT *Health and Beauty; or, Corsets and Clothing constructed in accordance with the Physiological Laws of the Human Body.* By Madame R. A. Caplin. pp. 1245—46.
OLT *The Draper in Australia.* p. 1246.

Oct. 18
NN (whole section) *Tender and True: a Colonial Tale.* By the Author of 'Clara Morison.' [Catherine Helen Spence] 2 vols. pp. 1272—73.
NN *The Double Coronet: A Novel.* By the Author of 'Charles Auchester.' [Elizabeth Sarah Sheppard] 2 vols. p. 1273.

Oct. 25
OLT *Old Memories: a Novel.* By Julia Melville. 3 vols. p. 1307.

Nov. 1
MINOR MINSTRELS (all) pp. 1334—35.
The Lonely Man of the Ocean: a Tale. By the Author of 'The Feast of Belshazzar.'
Vestigia. By One of the Million.
The Shadow of the Yew, and other Poems. Dedicated to the Author of 'Proverbial Philosophy.' By Norman B. Yonge.
Troubled Dreams: being Original Poems. By John Hautleigh.
Vernon: a Tale of the Sea. By Henry Bate.
David and Goliath: a Martial Lyric in Sixty-six Verses. By Thomas Henry Glamorgan.
The Fall of Sebastopol. By J. N. Crampton.
Pebbles from Parnassus.
A Summer Day Dream, and other Poems. By Theta.
The Cross Road: an Allegory. By H. F. Darwell.
Flowers and Fancies. By John Blackman.

Sequel to Neddy and Sally; or, Love and Glory. By John Brown.
Poems. By James Sykes.

Nov. 8
Mr. Arle: a Novel. [Emily Jolly] 2 vols. pp. 1368—69.
Kathie Brande: a Fireside History of a Quiet Life. By Holme Lee. [Harriet Parr] 2 vols. p. 1369.

Nov. 15
OLT *The City Banker.* By the Author of "Whitefriars" & c. [Emma Robinson] p. 1401.
OLT *The Story of my Wardship.* By Mary Catherine Jackson. 3 vols. pp. 1401—02.

Nov. 29
NN (whole section) *The Mildmayes; or, the Clergyman's Secret.* By Danby North. 3 vols. p. 1464.
NN *My Parish; or, 'The Country Parson's' Visits to his Poor.* By the Rev. Barton Bouchier, A. M. p. 1464.
NN *Ivors.* By the Author of 'Amy Herbert,' &c. [Elizabeth Sewell], p. 1464.

Dec. 6
BOOKS FOR CHILDREN (all)
Granny's Wonderful Chair. By Frances Brown. p. 1497.
Snow-Flakes and Sunbeams; or, the Young Fur Traders. By Robert Michael Ballantyne, Esq. p. 1497.
Gruffel Swilendrinken. By Alfred Crowquill. p. 1497.
Our Eastern Empire; or, Stories from the History of British India. By the Author of 'The Martyr Land,' & c. p. 1497.
Pictures from the Pyrenees; or, Agnes' and Kate's Travels. By Caroline Bell. p. 1497.
Julia Maitland; or, Pride goes before a Fall. By Mary and Elizabeth Kirby. p. 1497.
The Months: a Book for all Seasons. By George Frederick Pardon. p. 1497.
The Farm of Aptonga. By the Rev. J. M. Neale p. 1497.
Laugh and grow Wise. By the Senior Owl of Ivy Hall. p. 1497.

Dec. 13

NN *Prue and I.* By G. W. Curtis. p. 1534.

NN *What might have been; or, the Old Love and the New.* By the Author of 'Cross Purposes.' A Novel. 3 vols. p. 1534.

NN *The Myrtle and the Heather: a Tale.* By A. M. Goodrich. 2 vols. p. 1534.

Dec. 20

OLT *Jonathan Oldaker; or, Leaves from the Diary of a Commercial Traveller.* By J. Crawford Wilson. p. 1569.

OLT *Oliver Cromwell England's Great Protector.* By H. W. Herbert. p. 1569.

OLT *The Paragreens on a Visit to the Paris Universal Exhibition.* By the Author of 'Lorenzo Benoni,' & c. [Giovanni Ruffini] pp. 1569—70.

1857

Jan. 3

OLT *Sketches from Life.* By Harriet Martineau. pp. 14—15-

OLT *Saxelford: a Story for the Young.* By E. J. May. p. 15.

Jan. 17

MINOR MINSTRELS

The St. Lawrence and the Sanqenay. By Charles Sangster. pp. 79—80.

Lays of Memory, Sacred and Social. By a Mother and a Son. p. 80.

The Poetical Works of the late Alfred Johnstone Hollingsworth. Vol. I. pp. 79—80.

The Lee Shore. By Hamilton Moore, Esq., R. N. p. 80.

The Magic Word. By Alton. p. 80.

On Truth and Error. By John Hamilton. p. 80.

Jan. 24

OLT *The Early Dawn, or, Stories to think about.* By a Country Clergyman. p. 116.

Jan. 31

NN *Oliver Cromwell.* By Charles Edward Stewart. 2 vols. p. 148.

NN *The Old Home: a Tale.* By Mrs. Mackenzie Daniel[s]. 3 vols. p. 148.

NN *The Education of Character; with Hints on Moral Training.* By Mrs. Ellis. p. 149.

Feb. 7

OLT *Ernest Milman: a Tale of Manchester Life.* By Powys Oswyn. pp. 180—81.

Feb. 21

NN *Giulio Branchi: a Story of a Tuscan.* By Alfred Elwes. p. 243.

NN *Julia; or, the Neapolitan Marriage.* By Margaret Tullok. p. 243.

NN *Mormon Wives: a Narrative of Facts stranger than Fiction.* By Meta Victoria Fuller p. 243.

OLT *Whaling and Fishing: the Sequel to 'A Boy's Voyages.'* p. 244.

Feb. 28

Incidents of Travel and Adventure in the Far West. By N. S. Carvalho. pp. 272—73.

OLT *Autobiography of the Blind James Wilson.* By John Bird p. 278.

OLT *Joseph the Jew: a Tale founded on Facts.* By the Author of 'Mary Mathieson.' [Mrs. Scott] p. 278.

March 14

OLT *The Feminine Soul: its Nature and Attributes.* By Elizabeth Strutt. p. 341.

March 21

OLT *Western Border Life; or, What Fanny Hunter Saw and Heard in Kansas and Missouri.* p. 372.

OLT *Morning Clouds.* [Anne Judith Penny] p. 372.

March 28

NN *A Twine of Way-side Ivy.* By Margaret Casson. p. 405.

NN *The Burnish Family.* Prize Tale. p. 405.

OLT *Aldershot, and all about it.* By Mrs. Young. p. 405.

April 4

Anthony Burns: A History. By Charles Emery Stevens.

Autobiography of a Female Slave. [Mattie Griffiths]

Kansas; its Interior and Exterior Life. By Sara T. L. Robinson. pp. 433—34.

April 18
NN *Photo, the Suliote: a Tale of Modern Greece.* By D. R. Morier. Esq. 3 vols. p. 499.
NN *Marguerite's Legacy: a Novel.* 3 vols. By Mrs. T. F. Steward. pp. 499—500.
NN *The Star and the Cloud; or, a Daughter's Love.* By A. S. Roe. p. 500.
OLT *The Mormons: the Dream and the Reality.* Edited by a Clergyman. p. 500.

April 18
OLT *Deborah; or, Fireside Readings for Household Servants.* By the Rev. N. Macleod. p. 500.

May 9
OLT *Glenwood Manor House. A Novel.* By Esther Bakewell. p. 594.

May 23
Catherine de Vere: a Tale. By H. M. W. p. 661.
NN *The Rival Suitors: a Novel.* By Mrs. Hubback. 3 vols. pp. 661—62.
NN *The Wreckers.* By the Author of 'Smugglers and Foresters.' & c. [Mary Rosa Kettle] 3 vols. p. 662.
NN *The Sisters of Charity.* By Mrs. [Annie Emma] Challice. 2 vols. p. 662.
NN *Under the Lime Tree.* By Caroline Ricketts. p. 662.

June 13
OLT *Over the Sea; or, Letters from an Officer in India to his Children at Home.* p. 757.
OLT *The Unprotected; or, Facts in Dressmaking Life.* By a Dressmaker. [Marie Guignard] p. 757.
OLT *The Bay Path: a Tale of New England Colonial Life.* By J. G. Holland. p. 757.
OLT *Nightshade: a Novel.* By William Johnstone, M. A. pp. 757—58.

June 20
NN *Mothers and Sons: a Story of Real Life.* By William Platt, Esq. 3 vols. p. 789.

NN *Sivan the Sleeper: a Tale of all Time.* By the Rev. H. C. Adams. p. 789.
NN *Theodora Phranza; or, the Fall of Constantinople.* By the Rev. J. M. Neale, M. A. p. 789.
NN *Helen and Olga.* [Anne Manning] p. 789.
OLT *Gracie Amber.* By Mrs. W. C. Denison. p. 790.
OLT *Life Pictures from a Pastor's Note-Book.* By Robert Turnball p. 790.

June 27
OLT *Grace Truman; or, Love and Principle.* By Mrs. Sallie Rochester Ford. p. 819.
OLT *The Olive Branch; or, White oak Farm.* By A.L.O.E. [Miss Charlotte Maria Tucker] p. 819.

July 4
OLT *The Two Aristocracies: a Novel.* By Mrs. Gore. 3 vols. p. 852.
OLT *Pictures of the Olden Times, as shown in the Fortunes of a Family of Pilgrims.* By Edmund H. Lears. p. 852.
OLT *Dearforgil.* By the Author of the 'Last Earl of Desmond.' [Rev. Charles Bernard Gibson] p. 853.

July 18
OLT *Cuthbert St. Elme, M. P.; or, Passages in the Life of a Politician.* 3 vols. p. 908.
OLT *The Hobbies: a Novel.* By Morgan Kavanagh. 3 vols. p. 909.
OLT *Fides.* By the Author of 'Gabrielle; or, the Sisters,' & c. p. 909.
OLT *Sunshine after Rain; or, the Sister's Vow: a Tale.* 2 vols. p. 909.

Aug. 1.
NN (whole section) *A Woman's Story.* By Mrs. S. C. Hall. 3 vols. p. 971.
NN *Guy Livingstone; or, 'Thorough'.* [George Alfred Lawrence] p. 971.
NN *Jane Hardy; or, the Withered Heart.* By T. S. Arthur. pp. 971—72.

Aug. 29
The Coronet and the Cross. Compiled

from Authentic Documents, by the Rev. Alfred H. New. pp. 1079—80.

Sept. 5
NN *Orange Blossoms.* Edited by J. S. Arthur. p. 1112.
NN *Abbey Lands: a Tale.* By William Smyth Rockstro. p. 1112.
NN *Quits! a Novel.* By the Baroness Tautphoeus. 3 vols. p. 1112.
NN *Emeline Latimer: a Novel.* [Sarah Dunn] 3 vols. p. 1112.
NN *Labour and Live: a Story.* By the Author of 'Blenheim.' [Mrs. Ellen Epps] p. 1112.

Sept. 26
OLT *St. Eustace.* By Vance Ireton St. John. 3 vols. p. 1210.
OLT *The Refugee: a Novel founded on Phrenological Observations.* By Alfred Godwine, Ph. D. p. 1210.
OLT *Recollections of Mrs. Hester Taffetas.* Edited by Her Granddaughter. p. 1210.
OLT *A Cyclopaedia of Female Biography.* Edited by Sarah Adams. p. 1210.
OLT *A Lord of the Creation.* By the Author of 'Ethel.' [Marian James] p. 1210.

Oct. 3
OLT *Lucian Playfair.* By Thomas Mackern. 3 vols. pp. 1237—38.
OLT *The Wolf-Boy of China.* By William Dalton. p. 1238.
OLT *Rose Morison; or, Sketches of Home Happiness.* p. 1238.
OLT *Violets and Jonquils.* [Thomas Henry Wilkins] 2 vols. p. 1238.

Oct. 24
The Garies and their Friends. By J. Frank Webb. p. 1320.
Mabel Vaughan. By the Author of 'The Lamplighter.' [Maria Susanna Cummins] Edited by Mrs. Gaskell. p. 1320.

Nov. 7
OLT *The Laird of Restalrig's Daughter.* p. 1389

Nov. 21
OLT *Love in Light and Shadow.* 2 vols. —*Katherine Evering,* by the Author of 'Mr. Arle.' [Miss Emily Jolly]—*Sister Anne,* by the Author of 'Ethel.' [Marian James] p. 1452.
OLT *Blanche's Wanderings.* By Mary Stuart Hall. pp. 1452—53.
OLT *Court Secrets: a Novel.* 3 vols. By Mrs. Thomson. p. 1453.
OLT *Kiama: a Tradition of Hawaii.* By James J. Jarves. p. 1453.
OLT *The Highlanders of Glen Ora.* By James Grant. p. 1453.

Nov. 28
A Woman's Preaching for Woman's Practice. By Augusta Johnstone.
Industrial and Social Position of Women in the Middle and Lower Ranks. [John Duguid Milne] p. 1479.
OLT *Mauleverer's Divorce: a Story of Woman's Wrongs.* By the Author of 'Whitefriars,' &c. [Miss Emma Robinson] 3 vols. pp. 1485—86.
OLT *Almost; or, Crooked Ways: a Tale.* By Anna Lisle. p. 1486.
OLT *The Lady of Glynne.* By the Author of 'Marguerite and her Bridesmaids.' [Anne Marsh Caldwell] 3 vols. p. 1486.

Dec. 5
OLT *The Forsters: a Novel.* By Marguerite A. Power. 2 vols. p. 1516.
OLT *Moss-Side.* By Marion Harland. p. 1516.
OLT *Dissimulation: a Novel.* 3 vols. By the Author of 'The Wilderness of the World.' [Eustace Mitford] p. 1516.

Dec. 12
OLT *Howard Plunkett; or, Adrift in Life. A Novel.* By Kinhahan Cornwallis. 2 vols. pp. 1550—51.

Dec. 19
NN (whole section) *Riverston.* By Georgina [sic] M. Craik. 3 vols. p. 1586.
NN *The Gables: A Story of a Life.* By Julia Melville. 3 vols. p. 1586.
NN *Northwode Priory.* By the Author of 'Everley.' [Miss Cornish] 2 vols. p. 1586.

NN *The Ruling Passion*. By Rainey Hawthorne [Mrs. J. H. Riddell] p. 1586.
NN *Early Struggles*. By Mrs. A. Crawford. 3 vols. p. 1586.

Dec. 26
OLT *The Three Clerks: a Novel*. By Anthony Trollope. 3 vols. p. 1621.
OLT *The Game of Life. By 'Waters.'* [William Russell] p. 1622.

1858
Jan. 2
NN *Caste*. By the Author of 'Mr. Arle.' [Emily Jolly] 3 vols. p. 16.
NN *The Handwriting on the Wall: a Story*. By Edwin Atherstone. 3 vols. pp. 16—17.
NN *The Prisoner of the Border: a Tale of 1838*. By Hamilton Myers. p. 17.
OLT *The Rival King; or, Overbearing*. By the Author of 'Sidney Grey,' & c. [Miss Annie Kearie] pp. 17—18.
OLT *The Youth's Companion*. Edited by William Chambers. p. 18.

Jan. 9
OLT *Clara Hope*. By Elizabeth Milner p. 48.

Jan. 16
OLT *Constance and Edith; or, Incidents of Home Life*. By a Clergyman. p. 81.

Jan. 30
NN *Orphans: a Chapter in Life*. By the Author of 'Margaret Maitland,' & c. [Margaret Oliphant] p. 144.
NN *Sir Henry Appleton*. By the Rev. W. E. Heygate. p. 144.
NN *Captain Molly: the Story of a Brave Woman*. By Sheare Salmon. p. 144.
NN *Dauntless*. By the Author of 'Hands, not Hearts,' & c. [Janet. W. Wilkinson] 2 vols. p. 144.
NN *The White House by the Sea: a Love Story*. By M. Betham Edwards. 2 vols. pp. 144—45.
NN *Self-Mastery; or, Kenneth and Hugh*. By Catherine D. Bell. p. 145.
NN *Frank Millward: a Novel*. By W. Kenrick, Esq. 2 vols. p. 145.

NN *The Story of a Stolen Heir: a Novel*. By James G. Bertram. 3 vols. p. 145.
NN *Dawn and Twilight: a Tale*. By the Author of 'Amy Grant,' & c. [Miss Hopton or C. B. Dogett] 2 vols. p. 145.
NN *The Heirs of the Farmstead*. By the Author of 'Orphan Upton.' p. 145.
NN *The Coral Island: a Tale of the Pacific Ocean*. By Robert Michael Ballantyne. p. 145.

Feb. 6
NN *Adèle: a Tale*. By Julia Kavanagh. 3 vols. pp. 176—77.
NN *The Year Nine: a Tale of the Tyrol*. By the Author of 'Mary Powell.' [Anne Manning] p. 177.
NN *The Plant Hunters*. By Capt. Mayne Reid. p. 177.
NN *Ungava: a Tale of the Esquimaux*. By Robert Michael Ballantyne. p. 177.
OLT *A Woman's Thoughts about Women*. By the Author of 'John Halifax, Gentleman.' [Dinah Maria Mulock Craik] p. 177.

Feb. 13
NN *The Noble Traytour: a Chronicle*. By Thomas of Swarraton, Armiger. 3 vols. p. 207.
NN *The Exiles of Italy*. By G.C.H. [Henry G. Curran] p. 207.
NN *The Wild Tribes of the North: a Tale of Adventures*. By Anna Bowman. p. 207.
NN *Vendgiad*. p. 207.
NN *Bertram Noel: a Story for Youth*. By E. J. May p. 207.
OLT *The Rights, Duties, and Relations of Domestic Servants, their Masters and Mistresses*. By T. H. Bayliss, p. 208.
OLT *The Gloaming of Life: a Memoir of James Stirling*. By the Rev. Alexander Wallace. p. 208.
OLT *Stenelaus and Amylda: a Christmas Legend for Children of a Larger Growth*, p. 208.

Feb. 20
OLT *Charles Oliphant: a Novel*. By W. James, Esq. 3 vols. p. 238.

OLT *The Mohawk Chief.* By the Author of 'The Fall of the Nan Soung.' 3 vols. p. 238.

March 13
OLT *Memoirs of the Queens of Prussia.* By Emma Willsher Atkinson. p. 303.
OLT *The Stage and the Company: a Novel.* By Mrs. Hubback. 3 vols. p. 303.
OLT *The Royal Sisters; or, Pictures of a Court.* By Mrs. Robert Cartwright. 2 vols. p. 303.
OLT *Margaret Hamilton: a Novel.* By Mrs. C. J. Newby. 3 vols. p. 303.
OLT *Ran away to Sea: an Autobiography for Boys.* p. 303.
NN *The Coquette: a Novel.* By Biddulp Warner, Esq. p. 335.
NN *The Colonel's Daughters.* By Mrs. Clere. p. 335.

March 27
NN *Gaston Bligh.* By L. S. Lavanu. 2 vols. p. 399.
NN *Baffled: a Tale.* 2 vols. p. 399.
NN *The Old Palace.* By Julia Tilt. 2 vols. p. 399.
NN *A Lord for a Rival.* By J. Airey Aldercliffes. p. 399.
NN *Uncle Ralph: a Tale.* By the Author of 'Dorothy.' [Margaret Agnes Paul], pp. 399—400.
NN *The Moors and the Fens.* [Charlotte Riddell] 2 vols. p. 400.

April 3
NN *The Wayfarers: or, Toil and Rest.* By Mrs. P. M. Latham pp. 432—33.
NN *What You Will: an Irregular Romance.* p. 433.
NN *Masters and Workmen: a Tale for the Times.* By Sarah Elizabeth B. Patterson. p. 433.
OLT *Castle Rag and its Dependencies.* By M. A.J. Barber p. 433.

April 10
OLT *Aspirations of Nature.* By J. T. Hecker. p. 466.

April 24
NN (whole section) *Ursula: a Tale of Country Life.* By the Author of 'Amy Herbert,' & c. [Elizabeth Sewell] 2 vols. pp. 529—30.
NN *Gerald Fitzgerald: a Novel.* By George Herbert. 3 vols. p. 530.
NN *The Two Brothers.* By the Author of 'The Discipline of Life,' & c. [Lady Emily Ponsonby] 3 vols. p. 530.
NN *The Netherbys of Otterpool: a Novel.* [Mrs. Jane Carr Bateman] 3 vols. p. 530.
NN *The Red Rose: a Legend of St. Alban's Abbey.* p. 530.
NN *The Heiress of Vernon Hall.* p. 530.

May 8
NN (whole section) *The Cruelest Wrong of All.* By the Author of 'Marguerite; or, Prejudice at Home.' [Annie Tinsley] pp. 592—93.
NN *Violet Bank and its Inmates.* [Mrs Henrietta Camilla Jenkin] 3 vols. p. 593.
NN *Sir Guy d'Esterre.* By Selina Bunbury. 2 vols. p. 593.
NN *William and James, or the Revolution of 1688.* By a Lady. p. 593.

May 15
OLT *One-and-Twenty.* By the Author of 'Wildflower.' [Frederick William Robinson] 3 vols. p. 625.
OLT *Likes and Dislikes; or, Some Passages in the Life of Emily Marsden.* p. 625.

May 22
NN *The Rich Husband: a Novel of Real Life.* By the Author of 'The Ruling Passion.' [Rainey Hawthorne —pseud. for Mrs. J. H. Riddell] 3 vols. pp. 655—56.
NN *The Web of Life.* By Allan Park Paton. p. 656.

May 29
NN (whole section) *The Passionate Pilgrim; or, Eros and Anteros.* By Henry J. Thurstan. pp. 686—87.
NN *For and Against; or, Queen Margaret's Badge.* By Francis M. Wilbraham. 2 vols. p. 687.

NN *The Two Buccaneers: a Tale of the Sea.* By C. F. Armstrong, Esq. 3 vols. p. 687.

NN *Easton and its Inhabitants.* By L. E. [Hon. Eleanor Eden] p. 687.

NN *Urling: a Novel.* 3 vols. p. 687.

OLT *Practical and Economical Cookery, with a Series of Bills of Fare.* By Mrs. Smith. p. 687.

June 5

Intellectual Education, and its Influence on the Characters and Happiness of Women. By Emily Shirreff. pp. 714—15.

NN (whole section) *Doctor Thorne: a Novel.* By Anthony Trollope. 3 vols. p. 719.

NN *Heckington: a Novel.* By Mrs. Gore. 3 vols. p. 719.

NN *The Gilberts and their Guests: a Story of Homely English Life.* By Julia Day. 3 vols. p. 719.

June 12

OLT *Memorials of an only Daughter.* By her Mother, the Authoress of 'The Shady Side.' [Mrs. Martha Stone Hubbell] p. 752.

June 19

OLT *The Heirs of Cheveleigh.* By Gervaise Abbot. 3 vols. p. 783.

OLT *Hand and Glove.* By Amelia B. Edwards. p. 783.

OLT *The Poor Relation: a Novel.* By Miss Pardoe. 3 vols. pp. 783—84.

June 26

OLT *Ida; or, the Last Struggles of the Welsh for Independence.* By Alice Somerton. p. 818.

OLT *Boernice.* By Mrs. Charles Clacy. p. 818.

July 3

OLT *Hartley Hall.* p. 17.

OLT *Will He Marry Her?* By the Author of 'Too Clever by Half.' [John Lang] p. 17.

OLT *Edith; or, Life's Changes.* p. 17.

OLT *The House of Camelet: a Tale of the Olden Times.* By Mary Linwood. 2 vols. p. 17.

July 31

NN (whole section) *Philip Paternoster: a Tractarian Love Story.* By an ex-Puseyite. [Rev. Charles Maurice Davies] 2 vols. p. 137.

NN *Which? or, Eddies round the Rectory.* By Owen Varra. 2 vols. p. 137.

NN *Langton Manor House; or, Love and its Shadows: a Sketch.* By Puss-in-the Corner. p. 137.

NN *Garestone Hall. A Tale.* p. 137.

NN *An English Girl's Account of a Moravian Settlement in the Black Forest.* Edited by the Author of 'Mary Powell.' [Anne Manning] p. 137.

Aug. 7

OLT *Confession: a Tale of the Stars and Clouds.* By S. Hancock. pp. 167—68.

OLT *The Scholar and the Trooper; or, Oxford during the Great Rebellion.* By the Rev. W. E. Heygate, M. A. p. 168.

Aug. 14

The Private Journal and Literary Remains of John Byrom. Edited by Richard Parkinson, D. D. Vol. II., Part II.

Miscellanies, being a Selection from the Poems and Correspondence of the Rev. Thomas Wilson. By the Rev. F. R. Raines. pp. 198—99.

Aug. 21

NN *A Friend in Need: a Romance.* [Mrs. T. E. Freeman] 3 vols. p. 231.

NN *Framleigh Hall: a Novel.* [Julia Wedgwood] 3 vols. pp. 231—32.

Sept. 4

NN (whole section) *Five Years of It.* 2 vols. By Alfred Austin. p. 296.

NN *Ethel Beranger: a Novel.* 2 vols. By Caroline Giffard Phillipson. p. 296.

NN *Theodosia Ernest; or, the Heroine of Faith.—Theodosia Ernest; or, Ten Days' Travel in Search of the Church.* p. 296.

Sept. 18

The Daughter of the Cedars.—[La Fille des Cedres]. By the Author of 'Pericles.'

Woman, her Mission and her Life. By Adolphe Monod. D. D.
Select Discourses. By Adolphe Monod. p. 360.
NN (whole section) *Eva Desmond; or, Mutation.* 3 vols. pp. 360—61.

Oct. 16
The Evils of Wet-Nursing: a Warning to Mothers.—How to Manage a Baby.— Why do not Women Swim? a Voice from many Waters.—How to Feed a Baby with the Bottle. Ladies' National Association for the Diffusion of Sanitary Knowledge. pp. 483—84.

Nov. 13
NN *Sylvan Holt's Daughter.* By Holme Lee. [Harriet Parr] 3 vols. p. 616.
NN *Checkmate: a Tale.* [Martin Francis Mahony] p. 616.

Nov. 27
The Afternoon of Unmarried Life. By the Author of 'Morning Clouds.' [Mrs. S. J. Penny] p. 676.
NN (whole section) *The Laird of Norlaw.* By the Author of 'Margaret Maitland,' &c. [Margaret Oliphant] 3 vols. p. 682.
NN *Maud Bingley.* By Frederica Graham. 2 vols. p. 682.
NN *Redmarsh Rectory: a Tale of Life.* By Nona Bellairs. 3 vols. p. 682.

Dec. 4
NN (whole section) *Fellow Travellers; or, the Experience of Life.* By the Author of 'Margaret; or, Prejudice at Home.' [Annie Tinsley] 3 vols. pp. 717—18.
NN *Gordon of Duncairn: a Novel.* [Mrs. Ph. Solms Boosey] 2 vols. p. 718.
NN *My Lady: a Tale of Modern Life.* 2 vols. p. 718.
NN *The Secret of a Life.* By M. M. Bell. p. 718.
NN *Unrequited Love: a Romance founded on Incidents of Real Life.* By J. P. Nagle. p. 718.
NN *Rest and Unrest; or, the Story of a Year.* By Catherine D. Bell. p. 718.

Dec. 11
NN *Mignonette: a Sketch.* By the Author of 'The Curate of Holy Cross.' [Ernest Richard Seymour] 2 vols. p. 757.
NN *The Master of Churchill Abbots and his Little Friends: a Tale.* By Florence Wilford. p. 757.
NN *Recollections of a Maiden Aunt.* p. 757.
NN *The Two Brides; or, the French Chateau and the English Home.* By F. Baldwin. p. 757.

Dec. 18
NN *Home and the Homeless: a Novel.* By Cecilia Mary Caddel. 3 vols. p. 797.

1859
Jan. 1
NN *Maiden Sisters: a Tale.* By the Author of 'Dorothy.' [Margaret Agnes Paul] p. 16.
NN *Florence: a Tale.* By M. E. Hammond. p. 16.
NN *Struggles in Falling.* By John Henry Lester. p. 16.

Feb. 5
NN *Father and Daughter.* By Fredrika Bremer. Translated by Mary Howitt. p. 185.
NN *Varium.* p. 185.
NN *An Old Debt.* By Florence Dashwood. 2 vols. pp. 185—86.

Feb. 12
NN *Yesterday: or, Mabel's Story.* pp. 220—21.
NN *A Few Out of Thousands: their Sayings and Doings.* By Augusta Johnstone. p. 221.

Feb. 19
NN *The Romance and its Hero.* By the Author of 'Magdalen Stafford.' 2 vols. p. 251.
NN *The Verneys; or, Chaos Dispelled.* By Miss Caroline Mary Smith. p. 251.
NN *The Two Mottoes.* By the Author of 'Summerleigh Manor.' [Margaret Roberts] pp. 251—52.

Feb. 26
NN *Adam Bede*. By George Eliot. 3 vols. p. 284.

March 5
NN *The Foster Brothers*. [James Payn] pp. 318—19.

March 12
NN *Lost and Won*. By Georgiana M. Craik. p. 354.
NN *Alfred Staunton: a Novel*. By J. Stanyan Bigg. p. 354.
NN *The Fate of Folly*. By Lord B*******. [Earl of Belfast] 3 vols. pp. 354—55.

March 26
(opens issue) *A Decade of Italian Women*. By T. Adolphus Trollope. 3 vols. pp. 413—14.
NN *The Bertrams: a Novel*. By Anthony Trollope. 3 vols. p. 420.
NN *Milly Warrener: a Tale of Country Life*. By the Author of 'Two Martyr Stories.' p. 420.
NN *Temptation and Atonement*. By Mrs. Gore. p. 420.

April 2
NN *"Creeds."* By the Author of 'The Morals of May Fair.' [Mrs. Annie Edwards] 3 vols. pp. 451—52.

April 9
NN *Gilbert Midhurst, M. P.* By Charles F. Howard. 2 vols. p. 483.
NN *Ellen Raymond; or, Ups and Downs*. By Mrs. Vidal. 3 vols. pp. 483—84.
NN *Blight; or, the Novel Hater*. By the Author of 'Good in Everything.' p. 484.
NN *Master and Pupil: a Tale*. By Mrs. Mackenzie Daniel[s]. 3 vols. p. 484.
OLT *Calipedry; or, Development of Beauty*. By Dr. Schreber. p. 485.

April 16
NN *Sir Gilbert: a Novel*. [Charles Henry Butcher] p. 514.
NN *Poplar House Academy*. By the Author of 'Mary Powell.' [Anne Manning] 2 vols. pp. 514—15.

NN *"The Julia": a Tale*. By the Author of 'Nelly of Truro.' [Jane Elizabeth Roscoe] p. 515.
NN *The Wife and the Ward; or, a Life's Error*. By Lieut.-Col. Edward Money. p. 515.

April 30
NN *The Broad Arrow*. By Oliné Keese. 2 vols. p. 580.
NN *Kitford: a Village Tale*. p. 580.
NN *False and True*. By the Hon. Lena Eden. p. 580.

May 7
NN (whole section) *Recollections of Geoffry Hamlyn*. By Henry Kingsley. 3 vols. pp. 610—11.
NN *The Old Plantation, and What I gathered there in an Autumn Month*. By James Hungerford. p. 611.
NN *The History of Moses Wimble: a Prose Dramatic and Lyrical Epic*. Written by Himself. p. 611.

May 14
NN *Life's Foreshadowings: a Novel*. [William German Wills] 3 vols. p. 644.

May 21
NN *The Dean; or, the Popular Preacher: a Tale*. By Berkeley Aiking. 3 vols. pp. 675—76.
NN *Ethel Woodville; or, Woman's Ministry: a Tale for the Times*. [Mrs. Hollings] 2 vols. p. 676.
NN *The Last of the Cavaliers*. [Rose Piddington] 3 vols. p. 676.
NN *Woodleigh*. By the Author of 'The House of Elmore,' & c. [Frederick William Robinson] 3 vols. p. 676.

May 28
NN (whole section) *The Man of Fortune: a Story of the Present Day*. By Albany Fonblanque. Esq. Jun. p. 710.
NN *Trust for Trust*. By A. J. Barrowcliffe. 3 vols. p. 710.
NN *Southwold: a Novel*. By Mrs. Lillie Devereux Umsted. p. 710.
NN *Holywood Hall: a Tale of 1715*. By James Grant. p. 710.

NN *Old and Young*. p. 710.
NN *The Rose of Ashurst*. By the Author of 'Emilia Wyndham.' [Anne Marsh Caldwell] p. 710.

June 4
Mothers of Great Men. By Mrs. [Sarah Stickney] Ellis.
Memorials of Eliza Hessel. True Womanhood. By Joshua Priestley. pp. 741—42.
NN (whole section) *Robert Mornay*. By Max Ferrer. p. 745.
NN *The Methodist*. By Miriam Fletcher. 2 vols. p. 745.
NN *Betty Westminster; or, the Worship of Wealth*. By William Platt, Esq. 3 vols. p. 746.
NN *Georgie Barrington: a Tale*. By Jeanette Browne. 3 vols. p. 746.
OLT *The Servant's Behaviour Book*. By Mrs. Motherly. p. 746.

June 11
OLT *Newton Dogvane: a Story of English Country Life*. By Francis Francis. 3 vols. p. 776.

June 18
OLT *Miriam Copley*. By J. C. Jeaffreson. 3 vols. p. 808
OLT *The Wife's Temptation: a Tale of Belgravia*. By the Authoress of 'The Sister of Charity.' [Annie Emma Challice] 2 vols. p. 808.
OLT *Reuben Sterling: a Tale of Scottish Life*. By Samuel Alfred Cox. 3 vols. p. 808.

June 25
OLT *A Tale for the Pharisees*. By the Author of 'Dives and Lazarus.' [William Gilbert] p. 839.

July 9
NN (whole section) *The Ordeal of Richard Feverel*. By George Meredith. 3 vols. p. 48.
NN *Through the Shadows*. By the Author of 'Sydney Grey.' [Annie Keary] 3 vols. pp. 48—49.
NN *A Mother's Trial*. By the Author of

'The Discipline of Life.' [Lady Emily Charlotte Mary Ponsonby] p. 49.
NN *Confidences*. By the Author of 'Rita.' [Hamilton Aidé] p. 49.

July 16
NN *Chances and Changes*. By the Author of 'My First Grief.' [Charles Beckett] p. 81.
NN *Hawksview: a Family History of our Own Times*. By Holme Lee. [Harriet Parr] p. 81.
NN *Emily Morton: a Tale. With Sketches from Life and Critical Essays*. By Charles Westerton. p. 81.

July 23
NN (whole section) *Cousin Stella*. By the Author of 'Violet Bank, and its Inmates.' [Mrs. Henrietta Camilla Jenkin] 3 vols. pp. 113—14.
NN *Confessions of a Too Generous Young Lady* p. 114.
NN *Helen Lindsay; or, the Trial of Faith*. By a Clergyman's Daughter. 2 vols. p. 114.
NN *Who is to Have It? A Novel*. By the Author of 'The Netherwoods of Otterpool.' [Mrs. J. C. Bateman] p. 114.

Aug. 6
A Life for a Life. By the Author of 'John Halifax, Gentleman,' & c. [Dinah Maria Mulock Craik] 3 vols. pp. 173—74.
Chateubriand and His Times.— [Chateaubriand et son Temps.] By the Count de Marcellus. p. 174.

Aug. 13
OLT *Women, Past and Present*. By John Wade.
The Laws of Life. With Special Reference to the Physical Education of Girls. By Elizabeth Blackwell, M. D., p. 208.

Aug. 20
NN (whole section) *Out of the Depths: the Story of a Woman's Life*. [Henry Gladwyn Jebb] pp. 240—41.
NN *The Parson and the Poor. a Tale of Hazlewood*. By Austyn Graham. 3 vols. p. 241.

NN *Alice Littleton: a Tale.* By Forester Fitz David. p. 241.

NN *The Exiles of the Cebenna.* By Aurelius Gratianus. p. 241.

NN *The Curate and the Rector: a Domestic Story.* By Elizabeth Strutt. p. 241.

Aug. 20

NN *Ernestin; or, the Heart's Longing.* By Aleth. p. 241.

Aug. 27

NN (whole section) *The Semi-Detached House.* Edited by Lady Theresa Lewis. p. 272.

NN *Millicent Neville: a Novel.* By Julia Tilt. 2 vols. p. 272.

NN *Frank Elliott; or, Wells in the Desert.* By James Challen. p. 272.

NN *The Dudleys.* By Edgar Dewsland. p. 272.

NN *Some Years After: a Tale.* p. 272.

Sept. 17

Some Memorials of Renée of France, Duchess of Ferrara. [Isabella M. Braikenridge] pp. 366—67.

Oct. 1

NN (whole section) *Almost a Heroine.* By the Author of 'Charles Auchester,' & c. [Miss Elizabeth Sarah Sheppard] 3 vols. p. 429.

NN *The Two Homes.* By William Mathews. 3 vols. p. 429.

Oct. 15

NN (whole section) *Raised to the Peerage: a Novel.* By Mrs. Octavius Freire Owen. 3 vols. p. 497.

NN *The Count de Perbruck: a Historical Romance.* By Henry Cooke. 3 vols. p. 497.

NN *Wreck and Ruin, or, Modern Society.* By Kinahan Cornwallis. 3 vols. p. 497.

NN *Freshfield.* By William Johnston, M. A. p. 497.

NN *The Dennes of Daundeleyon.* By Mrs. Charles J. Proby. 3 vols. p. 497.

Oct. 29

NN (whole section) *Wait and Hope.* By John Edmund Reade. 3 vols. p. 564.

NN *The Morning of Life.* By the Author of 'Gordon of Duncairn.' 2 vols. p. 564.

Nov. 12

NN (whole section) *Nut-Brown Maids.* [Henrietta Keddie] p. 631.

NN *Bentley Priory.* By Mrs. Hastings Parker. 3 vols. p. 631.

NN *The Campbells.* 3 vols. p. 631.

NN *Shifting Scenes in Theatrical Life.* By Eliza Winstanley, Comedian. p. 631.

Dec. 3

NN (whole section) *Misrepresentation: a Novel.* By Anna H. Drury. 2 vols. p. 738.

NN *The Quaker-Soldier.* [John Richter Jones] p. 738.

Henry St. John, Gentleman. By John Esten Cooke. p. 738.

OLT *Frank and Andrea; or, Forest Life in the Island of Sardinia.* By Alfred Elwes. p. 739.

OLT *Will Weatherhelm.* By William H. G. Kingston. p. 739.

OLT *The White Elephant.* By William Dalton. p. 739.

Dec. 10

NN *Against Wind and Tide.* By Holme Lee. [Harriet Parr] 3 vols. p. 773.

NN *Undercurrents: a Story of our own Day.* By Vane Ireton St. John. 3 vols. p. 773.

Dec. 24

NN *The Way of the World: a Novel.* 3 vols. By Alison Reid. p. 851.

NN *Now or Never: a Novel.* By M. Betham Edwards. p. 851.

OLT *Harry Hartley; or, Social Science for the Workers.* By J. W. Overton. p. 851.

1860

Jan. 14

NN *A Life Struggle.* By Miss Pardoe. 2 vols. p. 50.

Jan. 21

NN *Lucy Crofton.* By the Author of 'Margaret Maitland.' [Margaret Oliphant] p. 93.

NN *The Widow Green and her Three Nieces*. By Mrs. [Sarah Stickney] Ellis. p. 93.

Jan. 28
NN *Seven Years, and other Tales*. By Julia Kavanagh. 3 vols. p. 133.
NN *Life and its Lessons*. By Frederick W. B. Bouverie. p. 133.

Feb. 4
Undercurrents Overlooked. By the Author of 'Flemish Interiors.' [Mrs. William Pitt Byrne, née Julia Clara Busk] 2 vols.
The Missing Link; or, Bible Women in the Homes of the London Poor. By L. N. R. pp. 166—67.
NN *The Cousin's Courtship*. By John R. Wise. 2 vols. pp. 169—70.
NN *Aggesden Vicarage*. 2 vols. p. 170.
NN *The Day of Small Things*. By the Authoress of 'Mary Powell.' [Anne Manning] p.170.

Feb. 25
NN (whole section) *Elfie in Sicily*. 2 vols. p. 268.
NN *Atheline; or, the Castle by the Sea: a Tale*. By Louisa Stewart. 2 vols. p. 268.

March 3
NN *Yes and No, or, Glimpses of the Great Conflict*. [Rev. Henry Robert Reynolds] 3 vols. p. 300.
NN *The Marquis d'Hauterive; or, the Romance of a Poor Young Man*. By Octave Feuillet. p. 300.
NN *The Land of the Kelt: a Tale of Ierne in the Days of '98*. From an Unpublished MS, by Peter Paradox. M. D. 3 vols. pp. 300—01.
OLT *My Third Book: a Collection of Tales*. By Louise Chandler Moulton p. 302.

March 17
NN *Too Much Alone*. By G. F. Trafford. 3 vols. p. 373.
NN *The Earl's Cedars*. By the Author of 'Smugglers and Foresters,' & c. [Rosa Mackenzie Kettle] p. 373.

NN *Straight Forward*, and *Patience Hart; or, the Dissembler*. By F. C. Lefroy. p. 373.

March 24
NN (whole section) *Greymore: a Story of Country Life*. [Mrs. A. B. Church] pp. 406—07.
NN *Danesbury House: Prize Tale*. By Mrs. Henry Wood. p. 407.

March 31
NN (whole section) *The Man of the People*. By William Howitt. 3 vols. p. 441.
NN *Say and Seal*. By the Author of 'The Wide, Wide World.' [Elizabeth Wetherell pseud. for Miss Susan Warner] p. 441.
NN *The Washingtons*. By John Nassau Simpkinson. p. 441.

April 7
The Mill on the Floss. By George Eliot. 3 vols. pp. 467—68.

April 14
Woman's Right to Labour. By Caroline Dall. p. 504.

April 21
NN *The Great Experiment: a Novel*. By Miss Molesworth. 3 vols. p. 542.
NN *Which is Which? or, Miles Cassidy's Contract: a Picture Story*. By Robert B. Brough. 2 vols. p. 542.
NN *Tried in the Fire: a Tale*. By Mrs. Mackenzie Daniels. 3 vols. p. 542.
NN *Bengala; or, Some Time Ago*. By Mrs. Vidal. 2 vols. p. 542.
NN *One Trial: a Novel*. By H. R. C. [Henry Russell Cleveland] 2 vols. p. 542.
NN *Netley Hall; or, the Wife's Sister*. [William Davy Watson] p. 542.

May 5
NN *Hulse House: a Novel*. By the Author of 'Anne Grey.' [Harriet Cradock] 2 vols. p. 616.
NN *Influence; or, the Sisters*. By Albyn Locke. p. 616.
NN *The Living among the Dead: a Story founded on Facts*. [Mrs. Ellen Epps, née Elliott] p. 616.

NN *The Stepmother; or, Will She be a Nun?* By Florence [Mrs. France Sargent Osgood] p. 616.

May 12
NN (whole section) *Cathara Clyde: a Novel.* By Inconnu. p. 648.
NN *Stretton of Ringwood Chace: a Novel.* 3 vols. p. 648.

May 19
NN *Castle Richmond.* By Anthony Trollope. 3 vols. p. 681.
NN *Mary Bertrand.* By Francis Meredith. 3 vols. p. 681.
NN *Love and Labour; or, Work and its Reward.* By Kate Pyer. p. 681.

May 26
NN (whole section) *The First-Born; or, a Mother's Trials.* By the Author of 'My Lady.' 3 vols. p. 718.
NN *Sir Rohan's Ghost.* [Mrs Harriett Elizabeth Prescott Spofford] p. 718.
NN *Grandmother's Money.* By the Author of 'One-and-Twenty,' & c. [Frederick William Robinson] 3 vols. p. 718.
NN *Corvoda Abbey; or, Lights and Shadows of the Present Day.* p. 718.
NN *Alive or Dead? a Tale of St. Crispin's Parish.* By Charles Howel. p. 718.
NN *How could he Help it? or, the Heart Triumphant.* By A. S. Roe. p. 718.

June 2
NN *The Baddington Peerage.* By George Augustus Sala. 3 vols. p. 754.
NN *Steyne's Grief.* By the Author of 'Losing, Seeking and Finding.' p. 754.
NN *The Story of a Lost Life.* By William Platt. 3 vols. p. 754.
OLT *A Story about Riflemen and Rifles.* By Neyland Thornton. p. 755.
OLT *The Diary of a Poor Young Gentlewoman.* Translated from the German. By M. Anna Childs. p. 755.
OLT *My First Journal: a Book for the Young.* By Georgiana M. Craik. p. 755.

June 9
NN *El Fureidis.* By Maria S. Cummins. p. 788.
NN *Charley Nugent; or, Passages from the Life of a Sub.* [Janet Maughan] 3 vols. p. 789.
NN *The Wayward Heart: a Novel.* 3 vols. By Edward J. Branthwayt. p.789.

June 23
NN (whole section) *Mainstone's Housekeeper.* By Eliza Meteyard (Silverpen.) 3 vols. p. 852.
NN *Alice Lisle: a Tale of Puritan Times.* By the Rev. R. King, B. A. p. 852.
NN *Squires and Parsons: a Sketch for the Times.* p. 852.
NN *The Tin Box: a Story of the Last Century.* Edited by G. W. p. 852.
NN *Tinsel or Gold: a Fireside Story.* p. 852.
NN *Eleanor Morrison; or, Home Duties: a Tale.* By Lady Charles Thynne. p. 852.

July 7
Vice-Royalty; or, Counsel respecting the Government of the Heart. By Benjamin Smith. pp. 13—14.
NN (whole section) *Only a Woman: a Story in Neutral Tint.* By Capt. Lascelles Wraxall. 3 vols. p. 15.
NN *Country Landlords.* By E. M. S. 3 vols. p. 15.
NN *The Ironsides: a Tale of the English Commonwealth.* 3 vols. p. 15.

July 14
OLT *Chapters on Wives.* By Mrs. [Sarah Stickney] Ellis. pp. 52—53.
OLT *The New Priest in Conception Bay.* [Robert Traill Spence Lowell] p. 55.

July 28
NN (whole section) *The Queen's Pardon.* By Mary Eyre. pp. 123—24.
NN *After Many Days: a Tale of Social Reform.* By Seneca Smith. p. 124.

Aug. 4
NN (whole section) *Herbert Chauncey.* By Sir Arthur Hallam Elton, Bart. 3 vols. pp. 159—60.

NN *Adrift; or, the Fortunes of Connor Blake.* By Biddulph Warner. p. 160.
NN *Under a Cloud: a Novel.* By Frederick and James Greenwood. 3 vols. p. 160.

Aug. 11
NN (whole section) *The Nevilles of Garretstown.* 3 vols. Edited by the Author of 'Emilia Wyndham.' [Anne Marsh-Caldwell] pp. 193—94.
NN *The Two Households.* A Novel. By Terence Doyle. 2 vols. p. 194.
NN *Who shall be Duchess? or, the New Lord of Burleigh.* 2 vols. p. 194.
NN *Katherine Morris: an Autobiography.* By the Author of 'Step by Step.' p. 194.
NN *All Right; an Old Maid's Tale.* p. 194.
NN *The Chevaliers: a Tale.* By M. S. Birkinshow. p. 194.
NN *Aunt Dorothy's Will.* By Cycla. [for Mrs. Helen Clacy] 2 vols. p. 194.

Aug. 18
NN (whole section) *Scarsdale; or, Life on the Lancashire and Yorkshire Border Thirty Years Ago.* [Sir James Phillips Kay-Shuttleworth] 3 vols. pp. 225—26.
NN *From Hay-time to Hopping.* [Miss Coulton] p. 226.
NN *A False Step in Life.* By L. l. D. p. 226.
NN *High Church.* 2 vols. [Frederick William Robinson] p. 226.

Aug. 25
Englishwomen and the Age. By Mrs. Horace Roscoe St. John. *The English Woman's Journal.* pp. 248—50.
NN (whole section) *Bond and Free.* By the Author of 'Caste.' [Emily Jolly] 3 vols. p. 255.
NN *Ulic O'Donnell; an Irish Peasant's Progress.* By D. Holland. p. 255.

Sept. 1
NN (whole section) *Married; or not Married; that is the Question: a Novel.* By Augusta Huntingdon. 3 vols. p. 288.
NN *Passages from the Life of Agnes Home.* p. 288.
NN *Wedded and Winnowed; or, the Trials of Mary Gascoigne: a Tale for the Divorce Court.* By Marabel May. p. 288.

NN *Apelles and his Contemporaries: a Novel.* By the Author of 'Ernest Carroll.' [Henry Greenhough] p. 288.

Sept. 8
NN (whole section) *The Semi-Attached Couple.* By the Author of 'The Semi-Detached House.' [Hon. Emily Eden] 2 vols. p. 321.

Sept. 15
NN (whole section) *Rutledge.* [Mrs. Miriam Harris] *The Household of Bouverie; or, the Elixir of Gold: A Romance.* By a Southern Lady. [Mrs. Catherine Ann Warfield] 2 vols. pp. 352—53.
NN *Captain Brand, of the Centipede, a Pirate of Eminence in the West Indies.* By Lieut. H. A. Wise. U. S. N. (Harry Gringo) p. 353.

Sept. 22
NN *The Man of Destiny: a Romance of Modern History.* By L. A. Chamerovzow. 2 vols. p. 383.

Sept. 29
(opens issue) *Report of the Association for Promoting the General Welfare of the Blind.* pp. 407—08.

Oct. 6
NN *Over the Cliffs.* By Charlotte Chanter. 2 vols. p. 449.
NN *My Wife's Pin-Money; or, Marriage in Extremis.* By M. E. E. Nelson p. 449.
NN *The Emigrant's Daughter.* By M. E. E. Nelson. p. 449.
NN *Helen: a Romance of Real Life.* By Raymond Lock. p. 449.

Oct. 13
(opens issue) *William Grimshaw, Incumbent of Haworth.* By R. Spence Hardy. pp. 473—74.

Nov. 10
NN (whole section) *The Skeleton in the Cupboard.* 2 vols. By Lady Scott. p. 628.
NN *Gladys the Reaper.* By the Author of 'Simplicity and Fascination.' [Annie Beale] 3 vols. pp. 628—29.

NN *The Valley of a Hundred Fires*. By the Author of 'Margaret and her Bridesmaid.' [Anne Marsh-Caldwell] 3 vols. p. 629.

Nov. 17
Home Life of English Ladies of the Seventeenth Century. By the Author of 'Magdalen Stafford.' pp. 664—65.
NN *Wearing the Willow; or, Bride Feilding*. By the Author of 'Nut-Brown Maids.' [Henrietta Keddie] p. 668.
NN *The Wortlebank Diary; and Some Old Stories from Kathie Brande's Portfolio*. By Holme Lee. [Harriet Parr] 3 vols. p. 668.
NN *The Manse of Mastland*. Translated from the Dutch, by Thomas Keightley. pp. 668—69.
NN *The Evil Eye; or, the Black Spectre: a Romance*. By William Carleton. p. 669.
NN *The Osbornes of Osborne Park: a Tale*. By George Rate. p. 669.
My Life, and What shall I do with It? a Question for Young Gentlewomen. By an Old Maid. [Miss L. F. March Phillips] pp. 702—03.
NN *Keeping up Appearances: a Novel of English Life*. By Cyrus Redding. 3 vols. pp. 708—09.
OLT *Digby Heathcote; or, the Early Days of a Country Gentleman's Son and Heir*. By William Kingston, Esq. p. 709.
OLT *Hannah Lavender; or, Lady Hall*. p. 709.

Dec. 1
NN *The House on the Moor*. By the Author of 'Margaret Maitland,' & c. [Margaret Oliphant] 3 vols. p. 749.
OLT *Old Friends and New Acquaintances*. By Agnes Strickland. p. 750.
OLT *Head and Hand; or, Thought and Action in relation to Success and Happiness*. By the Rev. R. W. Fraser, M. A. p. 750.
OLT *Roughing It with Alick Baillee*. By William J. Stewart. p. 750.
OLT *Chapters from the Life of James Tacket*. p. 750.
OLT *Henry and Mary; or, the Little Orphans*. By Susan Corbett. p. 750.

Dec. 8
NN *High Places*. By G. T. Lowth, Esq. 3 vols. p. 789.

Dec. 15
The Conduct of Life. By Ralph Waldo Emerson. pp. 824—25.
OLT *Woman and her Wants: Four Lectures to Ladies on the Female Body and Clothing*. By Madame Roxey Ann Caplin. p. 829.

Dec. 22
NN *Hope Evermore; or, Something to do*. By the Author of 'Left to Themselves.' [Mrs. Yorick Smythies, née Gordon] 2 vols. pp. 869—70.

Dec. 29
NN *Magdalen Havering*. By the Author of 'The Verneys.' [Caroline Mary Smith] pp. 908—09.
NN *The World's Furniture: a Novel*. 3 vols. p. 909.

1861
Jan. 26
NN (whole section) *The World's Verdict*. By the Author of 'Morals of May Fair.' [Mrs. Annie Edwards] 3 vols. p. 119.
NN *Fit to be a Duchess*. By Mrs. G. Smith. p. 119.
NN *A Christmas Story*. By the Author of 'Grandmother's Money.' [Frederick William Robinson] p. 119.
NN *The Twickenham Papers*. By a Society of Novelists. 2 vols. p. 119.

Feb. 2
NN *Perpetua: a Love Tale*. By E. G. P. p. 155.
NN *Miss Gilbert's Career: an American Story*. By J. G. Holland. p. 155.

Feb. 9
NN *Claudia and Pudens*. By the Rev. Samuel Lysons, M. A. p. 193.

March 2
NN *Change; or, some Passages in the Life of Basil Rutherford*. By Emily Cuyler. p. 292.
NN *Burrowdale: a Tale*. p. 292.

NN *The Squire: a Biographic Sketch.* pp. 292—93.

NN *Minnie's Love.* By the Author of 'A Trap to Catch a Sunbeam,' & c. [Mrs. Matilda Anne Mackarness] p. 293.

March 9
NN *The Wild Huntress.* By Captain Mayne Reid. 3 vols. p. 324.
NN *The Sunbeam; or, the Misused Gift.* By the Author of 'My Christmas Hour.' p. 324.

March 30
NN *Struggle for Life.* By the Author of 'Seven Stormy Sundays,' & c. [Lucretia Peabody Hale] p. 430.
NN *Rose Mary; or, Life and Death.* By J. Vincent Huntingdon. p. 430.

April 6
NN *Silas Marner, the Weaver of Raveloe.* By George Eliot. pp. 464—65.

April 27
NN *Elsie Venner: a Romance of Destiny.* By Oliver Wendell Holmes. pp. 559—60.

May 11
NN *La Beata.* By T. Adolphus Trollope. 2 vols. p. 628.
NN *All for the Best: a Story of Quiet Life.* 3 vols. pp. 628—29.
NN *The Moor Cottage: a Tale of Home Life.* By May Beverley. p. 629.
OLT *The Shilling Kitchiner; or, Oracle of Cookery for the Million.* By the Editor of 'The Dictionary Daily Wants.' p. 629.
OLT *The Dictionary of Daily Wants.* By the Editor of 'Enquire Within upon Everything.' [Robert Kemp Philp] p. 629.

May 18
OLT *The Tragedy of Life.* By John H. Brenton. 2 vols. p. 660.

May 25
English Puritanism and its Leaders: Cromwell, Milton, Baxter, Bunyan. By John Tulloch, D. D. pp. 688—89.
NN (whole section) *Crispin Ken.* By the Author of 'Miriam May.' [Rev. Arthur Robins] 2 vols. p. 692.

NN *City and Suburb.* By G. F. Trafford. 3 vols. p. 692.
NN *Wheel within Wheel.* By Noel Radcliffe. 3 vols. pp. 692—93.

June 1
OLT *The Near and the Heavenly Horizons.* By Madame de Gasparin. p. 726.

June 8
NN *Trumps: a Novel.* By George William Curtis. Illustrated by Augustus Hoppin. p. 761.
OLT *Dictionary of Useful Knowledge, A to F* [Robert Kemp Philp] p. 762.

June 22
NN *Who Breaks—Pays: Italian Proverb.* By the Author of 'Cousin Stella.' [Mrs. Charles Jenkin] 2 vols. pp. 828—29.
NN *Ruth Baynard's Story.* [Mrs. Gertrude Parsons] p. 829.

June 29
NN (whole section) *Homeless; or, a Poet's Inner Life.* By M. Goldsmith. 3 vols. pp. 859—60.
NN *Manordean: a Novel.* By Herbert Steele. p. 860.
NN *The Step-Sisters.* By the Author of 'Heatherbrae.' [Sarah Dunn] 2 vols. p. 860.
NN *Our Brother Paul: a Novel.* By Mrs. Mackenzie Daniels. 3 vols. p. 860.
NN *Aunt Agnes; or, the Why and the Wherefore of Life.* By a Clergyman's Daughter. p. 860.

July 6
NN (whole section) *Oliver Ellis; or, The Fusileers: a Tale.* By James Grant, Esq. pp. 16—17.
NN *Cruise of the Daring: a Tale of the Sea.* By C. F. Armstrong. 3 vols. p. 17.
NN *The Broken Troth, from the Italian.* By Phillip Ireton. 2 vols. p. 17.
NN *Forgiveness: a Novel.* By J. C. Bateman. 3 vols. p. 17.
NN *May Blossom; or, Shadow across the Hearth.* By Austyn Graham. 2 vols. p. 17.

OLT *Uphill Work.* By Mrs. Clara Lucas Balfour. p. 18.
OLT *Climbing: a Manual for the Young.* By Benjamin Smith. p. 18.

July 13
NN (whole section) *Loving, and being Loved.* By Annette Marie Maillard. 2 vols. p. 49.
NN *Under the Spell.* By the Author of 'Grandmother's Money, & c.' [Frederick William Robinson] 3 vols. p. 49.
NN *Baby Bianca; or, the Venetians.* By Mrs. Richard Valentine. pp. 49—50.
NN *Side Winds.* By Morton Rae. p. 50.
NN *Retribution: a Novel.* By Mrs. Augustus Peel. 3 vols. p. 50.
NN *Edmondale; or, a Family Chronicle.* p. 50.
NN *The Tablette Booke of Ladye Mary Keyes.* p. 50.

July 20
NN *Court Life at Naples in our own Times.* By the Author of 'La Cava.' 2 vols. p. 81.
OLT *From Death to Life: Bible Records of Remarkable Conversions.* By the Rev. Adolph Sadlier. p. 82.

Aug. 3
NN *Paul Foster's Daughter.* By Dutton Cook. 3 vols. p. 150.
NN *The Leighs; or, the Discipline of Daily Life.* By Miss Palmer. p. 150.
NN *Life in the Land of the Fire Worshippers.* By Charles de H****. Edited by Fredrika Bremer. 2 vols. p. 185.
NN *My Heart's in the Highlands.* By the Author of 'Nut-Brown Maids.' [Henrietta Keddie], p. 185.
NN *The Bank Parlour; or, Experiences in the Life of a Late Banker.* By A. B. Blackie. p. 185.

Aug. 17
NN *Adrift; or, the Rock on the South Atlantic.* Edited by Frank Fowler. p. 217.

Aug. 24
Gazida. Par Xavier Marmier. pp. 241—42.

OLT *The Family Save-All, a System of Secondary Cookery.* By the Editor of 'Enquire Within' [Robert Kemp Philp] p. 248.

Aug. 31
(opens issue) *Memoirs and Correspondence of King Jerome and Queen Catherine*—[Mémories et Correspondance du Roi Jérome et de la Reine Catherine]. Première Partie. pp. 271—73.
The Book of Good Counsels: from the Sanskrit of the Hitopadesa. By Edwin Arnold, M. A. pp. 278—79.

Sept. 7
Practical Illustration of Woman's Right to Labour. Edited by Caroline H. Dall.
Treatise on Deportment, Dancing and Physical Education for Young Ladies. By Madame D'Egville Michau. pp. 304—05.
Memoir of the Life and Writings of William Tennant, L. L. D. By Matthew Foster Conolly. pp. 310—11.

Sept. 21
On Food: being Lectures delivered at the South Kensington Museum. By E. Lankester, M. D.
The Cook's Guide and Housekeeper's and Butler's Assistant. By Charles Elmé Francatelli. p. 368.

Oct. 12
OLT *The Huntley Casket.* By A. Crawford. pp. 477—78.

Nov. 2
NN (whole section) *The Cloister and the Hearth: a Tale of the Middle Ages.* By Charles Reade. 4 vols. pp. 576—77.

Nov. 9
NN *The Romance of a Dull Life.* By the Author of 'Morning Clouds.' [Mrs. A. J. Penny] p. 615.

Dec. 7
Lovel the Widower. By W. M. Thackeray. p. 758.

Dec. 14
CHILDREN'S BOOKS
The Wonderful Adventures of Tuflongbo.
By Holme Lee [Harriet Parr] p. 805.

Dec. 28
(opens issue) *Woman's Rights under the Law. In Three Lectures, delivered in Boston in 1861.* By Caroline H. Dall.
Experiences of an English Sister of Mercy. By Margaret Goodman. pp. 873—74.
NN (whole section) *White and Black: a Story of the Southern States.* [Caroline Ashurst Biggs] 3 vols. pp. 877—78.
NN *The Seven Sons of Mammon: a Story.* By George Augustus Sala. 3 vols.
NN *Norman Sinclair.* By W. Edmonstone Aytoun, D. C. L. 3 vols. p. 878.
OLT *Old Vauxhall: a Romance.* By W. H. Marshall, Esq. 3 vols. p. 881.

1862
Jan. 4
Domestic Life in Palestine. By Mary Eliza Rogers.
Travels in the Holy Land. By Fredrika Bremer. Translated by Mary Howitt. 2 vols. pp. 15—16.

Jan. 18
OLT *The Frigate and the Lugger: a Nautical Romance.* 3 vols. p. 81.

Jan. 25
The Lady's Guide to the Ordering of her Household. By a Lady.
Dinners and Dinner-givers. pp. 109—10.

Feb. 1
Olive Blake's Good Work: a Novel. By John Cordy Jeaffreson. 3 vols. pp. 149—50.

Feb. 8
Memoirs of Queen Hortense, Mother of Napoleon III. Compiled by Lascelles Wraxall and Robert Wehrhan. 2 vols. pp. 186—88.

March 22
Galileo Galilei.—[Gailileo Galilei: sa Vie, son Proces et ses Contemporaines, d'après

les Documens Originaux, par Philarete Chasles] pp. 389—91.

April 19
Can Wrong be Right? a Tale. By Mrs. S. C. Hall, 2 vols. pp. 523—24.

May 10
Carr of Carrlyon: a Novel. [Hamilton Aidé] 3 vols. p. 624.

May 24
OLT *The Cotton Lord.* By Herbert Glynn. 2 vols. p. 691.

June 14
(opens issue) *The Autobiography of a Working Man.* Edited by the Hon. Eleanor E. Eden. p. 781.

June 21
NN *La Belle Marie: a Romance.* By the Author of 'Smugglers and Foresters,' & c. [Rosa Mackenzie Kettle] 2 vols. p. 818.
NN *Mrs. Blake: a Story of Twenty Years.* By Mrs. Newton Crosland. 3 vols. p. 818.
OLT *Yorke House: a Novel.* 3 vols. By William Platt p. 822.
OLT *Carine Steinburgh: an Autobiography.* [Elodie Lawton Miyatovic] p. 822.
OLT *The Crawfords: a Tale.* By Caroline Ricketts. p. 822.

June 28
NN *Marrying for Money: a Novel.* By Mrs. Mackenzie Daniels. 3 vols. p. 851.

July 5
OLT *Sirenia; or, Recollections of a Past Existence.* [Benjamin Lumley] p. 17.

July 12
The Queen's Maries: a Romance of Holyrood. By G. J. Whyte Melville. pp. 45—46.

July 19
Mrs. Beeton's Book of Household Management.
Plain Cookery-Book for the Working Classes. By Charles Elmé Francatelli.
Handbook of Domestic Recipes.
Everybody's Pudding Book.

Passages in the Life of a Young House-keeper related by Herself. pp. 78—80.
OLT *The Master.* By Mrs. Mary Denison p. 80.

Aug. 2
Woman: what she has been, what she is, what she will be, or what she ought to be—[La Femme: ce qu'elle fut, ce qu'elle est, ce qu'elle sera, ou ce qu'elle devrait être, par J. T. L.] p. 139.

Aug. 9
Selections from the Poetry of the Afghans. By Capt. H. G. Raverty pp. 175—76.

Aug. 16
OLT *A Loss Gained.* By Philip Cresswell. p. 209.
OLT *Baronscliffe; or, a Deed of other Days.* By Mrs. P. M. Latham. p. 209.
OLT *Childhood and Youth. a Tale.* By Count Nicola Tolstoi. Translated from the German by M. von Meysenbug. p. 209.

Aug. 23
OLT *Poems from the German.* By Richard Garnett. pp. 241—42.

Sept. 6
Two Lives. By Blanchard Jerrold. 2 vols. pp. 296—97.
Adventures of Baron Wenceslas Wratislaw. By A. H. Wratislaw. M. A. pp. 298—301.
OLT *Hearths and Watchfires.* By Capt. Colomb, R. A. 3 vols. p. 305.
OLT *The Last Days of a Bachelor: an Autobiography.* By James M'Gregor Allan. 2 vols. p. 305.
OLT *The Haunted Castle.* By M. and R. Meehan. p. 305.

Sept. 13
Fern Vale; or, the Queensland Squatter. A Novel. By Colin Munro. 3 vols. p. 333.

Sept. 20
The Royal English and Foreign Confectioner. By Charles Elmé Francatelli. pp. 361—62.

NN *Footsteps behind Him: a Novel.* By William F. Stewart. 3 vols. p. 365.
OLT *Raising the Veil.* By John Pomeroy. 2 vols. p. 370.
OLT *All's Well that Ends Well.* By Cyrus Redding. 3 vols. p. 370.
OLT *The Red Track: a Story of Social Life in Mexico.* By Gustave Aimard p. 370.

Sept. 27
Studies of the Manners and Literature of Germany in the Nineteenth Century—[Trente Années de Critique: Etudes sur l'Allemagne au Dix-neuvième Siècle, par M. Philarete Chasles]—pp. 395—96.

Oct. 4
OLT *Measure for Measure: a Novel.* By the Author of 'Greymore.' [Mrs. A. B. Church] 3 vols. p. 431.
OLT *Janet, one of Many: a Story in Verse.* By Mrs. [Sarah Stickney] Ellis. p. 431.

Oct. 11
OLT *Aunt Judy's Letters.* By Mrs. Alfred Gatty. Illustrated by Clara S. Lane. p. 460.

Oct. 25
English Women of Letters: Biographical Sketches. By Julia Kavanagh. 2 vols. pp. 527—28.

Nov. 8
Our Last Years in India. By Mrs. John B. Speid. pp. 587—88.

Nov. 15
OLT *Jane Grey.* Par Alphonse Bret. p. 627.
OLT *Honey and Gall: a Poetical Miscellany.—[Miel et Fiel: Mélanges Poétiques,* par Adrian Saintour]. pp. 627—28.

Nov. 22
NN *The Church in the World.* 3 vols. pp. 657—58.
OLT *Roxana, the Spanish Maid; a Tale of Modern Times.* pp. 695—96.

Dec. 6
OLT *Stories from the Shores of the Rhine—[Contes du Bords Du Rhin,* par Erckmann Chatriau]. p. 734.

OLT *Unedited Stories of Edgar Poe—* [*Contes Inédits d'Edgar Poe*, traduits de l'Anglais par William Hughes]. p. 734.

Dec. 13
Praying and Working; being an Account of what Men can do in Earnest. By the Rev. W. Fleming Stevenson. pp. 764—65.

Dec. 20
OLT *The Prophecy.* By Lady Rachel Butler. 2 vols. p. 805.
OLT *Normanton.* By A. J. Barrowcliffe. p. 805.

Dec. 27
OLT *The Mountain Refuge; or, Sure Help in Time of Need: a Tale of the Vaudois of the Sixteenth Century.* p. 844.

1863

Jan. 10
FRENCH NOVELS
Lady Fortune—[*Dame Fortune*, par Paul Perret]—p. 48.
The Trial of Handsome William—[*La Cause du Beau Guillaume Durant*]. pp. 48—49.
The Conquest of a Soul—[*La Conquête d'une Ame*, par Eugène Lataye]. p. 49.

Jan. 17
OLT *Thoughts on the Dwellings of the People.* By Thomas Hare, p. 85.
OLT *Counsels of an Invalid: Letters on Religious Subjects.* By George Wilson, M. D. p. 85.

Jan. 24
OLT *Aims and Ends: a Novel.* 3 vols. By C. C. G. [Mrs. Thomas Sheridan] p. 119.

Feb. 14
Sisterhoods in the Church of England. By Margaret Goodman. pp. 221—22.
FRENCH BOOKS
The Religion of Fools—[*La Religion des Imbéciles*, par Henri Monnier]. p. 226.
Railways and the Credit of France—[*Les Chemins de Fer et le Crédit de France*, par G. Pougard'hieu]. p. 226.

Lovers of the Present Day—[*Les Amants d'Aujourd'hui*, par Arnould Fremy]. p. 226.
Women in the Provinces—[*Les Femmes de Province*]. p. 226.
Brazil as it is—[*Brésil tel qu'il est*, par Charles Expilly]. p. 226.
The Wild Sports of India—[*Les Chasses Sauvages de l'Inde*, par Germain de Lagny], p. 226.
The Wedding Present—[*Le Présent de Noces*, par M. Arthur Ponroy]. p. 226.
A Young Girl's First Love—[*Le Premier Amour d'une Jeune Fille*, par Lardin et Mie d'Aghonne]. p. 226.
Les Demi-Dots, par M. Audeval. p. 226.
Conversations of Goethe with Eckerman.—[*Entretiens de Goethe et d'Eckerman: Pensées sur la Littératur, les Moeurs et les Arts*, traduits, pour la première fois, par J. N. Charles]. p. 226.
The Tropic Land: Scenes of Mexican Life—[*La Terre Chaude: Scènes de Moeurs Mexicaines*, par Lucien Béart.] pp. 226—27.

Feb. 28
NN *Sylvia's Lovers.* By Mrs. Gaskell. 3 vols. p. 291.

March 7
FRENCH BOOKS
Acts and Gestes of Garin de Loherain—[Garin de Loherain: Chanson de Geste] p. 329.
The Pirate of St. Laurent—[*Le Pirate de Saint-Laurent,* par H. Emile Chevalier]. pp. 329—30.

March 14
NN (whole section) *True as Steel.* By Walter Thornbury. 3 vols. p. 360.
NN *A Daughter of Eve: a Novel.* By Hain Friswell. 2 vols. p. 360.
Such Things Are. By the Author of 'Recommended to Mercy.' [Mrs. Margaret Houstoun] 3 vols. p. 360.
NN *Ada Fortescue: a Novel.* [Sibella Jones] 3 vols. p. 360.

NN *A Prodigal Son.* By Dutton Cook. 3 vols. pp. 360—61.

NN *The Mistakes of a Life: a Novel.* By Mrs. J. Hubback. 3. vols. p. 361.

NN *Christmas at the Cross Keys.* By Kenner Deane. p. 361.

March 28
Live It Down: a Story of Light Lands. By J. C. Jeaffreson. 3 vols. pp. 419—20.

April 11
NN *Nobly False: a Novel.* By James M'Grigor Allan. 2 vols. pp. 489—90.

April 18
OLT *Burton Abbots: a Woman's Story, in Four Books.* 3 vols. p. 521.

April 25
John Leifchild, D. D.: his Public Ministry, Private Uefulness, and Personal Characteristics. By J. R. Leifchild, A. M. pp. 550—52.

NN (whole section) *The Story of Elizabeth.* [Anne Isabella Thackeray] pp. 552—53.

NN *Deep Waters: a Novel.* By Anna H. Drury. 3 vols. p. 553.

NN *The Deserted House of Hawksworth.* 3 vols. p. 553.

May 23
NN *Up and Down in the World.* By Blanchard Jerrold. 3 vols. p. 680.

NN *Skirmishing.* By the Author of 'Cousin Stella.' [Mrs. Charles Jenkin] p. 680.

NN *The Poachers: a Tale.* By the Rev. E. H. Maclachlan, M. A. p. 680.

NN *Willie Heath and the House-Rent.* By the Rev. Dr. Leask. p. 680.

May 30
NN (whole section) *Giulio Malatesta: a Novel.* By T. A. Trollope. 3 vols. pp. 707—08.

NN *A Dark Night's Work.* By Mrs. Gaskell. p. 708.

June 6
NN *Heart and Cross.* By the Author of

'Margaret Maitland.' [Margaret Oliphant] pp. 743—44.

NN *Arrows in the Dark.* By the Author of 'Said and Done.' p. 744.

NN *Bertha's Repentance: a Tale.* By J. Frazer Corkran. p. 744.

NN *Wayfe Summers: the Story of an Inner and an Outer Life.* By Thomas Archer. 2 vols. p. 744.

NN *Mildrington, the Barrister: a Romance.* [Percy Hetherington Fitzgerald] 2 vols. p. 744.

NN *Charlie Thornhill; or, the Dunce of the Family: a Novel.* By Charles Clarke. 3 vols. p. 744.

NN *Grace of Glenholme.* 3 vols. By William Platt. p. 776.

June 20
NN (whole section) *Rough and Smooth: a Tale of Our Own Time.* By Lieut.-Col. R. D. Clephane. p. 810.

NN *The First Temptation.* Translated from the German, by Mrs. William R. Wilde. 3 vols. p. 810.

NN *A Simple Woman.* By the Author of 'Nut Brown Maids.' [Henrietta Keddie] p. 810.

NN *Tried and True: a Tale.* By Alton Clyde. p. 810.

NN *Snowed Up.* By Mrs. Octavius Freire Owen. 3 vols. p. 810.

NN *Manxland: a Tale: with an Introductory Sketch of a Manx Home Mission.* By B. Stowell. p. 810.

NN *Joan Carewe: a Novel.* By E. M. O. L. 3 vols. p. 810.

OLT *Legends of the Lintel and the Ley.* By W. C. Dendy. p. 811.

June 27
NN (whole section) *Respectable Sinners.* By Mrs. Brotherton. 3 vols. p. 839.

NN *Chesterford, and some of its People.* By the Author of 'A Bad Beginning.' [Katherine S. Macquoid] p. 839—40.

July 11
NN *Romola.* By George Eliot. 3 vols. p. 46.

NN *Church and Chapel.* By the Author of 'High Church.' [Frederick William Robinson] 3 vols. pp. 46—47.

NN *Sir Everard's Daughter.* By John Cordy Jeaffreson. p. 47.

July 18
NN *Dragon's Teeth.* By the Rev. James Pycroft. 3 vols. p. 81.

July 25
NN (whole section) *Forbidden Fruit.* By I. T. 2 vols. pp. 110—11.

NN *Young Life; its Chances and Changes.* By the Author of 'Hidden Links.' [Charles Francis Liddell] 2 vols. p. 111.

Aug. 1
NN *Twice Lost: a Novel.* By the Author of 'Queen Isabel.' [Menella Bute Smedley] p. 146.

Aug. 8
NN *Altogether Wrong.* By the Author of 'The World's Furniture.' 3 vols. p. 172.

NN *Vicissitudes of a Gentlewoman.* 3 vols. pp. 172—73.

Aug. 15
NN *Mary Lindsay.* By the Lady Emily Ponsonby. 3 vols. p. 207.

NN *False Positions; or, Sketches of Character.* 2 vols. pp. 207—08.

OLT *Skating on Thin Ice: a Novel.* By the author of 'Reca Garland.' [Septimus Berdmore] 2 vols. p. 210.

Aug. 22
NN (whole section) *Martin Pole.* By John Saunders. 2 vols. p. 240.

NN *The Cream of a Life.* By a Man of the World. [Martin Archer Shee] 3 vols. p. 240.

NN *A Disputed Inheritance: a Tale of a Cornish Family.* By Thomas Hood. p. 240.

NN *Philip Lisle: a Novel.* By the Author of 'The Two Households.' [Terence Doyle] 3 vols. p. 240.

OLT *The Poet's Children.* By Mary Howitt p. 240.

Aug. 29
NN *Veronia.* 3 vols. pp. 266—67.

NN *Margaret Stourton; or, a Year of Governess Life.* p. 267.

OLT *Joseph Anstey; or, the Patron and the Protégé.* By D. S. Henry. p. 270.

OLT *Our County; or, Hampshire in the Reign of Charles the Second.* By Henry Moody p. 270.

Sept. 5
OLT *Ralph; or, St. Sepulchre's and St. Stephen's.* p. 301.

Sept. 19
Eleanor's Victory. By M. E. Braddon. 3 vols. pp. 361—62.

OLT *A Country Visit.* By Charlotte Hardcastle. 3 vols. p. 366.

Oct. 10
OLT *Shirley Hall Asylum; or, Memoirs of a Monomaniac.* Edited by the Author of 'Dives and Lazarus.' & c. [William Gilbert] p. 465.

Oct. 31
NN *After Long Years: a Novel.* By Mrs. Mackenzie Daniels. 2 vols. pp. 566—67.

Nov. 21
NN *Queen Mab.* By Julia Kavanagh. 3 vols. pp. 675—76.

Nov. 28
The Principles of Charitable Work, as set forth in the Writings of Amelia Wilhelmina Sieveking.
Life of Amelia Wilhelmina Sieveking. Edited by Caroline Winkworth. pp. 712—13.

Dec. 5
NN *Leo: a Novel.* By Dutton Cook. 3 vols. pp. 752—53.

1864

Jan. 2
OLT *A Treatise on the Fishery Laws of the United Kingdom.* By James Paterson. p. 18.

OLT *Mr. Wind and Madam Rain.* By Paul de Musset. pp. 18—19.

OLT *Tales of Many Lands.* By M. Fraser Tytler p. 19.

OLT *Bygone Days in our Village.* By J. L. W. [Jean L. Watson] p. 19.

OLT *Florian's Husband.* [Barbara Gunn] 3 vols. p. 19.

Jan. 9

The Wife's Evidence. By W. G. Wills. 3 vols. pp. 46—47.

Jan. 23

NN *Annis Warleigh's Fortunes.* By Holme Lee. [Harriet Parr] 3 vols. pp. 118—19.

NN *Not an Angel.* By the Author of 'Ethel,' & c. [Marian James] 2 vols. p. 119.

NN *Maud Winthrop's Life Charge: a Novel.* By Mace Anstruther. 2 vols. p. 119.

NN *The Shadow of Ashlydyat.* By Mrs. Henry Wood. 3 vols. p. 119.

Jan. 30

NN *Meadowleigh: a Tale of English Country Life.* By the Author of 'The Ladies of Bever Hollow.' [Miss Anne Manning] 2 vols. p. 154.

NN *The Mortons of Bardom: a Lancashire Tale.* 3 vols. p. 154.

NN *Keeping Afloat; or, the Meeting at the Morgue: a Novel.* pp. 154—55.

Feb. 6

The Queens of the Foot-lights.—[*Les Reines de la Rampe,* par L. de Montchamp et Ch. Monsont]. pp. 189—90.

NN *Wild Fire.* By Walter Thornbury. 3 vols. pp. 192—93.

Feb. 13

NN *Lloyd Pennant: a Tale of the West.* By Ralph Neville. 2 vols. pp. 227—28.

Feb. 20

NN *The Life of Sir Timothy Graceless, Bart.* Written by Himself. Edited by Omega. 2 vols. p. 262.

March 5

NN *Beppo the Conscript: a Novel.* By T. Adolphus Trollope. 2 vols. pp. 330—31.

OLT *Horrors of the Virginian Slave Trade.* By John Hawkings Simpson. pp. 336—37.

March 12

NN (whole section) *Madeleine Graham.* By the Author of 'Whitefriars,' & c. [Miss Jane or Emma Robinson] 3 vols. p. 371.

NN *Wylder's Hand: a Novel.* By Joseph Sheridan Le Fanu. 3 vols. pp. 371—72.

March 19

NN *The Town of the Cascades.* By Michael Banim, survivor of the O'Hara Family. 2 vols. p. 405.

NN *Peculiar: a Tale of the Great Transition.* By Epes Sargent. Edited by William Howitt. 3 vols. p. 405.

March 26

NN *The Small House at Allington.* By Anthony Trollope. With Illustrations. pp. 437—38.

April 2

NN *Miriam's Sorrow.* By Mrs. Mackenzie Daniel[s]. 2 vols. pp. 472—73.

April 23

OLT *Autobiography of Maude Bolingbroke.* By Emma Jane Macintosh. p. 577.

OLT *Diary of George Deru; or, Jottings of a Year of Middle Life.* p. 577.

OLT *Trial and Trust; or, Ellen Morden's Experience of Life.* p. 577.

April 30

NN *Emilia in England.* By George Meredith. 3 vols. pp. 609—10.

NN *Clara Vaughan: a Novel.* [Richard Doddridge Blackmore] 3 vols. pp. 610—11.

May 14

NN *Rathlynn.* By the Author of 'The Saxon in Ireland.' [John Hervey Ashworth] 3 vols. p. 675.

NN *Dorothy Dovedale's Trials.* By Thomas Miller. 2 vols. p. 675.

May 21
Diaries of a Lady of Quality from 1797 to 1844. Edited with Notes, by A. Hayward, pp.705—06.

May 28
Not Dead Yet. By J. C. Jeaffreson. 3 vols. pp. 735—36.

June 4
NN *Late Laurels.* By the Author of 'Wheat and Tares.' 2 vols. [Sir Henry Stewart Cunningham] p. 773.
NN *The Danes sketched by Themselves.* Translated by Mrs. Bushby. 3 vols. pp. 773—74.
NN *The Goldsworthy Family; or, the Country Attorney.* By William Gilbert. 2 vols. p. 774.

June 11
NN *John Greswold.* By the Author of 'Paul Ferroll.' [Mrs. Caroline Clive] 2 vols. pp. 803—04.
NN *Hester Kirton.* By the Author of 'A Bad Beginning & c.' [Katherine S. Macquoid] 3 vols. p. 804.
NN *Lost Sir Massingberd: a Romance of Real Life.* [James Payn] 2 vols. p. 804.

June 18
NN *Too Strange not to be True: a Tale.* By Lady Georgiana Fullerton. 3 vols. p. 834.

June 25
NN *Barbara Home.* 3 vols. By Margaret Blount. pp. 868—69.

July 2
NN *Blythe House.* By R. F. H. [Rosa F. Hill] p. 17.
NN *Maurice Dering.* By the Author of 'Guy Livingstone.' [George Alfred Lawrence] p. 17.

July 9
OLT *The Layrock of Langley Side: a Lancashire Story.* By Benjamin Brierly. p. 50.
OLT *Brothers and Sisters; or, True of Heart: a Story of Home Life.* By Emma Marshall. p. 50.

July 23
NN *Mattie: a Stray.* By the Author of 'High Church.' [Frederick William Robinson] 3 vols. pp. 111—12.
NN *Haunted Hearts.* By the Author of 'The Lamplighter.' [Maria Susanna Cummins] 2 vols. p. 112.
NN *Rington Priory: a Tale.* By Ethel Hone. 3 vols. p. 112.
NN *Frederick Rivers; Independent Parson.* By Mrs. Florence Wilson. pp. 112—13.

Aug. 13
The History of the Cotton Famine. By R. A. Arnold. pp. 202—04.
NN *Dangerous Connexions: a Novel.* By Charles Gibbon. 3 vols. p. 209.
NN *The Trial; or, More Links in the Daisy Chain.* By the Author of 'The Heir of Redclyffe.' [Charlotte Yonge] 2 vols. p. 209.
NN *Breakers Ahead.* By Ralph Vyvyan. [Sir Henry Denis Le Marchant] 2 vols. pp. 209—10.
NN *Second to None: a Military Romance.* By James Grant. 3 vols. p. 210.
NN *Roger Whatmough's Will: a Novel.* By John Bradford. 2 vols. p. 210.

Aug. 20
NN *Wanted, a Home.* By the Author of 'Morning Clouds.' [Mrs. A. J. Penny] 3 vols. p. 240.
NN *Black Moss: a Tale by a Tarn.* By the Author of 'Miriam May.' [Rev. Arthur Robins] 2 vols. p. 240.
NN *Father Sterling: a Novel.* 2 vols. By James M'Grigor Allan. p. 241.
NN *A Fatal Error; or, the Vyviannes.* By J. Masterman. 2 vols. p. 241.
OLT *Thoughts from a Girl's Life.* By Lucy Fletcher. p. 242.
OLT *Mr. Christopher Katydid of Casconia: a Tale.* Edited by Mark Hayward. 2 vols. p. 242.

Aug. 27
NN (whole section) *The Man in Chains.* By C. J. Collins. 3 vols. p. 272.

NN *Alice Hythe: a Novel.* By William Platt. 3 vols. p. 272.

Sept. 3
OLT *Thoughts of Home; or, Counsel and Consolation for Expatriated Invalids.* By Lady Charlotte Maria Pepys. p. 305.
OLT *Above Rubies; or, Memorials of Christian Gentlewomen.* By Miss Brightwell. p. 305.

Sept. 10
NN *Sibylla Lockwood.* By Noell Radecliffe. 3 vols. pp. 336—37.
NN *Zoe's Brand.* By the Author of 'Recommended to Mercy.' [Mrs. Margaret Houstoun] 3 vols. p. 337.
NN *Rosa: a Tale of Spain in the Seventeenth Century.* By Derwent Tremorne. p. 337.

Sept. 17
OLT *Ten Days in a French Parsonage in the Summer of 1863.* By George Musgrove, M. A. 2 vols. p. 368.

Oct. 1
(open issue) *The Maori King; or, the Story of our Quarrel with the Natives of New Zealand.* By J. E. Gorst. M. A. pp. 423—25.

Oct. 22
NN *Abbots Cleve; or, Can it be proved? a Novel.* [Ross Neil (Miss Isabella Harwood)] 3 vols. pp. 526—27.

Nov. 5
Cookery for English Households. By a French Lady.
The English and Australian Cookery-Book. By an Australian Aristologist. [Hon. Edward Abbott, of Tasmania] pp. 595—96.
NN *The Queen of the County.* By the Author of 'Margaret and her Bridesmaid,' & c. [Mrs. Anne Marsh Caldwell] 3 vols. pp. 598—99.
NN *The Wilmot Family.* By Mabel Sharman Crawford. 3 vols. p. 599.

Nov. 19
NN *Reverses.* By the Author of 'Angelo.' [Mrs Anne Marsh Caldwell] 2 vols. p. 670.
NN *Lion Hearted.* By the Author of 'The Gambler's Wife.' [Elizabeth Caroline Grey] 2 vols. p. 670.

Nov. 26
OLT *The Boyle Lectures for the Year 1846.* Delivered at the Chapel Royal, Whitehall, by Charles Merivale, B. D. p. 707.

Dec. 3
NN *Margaret Denzil's History.* Annotated by her Husband. [Frederick Greenwood] 2 vols. p. 743.
NN *Reaping the Whirlwind: a Novel.* 3 vols. By Mrs. Mackenzie Daniel. p. 743.
NN *Lord Lynn's Wife.* [John B. Harwood] 2 vols. pp. 743—44.

Dec. 10
NN *Black and Gold.* By Captain W. H. Patten-Saunders, K. C. G. 3 vols. p. 781.
OLT *What a Woman ought to be: Reflections on Education.* [Ce qu'une Femme doit être, & c.], par Madame Vve Leprince de Beaufort. p. 783.

Dec. 17
NN *Mr. Stewart's Intentions.* By Frederick William Robinson. 3 vols. pp. 818—19.

Dec. 24
(opens issue) *History of Lace.* By Mrs. Bury Palliser. pp. 851—52.
NN *Blount Tempest.* By the Rev. J. C. M. Bellew. 3 vols. p. 859.
NN *Oswald Cray.* By Mrs. Henry Wood. 3 vols. p. 859.

Dec. 31
(opens issue) *Report of the Superintendent and Schoolmistress of the Children's Establishment, Limehouse.* pp. 885—86.
NN *The Ordeal for Wives.* By the Author of 'The Morals of May Fair.' [Mrs Annie Edwards] 3 vols. p. 891.
NN *The Aarbergs.* By Rosamond Hervey. 2 vols. p. 892.

NN *Maud Neville*. 2 vols. p. 892.

NN *The Queen of the Seas: a Tale of Sea and Land*. 3 vols. By C. F. Armstrong. p. 892.

OLT *Thornycorft Hall. Its Owners and its Heirs*. By Emma Jane Worboise. p. 893.

1865

Jan. 7

NN *Uncle Silas: a Tale of Bertram-Haugh*. By J. S. Le Fanu. 3 vols. pp. 16—17.

NN *Melbourne House*. By the Author of 'The Wide, Wide World.' [Elizabeth Wetherell pseud. for Susan Warner] p. 17.

NN *Nelly Deane: a Story of Every-Day Life*. [Mrs. Benson] 2 vols. pp. 17—18.

Jan. 14

NN *Cecil Forrester: a Novel*. By Frederick Sheridan. 2 vols. p. 51.

NN *By the Trent*. By Mrs. E. S. Oldham. p. 51.

Jan. 28

NN *De Profundis: a Tale of Social Deposits*. By William Gilbert. 2 vols. p. 124.

Feb. 18

NN (whole section) *Kinkora; an Irish Story*. By the Hon. Alfred Canning. 2 vols. p. 232.

NN *Christian's Mistake*. By the Author of 'John Halifax, Gentleman.' [Dinah Mulock Craik] pp. 232—33.

NN *Dorothy Firebrace*. By the Author of 'Whitefriars,' & c. [Miss Emma Robinson] 3 vols. p. 233.

NN *George Geith of Fen Court: a Novel*. By F. G. Trafford. 3 vols. p. 233.

NN *Lynn of the Craggs: a Novel*. By Charlotte Smith. 3 vols. p. 233.

Feb. 25

NN *The Three Watches*. By W. G. Wills. 3 vols. p. 272.

March 4

NN *Shattered Idols*. 3 vols. p. 311.

March 18

Homely Rhymes, Poems, and Reminiscences. By Samuel Bamford. pp. 379—80.

NN *Look Before You Leap*. [Mrs Annie French] 2 vols. p. 382.

March 25

NN *Carry's Confession*. By the Author of 'High Church,' & c. [Frederick William Robinson] 3 vols. pp. 419—20.

NN *Avila Hope*. 2 vols. p. 420.

April 1

NN *Once and Again: a Novel*. By the Author of 'Cousin Stella.' [Mrs. Charles Jenkins] 3 vols. pp. 454—55.

NN *Miss Mackenzie*. By Anthony Trollope. 2 vols. p. 455.

NN *Dina; or, Familiar Faces*. [William Patrick Wilkie] 3 vols. p. 455.

OLT *After Business Jottings: Poems*. By R. R. Bealey. p. 455.

April 22

NN *Grey's Court*. Edited by Georgiana Lady Chatterton. 2 vols. pp. 551—52.

April 29

NN *Mercedes: a Romance*. By Sir C. F. Lascelles Wraxall. 3 vols. p. 585.

NN *The Angle-House: a Novel*. 3 vols. By Harry Neville p. 585—86.

NN *Bitter Sweets: a Love Story*. By Joseph Hatton. 3 vols. p. 586.

May 6

The Industrial Resources of the District of the Three Northern Rivers, the Tyne, Wear, and Tees. pp. 617—19.

NOVELS AND TALES

The Heiress of the Blackburnfoot: a Tale of Scottish Rural Life. [Miss Urquhart] p. 620.

N & T *Besom Ben*. By Edwin Waugh. pp. 620—21.

May 13

NN *Miles Buller; or, the Little World of Onniegate: a Novel*. 3 vols. p. 651.

NN *Blanche of Montacute: a Tale*. By Mrs. George Haly. 2 vols. p. 651.

May 20

NN *Violet Osborne*. By the Lady Emily Ponsonby. 3 vols. pp. 682—83.

NN *Who was to blame? a Novel.* By Joseph Verey. 2 vols. p. 683.

May 27
NN *Odd Neighbours.* By the Author of 'Lord Lynn's Wife.' [John Berwick Harwood] 3 vols. p. 717.

June 3
NN (whole section) *Our Charlie.* By Vere Haldane. p. 749.
NN *Alice Ferrars: a Novel.* 3 vols. p. 749.
NN *Aubrey Court: a Novel.* By Frank Lyfield. 3 vols. p. 749.

June 10
NN *Dharma; or, Three Phases of Love.* By E. Paulet. 3 vols. p. 777.

June 17
NN *Alec Forbes of Howglen.* By George M'Donald, M. A. 3 vols. p. 810.
OLT *Dunvarlick; or, Round about the Bush.* By David Macrae. p. 813.

July 1
NN *The Conscript: a Tale of the French War.* p. 13.

July 8
NN *A Woman's Way; or, the Chelsea Sisterhood.* By the Author of 'The Field of Life.' 3 vols. pp. 45—46.
NN *Wild Times: a Tale of the Days of Queen Elizabeth.* 3 vols. p. 46.

July 15
NN *Grasp your Nettle: a Novel.* By E. Lynn Linton. 3 vols. pp. 79—80.

July 29
Strathmore: a Romance. By Ouida. 3 vols. pp. 142—43.
Noel; or, It was to be. By Robert Baker and Skeleton Yorke. 2 vols. p. 143.

Aug. 5
NN (whole section) *Miss Russell's Hobby: a Novel.* 2 vols. p. 179.
NN *London Pilgrims.* 3 vols. p. 179.
NN *One against the World.* By John Saunders. 3 vols. pp. 179—80.

Aug. 12
NN *The Gayworthy:s a Tale of Threads and Thrums.* By the Author of 'Faith Gartney's Girlhood.' [Adelina D. Train Whitney] 2 vols. p. 210.

Aug. 19
The Lace-makers: Sketches of Irish Character. By Mrs. Meredith. pp. 241—42.

Sept. 2
NN *Can You Forgive Her?* By Anthony Trollope. With Illustrations. 2 vols. pp. 305—06.
NN *Andrew Ramsay of Errol.* By the Author of 'John Arnold' & c. [William Wilson] 3 vols. pp. 306—07.
OLT *Tales for the Marines.* By Walter Thornbury. 2 vols. p. 309.

Sept. 9
Principles of Education. By the Author of 'Amy Herbert.' [Elizabeth Sewell] 2 vols. p. 335.
NN *Hope Deferred: a Novel.* By Sybil. 2 vols. 337.

NN *Constance Sherwood: an Autobiography of the Sixteenth Century.* By Lady Georgiana Fullerton. 3 vols. pp. 366—67.

Oct. 7
NN *Miss Forrester: a Novel.* By Mrs. Edwards. 3 vols. p. 466.

Oct. 14
NN *Years Ago: a Tale of West Indian Domestic Life of the Eighteenth Century.* By Mrs. Henry Lynch. pp. 495—96.
NN *Sophy Laurie: a Novel.* By W. C. Hazlitt. 3 vols. p. 496.

Oct. 21
NN *Guy Deverell.* By J. S. Le Fanu. 3 vols. pp. 536—37.
NN *Sir Jasper's Tenant.* By the Author of 'Lady Audley's Secret.' [Mary Elizabeth Braddon] 3 vols. p. 537.
NN *The Holidays of the Countess*—[*La Vieille Roche. Les Vacances de la Comtesse,* par Edmond About]. pp. 537—38.

Oct. 28
NN *William Bathurst*. By Lewis Hough. 3 vols. pp. 574—75.
NN *The Bucklyn Shaig: a Tale of the Last Century*. By the Hon. Mrs. Alfred [Fanny Charlotte] Montgomery. 2 vols. p. 575.

Nov. 18
NN *Maxwell Drewitt: a Novel*. By G. F. Trafford. 3 vols. pp. 683—84.
NN *Doctor Harold*. By Mrs. Gascoigne. 3 vols. p. 684.

Nov. 25
NN *The Coming of Age of Mdlle. Bridot*. [*La Majorité de Mdlle. Bridot*. par Charles Deslys.] p. 724.

Dec. 2
NN *Snooded Jessaline; or, the Honour of a House*. By Mrs. T. K. Hervey. 3 vols. pp. 761—62.
NN *Marian Rooke*. By Henry Sedley. 3 vols. pp. 762—63.

Dec. 9
NN *The Clyffards of Clyffe*. By the Author of 'Lost Sir Massingberd.' [James Payn] 3 vols. p. 801.
OLT *The Red Shirt*. Episodes by Alberto Mario. p. 805.

Dec. 23
NN *Fides, the Beauty of Mayence*. Adapted from the German by Sir Lascelles Wraxall, Bart. 3 vols. pp. 884—85.

Dec. 30
NN *Adrienne Hope, the Story of a Life*. By Matilda M. Hays. 2 vols. p. 920.

1866
Jan. 20
NN *Common Sense: a Novel*. By Mrs. C. J. Newby. 3 vols. p. 89.
NN *Faith Unwin's Ordeal*. By Georgiana Craik. 2 vols. pp. 89—90.

Jan. 27
NN *Treason at Home: a Novel*. By Mrs. Greenhough. p. 131.

Feb. 17
NN *Woman against Woman*. By Florence Marryat. 3 vols. p. 233.

March 3
NN *A Noble Life*. By the Author of 'John Halifax.' [Dinah Mulock Craik] 2 vols. p. 296.
NN *Winifred Bertram and the World She Lived in*. By the Author of 'The Schönberg-Cotta Family.' [Elizabeth Charles] pp. 296—97.

March 10
NN *Falkner Lyle; or, the Story of Two Wives*. By Mark Lemon. 3 vols. p. 329.
NN *Walter Goring: a Story*. By Annie Thomas. 3 vols. p. 329.
NN *What Money Can't Do: a Novel*. By the Author of 'Altogether Wrong,' & c. 3 vols. pp. 329—30.

March 24
NN *The Grahams of Bessbridge House, Dydborough*. By Mrs. Trafford Whitehead. 2 vols. pp. 395—96.
NN *Chronicles of Dartmoor*. By Mrs. Marsh. 3 vols. p. 396.
NN *The Curse of the Claverings*. By Mrs. F. Graham. p. 396.

March 31
NN *Cerise: a Tale of the Last Century*. By C. J. Whyte Melville. 3 vols. p. 426.

April 7
NN *Jenny Bell: a Story*. By Percy [Hetherington] Fitzgerald. 3 vols. p. 457.
NN *St. Martin's Eve: a Novel*. By Mrs. Henry Wood. 3 vols. pp. 457—58.

April 14
A History of the Gypsies. By Walter Simson. Edited by James Simson. pp. 492—93.

April 21
NN *Beyond the Church*. [Frederick William Robinson] 3 vols. pp. 525—26.

May 5
NN *The Maitlands: a Tale of the Day*. By the Author of 'Three Opportunities.' 3 vols. p. 595.

May 12

NN *Rose Sinclair: a Novel*. By G. Blunt. 2 vols. p. 632.

May 19

NN (whole section) *The Dove in the Eagle's Nest*. By the Author of 'The Heir of Redclyffe.' [Charlotte Yonge] 2 vols. p. 667.

NN *Plain John Orpington*. By the Author of 'Lord Lynn's Wife,' & c. [John B. Harwood] 3 vols. p. 667.

NN *Hester's Sacrifice*. By the Author of 'St. Olave's' & c. [Eliza Tabor] 3 vols. pp. 667—68.

NN *Unconventional: a Novel*. By Thomas Sutton, B. A. 3 vols. p. 668.

May 26

NN *The Hidden Sin*. [Frances Browne] 3 vols. p. 699.

OLT *Fish, and How to Cook it*. By Elizabeth Watts. p. 704.

June 2

NN *The Lady's Mile*. By the Author of 'Lady Audley's Secret.' [Mary Elizabeth Braddon] 3 vols. p. 733.

June 9

NN (whole section) *Sir Owen Fairfax*. By Lady Emily Ponsonby. 3 vols. p. 765.

NN *A Son of the Soil*. [Margaret Oliphant] 2 vols. pp. 765—66.

NN *The Gain of a Loss*. By the Author of 'The Last of the Cavaliers.' [Rose Piddington] 3 vols. p. 766.

NN *The Talisman, the Opal*—[Le Talisman, l'Opale, par M. Jules Janin]. p. 766.

June 16

NN *Chandos: a Novel*. By Ouida. 3 vols. pp. 797—98.

NN *Phemie Keller*. By the Author of 'George Geith,' & c. [Mrs. Charlotte Elizabeth Lawson Riddell] 3 vols. p. 798.

June 23

NN *Felix Holt, the Radical*. By George Eliot. 3 vols. p. 828.

June 30

NN *All in the Dark*. By G. J. Sheridan Le Fanu. 2 vols. p. 860.

NN *Bound to the Wheel*. By John Saunders. 3 vols. p. 860.

NN *Ernest Graham: a Doctor's Story*. p. 861.

July 7

NN *Emily Foinder; or, the See-Saw of Life: a Novel*. By F. Devonshire, 3 vols. p. 13.

July 21

NN *Elster's Folly: a Novel*. By Mrs. Henry Wood. 3 vols. p. 76.

NN *The Romance of Mary Constant*. Written by Herself. p. 76.

NN *Lionel Merval: a Novel*. [William Bainbridge] 3 vols. pp. 76—77.

NN *An Old Man's Secret: a Novel*. 3 vols. By Frank Trollope. p. 77.

July 28

NN *A Troubled Stream: a Story*. By Charlotte Hardcastle. 3 vols. pp. 110—11.

Sept. 8

NN *The Second Mrs. Tillotson: a Story*. By Percy Fitzgerald, M. A. 3 vols. pp. 297—98.

OLT *Always in the Way: a Little Story*. By Thomas Jeans. p. 303.

Sept. 15

NN *The Shadows of Destiny: a Romance*. By Capt. Colomb. 2 vols. pp. 329—30.

Sept. 22

NN *The Race for Wealth: a Novel*. By Mrs. J. H. Riddell. 3 vols. pp. 363—64.

NN *Cradock Nowell: a Tale of the New Forest*. By Richard Doddridge Blackmore. 3 vols. p. 364.

Nov. 24

NN *Angelo Lyons: a Novel*. By William Platt. 3 vols. p. 674.

Brief Essay on the Position of Women. By Mrs. C. H. Spear. pp. 674—75.

Dec. 1

NN *Rachel's Secret.* By the Author of 'The Master of Marton.' [Eliza Tabor] 3 vols. pp. 709—10.

NN *Dacia Singleton.* By the Author of 'Altogether Wrong,' & c. 3 vols. p. 710.

NN *Sir Julian's Wife.* By Emma Jane Worboise. p. 710.

NN *Hetty Gouldworth: a Novel.* By George Macaulay. 2 vols. p. 710—11.

Dec. 8

NN *The Story of Nelly Dillon.* By the Author of 'Myself and my Relatives.' [Anne J. Robertson] 2 vols. p. 746.

Dec. 15

NN *Three Phases of Christian Love.* By Lady [May Elizabeth] Herbert. pp. 793—94.

Dec. 29

NN *Philip the Dreamer: a Novel.* 3 vols. p. 873.

1867

Jan. 12

NN *Played Out: a Novel.* By Annie Thomas. 3 vols. p. 44.

Jan. 19

NN *Leyton Hall, and other Tales.* By Mark Lemon. 3 vols. pp. 83—84.

Feb. 2

NN *Bent, not Broken: a Tale.* By George Manville Fenn. 3 vols. p. 154.

NN *Our Premier; or, Love and Duty.* By Frank Foster. p. 154.

Feb. 9

NN *The Master of Wingbourne: a Novel.* 2 vols. p. 186.

Feb. 23

NN *Vittoria.* By George Meredith. 3 vols. pp. 248—49.

March 2

NN *Idalia: a Romance.* By Ouida. 3 vols. p. 283.

OLT *Meta's Letters: a Tale.* By Mrs. Ensell. p. 289.

March 9

NN *Dumbleton Common.* By the Hon. Eleanor Eden. 2 vols. p. 317.

NN *Two Marriages.* By the Author of 'John Halifax, Gentleman.' [Dinah Mulock Craik] 2 vols. p. 317.

OLT *May and her Friends.* By E. M. B. With Illustrations by F. W. Lawson. p. 321.

March 16

NN *Jessie's Expiation: a Novel.* By Oswald Boyle. 3 vols. p. 349.

NN *Sir Cyrus of Stoneycleft: a Novel.* By Mrs. Wood. 3 vols. pp. 349—50.

March 23

NN *Lady Adelaide's Oath: a Novel.* By Mrs. Henry Wood. 3 vols. p. 383.

March 30

NN *Woodburn Grange: a Story of English Country Life.* By William Howitt. 3 vols. pp. 414—15.

NN *Maidenhood.* By Mrs. Sara Anna Marsh. 3 vols. p. 415.

April 6

NN *Off the Line.* By Lady Charles Thynne. 2 vols. pp. 450—51.

April 13

NN *The Loyalist's Daughter.* By a Loyalist. 4 vols. p. 481.

NN *The Chepford People: a Story about Themselves, their Pastors, Masters, and Neighbours.* 2 vols. p. 481.

NN *Emily's Choice: an Australian Tale.* By Maude Jeanne Franc. pp. 481—82.

NN *The Heir of Mabberley: a Novel.* By Henry George Stuckley, M. D. 2 vols. p. 482.

NN *Great Harefield.* p. 482.

April 20

NN *Cometh up as a Flower: an Autobiography.* [Rhoda Broughton] 2 vols. pp. 514—15.

April 27

NN *Armstrong Magney.* By Heraclitus Grey. p. 546.

NN *Which will Triumph? a Novel.* By A. B. Le Geyt. 3 vols. pp. 546—47.

OLT *The Word. The House of Israel.* By the Author of 'The Wide, Wide World.' [Elizabeth Wetherell pseud. for Susan Warner] p. 549.

OLT *Home Life of the Lancashire Factory Folk during the Cotton Famine.* By Edwin Waugh. pp. 549—50.

May 4

NN *Counting the Cost: a Novel.* By William Duthie. 3 vols. p. 585.

NN *A Wife and Not a Wife: a Novel.* By Cyrus Redding. 3 vols. p. 585.

OLT *The Journal of a Home Life.* By Elizabeth M. Sewell. p. 587.

May 11

NN *Ada Moore's Story: a Novel.* 3 vols. p. 619.

NN *Elinor Dryden's Probation.* By E. S. Macquoid. 3 vols. p. 619.

NN *Philo: a Romance of Life in the First Century.* By John Hamilton, M. A. Cantab. 3 vols. pp. 619—20.

NN *Marjorie Duddingstoune: a Tale of Old St. Andrews.* By William Francis Collier, LL. D. 2 vols. p. 620.

May 18

NN *Constance Rivers.* By Lady Barrett Lennard. 3 vols. p. 654.

NN *The Flying Scud: a Sporting Novel.* By the Author of 'Charlie Thornhill.' [Rev. Charles Clarke] 2 vols. pp. 654—55.

NN *More than a Match.* By the Author of 'Recommended to Mercy.' [Mrs. Margaret Houstoun] p. 655.

June 1

NN *Miss Jane, the Bishop's Daughter.* By John Harwood. 3 vols. pp. 720—21.

NN *The Means and the End; or, the Chaplain's Secret.* By Mrs. Henry H. B. Paul. p. 721.

June 8

NN *No Man's Friend.* By Frederick William Robinson. 3 vols. p. 753.

NN *Lillian's Inheritance: a Novel.* By Mrs. William Murray. 2 vols. pp. 753—54.

June 15

NN *The Claverings.* By Anthony Trollope. 2 vols. p. 783.

NN *Paul's Courtship: a Novel.* By Hesba Stretton. 3 vols. pp. 783—84.

NN *New Nobility: a Novel.* By Benedick Whippem. 3 vols. p. 784.

June 22

NN (whole section) *Begg'd at Court: a Legend of Westminster.* By Charles Knight. p. 815.

NN *Irene's Repentance.* By Christian Eyre. 2 vols. pp. 815—16.

NN *Playing on the Brink: a Novel.* By J. Frazer Corkran. 3 vols. p. 816.

OLT *Katie Lawford's Victory, and other Stories.* By L. C. M. p. 820.

OLT *Pomponia; or, the Gospel in Caesar's Household.* By Mrs. Webb. p. 820.

June 29

NN (whole section) *Far above Rubies: a Novel.* By Mrs. J. H. Riddell. 3 vols. pp. 850—51.

NN *Ersilia: or, the Ordeal.* p. 851.

NN *Idols of Clay: a Novel.* By Mrs. Gordon Smythies. 3 vols. p. 851.

OLT *The Young Man's Setting Out in Life.* By William Guest. p. 853.

July 13

NN *Artingale Castle.* By T. Adolphus Trollope. 3 vols. pp. 44—45.

July 20

Domestic Management; or, Hints on the Training and Treatment of Children and Servants. By Mrs. Charles Doig.

The Social and Political Dependence of Women. [Charles Anthony] pp. 73—74.

NN *The Little Rift: a Novel.* 2 vols. by A. W. p. 76.

NN *The House of Rochfort: a Novel.* By William Platt. 3 vols. p. 76.

Aug. 3
NN *Five Hundred Pounds Reward: a Novel.* By a Barrister. [William Knox Wigram] p. 140.
NN *The Last Chronicles of Barset.* By Anthony Trollope. 2 vols. p. 141.

Aug. 10
NN *The White Cockade; or, Faith and Fortitude.* By James Grant. 3 vols. p. 173.
NN *Is it a Blot? a Novel.* By the Author of 'The Cream of a Life.' [Charles Phillips] 3 vols. p. 173.

Aug. 31
OLT *The Diamond Rose: a Life of Love and Duty.* By Sarah Tytler. p. 272.

Sept. 7
The Enterprising Impresario. By Walter Maynard.
American and Italian Cantatrici. By Lucius. pp. 298—99.

Nov. 23
OLT *The Adventures of an Arcot Rupee.* By Major Charles F. Kirby. 3 vols. p. 683.
OLT *Lotta Schmitt, and other Stories.* By Anthony Trollope. pp. 683—84.

Dec. 7
OLT *Until the End: a Story of Real Life.* By John Pomeroy. p. 763.
OLT *Christian Heroes of the Army and the Navy.* By the Rev. Charles Rogers, LL. D. p. 763.

Dec. 14
NN *The Waterdale Neighbours.* By the Author of 'Paul Massie.' [Justin M'Cathy] 3 vols. pp. 800—01.

Dec. 28
NN *A Stormy Life: a Novel.* By Lady Georgiana Fullerton. 3 vols. p. 888.

1868
Jan. 11
NN *Hever Court.* By R. Arthur Arnold. 2 vols.
Forty Years Ago: a Novel. Edited by Mrs. C. J. Newby. 2 vols.

A Terrible Wrong: a Novel. By Ada Buisson. 2 vols. p. 54.
NN *Stung to the Quick: North Country Story.* By Mrs. G. Linnaeus Banks. 3 vols. pp. 54—55.

Jan. 18
OLT *Fetters of Iron—[Les Chaines de Fer, par Amédée Achard.]* p. 92.

Jan. 25
NN *Les Compéres du Roy.* Par Charles Deslys. p. 125.
By the Sea-Shore. By the Countess de Gasparin. Authorized Translation.
Camille. Authorized Translation.
The Family: its Duties, Joys and Sorrows. By Count A. De Gasparin. Translated from the French. pp. 127—28.

Feb. 15
The Epicure's Year-Book and Table Companion.
Warne's Model Cookery and Housekeeping Book.
The New Cookery Book and Complete Manual of English and Foreign Cookery. By Anne Bowman.
Le Livre de Cuisine, par Jules Gouffé. p. 246.
NN *Under Two Flags: a Story of the Household and the Desert.* By Ouida. 3 vols. pp. 248—49.

Feb. 29
NN *The White Rose.* By G. J. Whyte Melville. 3 vols. p. 317.

March 7
NN *Basil Godfrey's Caprice.* By Holme Lee. 3 vols. p. 354.
OLT *The Layman's Breviary.* From the German of Leopold Schefer, by C. T. Brooks. p. 357.

March 14
NN *Lord Falconberg's Heir: a Novel.* 2 vols. By Charles Clarke. pp. 385—86.

March 21
NN *Charlotte's Inheritance: a Novel.* By the Author of 'Lady Audley's Secret.' [Mary Elizabeth Braddon] 3 vols. p. 418.

April 11

NN *A Noble Woman*. By John Cordy Jeaffreson. 3 vols. p. 522.

NN *Alice Graeme: a Novel*. 2 vols. pp. 522—23.

NN *Country Coteries*. By Georgina Lady Chatterton. 3 vols. p. 523.

April 18

NN *Dora*. By Julia Kavanagh. 3 vols. pp. 553—54.

April 18

NN *The Wild Gazelle; and other Tales*. By C. F. Armstrong. 3 vols. p. 555.

April 25

NN *The Brownlows*. By Mrs. Oliphant. 3 vols. p. 587.

May 2

A Sister's Story. By Mrs. Augustus Craven. Translated from the French by Emily Bowles. 3 vols. pp. 621—22.

NN *Meg*. By Mrs. Eiloart. 3 vols. p. 622.

NN *Only Temper: a Novel*. By Mrs. C. J. Newby. 3 vols. p. 624.

OLT *The Shady Side and the Sunny Side: Two New England Stories*. By Country Ministers' Wives. p. 627.

May 9

NN *Grace's Fortune*. 3 vols. p. 658.

NN *Captain Balfour: a Novel*. By Caroline Agnes Drayton. 2 vols. pp. 658—59.

Lady Boluntiful's Legacy to her Family and Friends. Edited by John Timbs. pp. 659—60.

May 16

NN *Neighbours and Friends: a Novel*. By the Hon. Mrs. Henry Weyland Chetwynd. 3 vols. p. 693.

NN *The Rector's Homestead: a Simple Story*. 2 vols. pp. 693—94.

May 23

Memorials of the Rev. William V. B. Shrewsbury. p. 728.

May 30

NN *The Knave of Clubs: a Novel*. By Nannie Lambert. 2 vols. p. 757.

June 6

NN *The Dower House: a Story*. By Annie Thomas. 3 vols. pp. 793—94.

June 20

NN *The Dream Numbers: a Novel*. By T. Adolphus Trollope. 3 vols. pp. 856—57.

June 27

OLT *Medusa, and other Tales*. By the Author of 'A Week in a French Country House.' [Mrs. Adelaide Sartoris] p. 893.

July 4

NN *Robert Falconer*. By George Mac-Donald, LL. D. 3 vols. pp. 12—13.

July 11

NN *Ralph Redfern*. By the Author of 'The White Rose of Chayleigh.' 3 vols. p. 43.

NN *Time, Faith and Eternity: Passages in the Life of Geoffrey Walker*. pp. 43—44.

NN *Love's Matchless Might; or, Blanche—Her Choice*. By Henry Hopkinson. p. 44.

July 18

NN *Wallencourt*. By William Platt. 3 vols. pp. 77—78.

July 25

NN *The Moonstone: a Romance*. By Wilkie Collins. 3 vols. p. 106.

NN *Two French Marriages*. By Mrs. C. Jenkin. 3 vols. pp. 106—07.

NN *The Squire of Chapel Daresfield: a Novel*. By Whieldon Baddeley. 2 vols. p. 107.

NN *The Redcourt Farm: a Novel*. By Mrs. Henry Wood. 3 vols. p. 107.

Aug. 1

NN *Englewood House*. 3 vols. pp. 139—40.

NN *Francesca's Love*. By Mrs. Edward Pulleyne. 3 vols. p. 140.

Aug. 8

NN *The Ups and Downs of an Old Maid's Life*. By Jemima Compton. p. 172.

NN *Training for Life: a Novel*. By Oliver Hartshorne. p. 172.

Aug. 15

The Life, Letters and Posthumous Works of Fredrika Bremer. Edited by her sister, Charlotte Bremer. Translated from the Swedish by Frederick Milow. pp. 204—05.
NN *Ethel's Romance: a Novel*. By Matilda Homersham. 3 vols. pp. 205—06.
NN *Robert Chetwynd's Confession: a Novel*. By Elizabeth A. Murray. 3 vols. p. 206.
OLT *Wholesome Fare: a Manual of the Laws of Food and the Practice of Cookery*. By Edmund and Ellen J. Delamare.
Warne's Model Cookery and Housekeeping Book. Compiled and Edited by Mary Jewry. p. 209.
OLT *The Harvest: an Allegory*. By Mrs. Frederic Granville. Edited by the Very Rev. Walter Farquhar Hook. p. 209.

Aug. 22

NN *Flirts and Flirts; or, a Season at Ryde*. [Miss A. E. N. Bewicke] 2 vols. p. 236.

Sept. 5

NN *The Seabord Parish*. By George Macdonald. LL. D. 3 vols. p. 298.
NN *Violet Douglas; or, the Problems of Life*. By Emma Marshall. pp. 298—99.

Sept. 12

NN *Mildred*. By Georgiana M. Craik. 3 vols. pp. 329—30.

Sept. 26

Clarissa: a Novel. By Samuel Richardson. Edited by E. S. Dallas. 3 vols. pp. 393—94.

Oct. 10

NN *Pearl*. By the Author of 'Caste,' & c. [Miss Emily Jolly] 2 vols. pp. 458—59.
NN *A Screw Loose: a Novel*. By William P. Lancaster, M. A. p. 459.

Oct. 24

OLT *Youthful Impulse and Mature Reflection: Poems*. p. 531.

Oct. 31

NN *Aldersleigh: a Tale*. By Christopher James Reithmüller. 2 vols. p. 564.

NN *Anne Hereford: a Novel*. By Mrs. Henry Wood. 3 vols. p. 564.
NN *Roke's Wife: a Novel*. By Kenner Deene. 3 vols. p. 564.
OLT *At War with the World; or, Lucy Sutherland's Autobiography*. p. 567.

Nov. 28

NN *Laura's Pride: a Novel*. By the Author of 'Mary Constant.' 3 vols. pp. 711—12.

Dec. 5

NN *Olive Varcoe: a Novel*. By Francis Derrick. 3 vols. pp. 750—51.
NN *The Talk of the Town: a Novel*. 3 vols. p. 751.

BOOKS FOR CHILDREN

The Litte Gipsy. By Elie Sauvage. p. 753.
Sunbeam Stories. By the Author of 'A Trap to Catch a Sunbeam.' p. 753.
Heroes of the Crusades. By Barbara Hutton. p. 753.
Merry Tales for Little Folks. By Madame de Chatelain. p. 753.
Tales for the Toys, told by Themselves. By Frances Freeling Broderip. p. 753.

Dec. 12

NN *Realmah*. By the Author of 'Friends in Council.' [Sir Arthur Helps] 2 vols. pp. 790—91.
NN *The Mosaic-Worker's Daughter: a Novel*. By J.M. Capes. 3 vols. p. 791.
NN *Out of the Meshes: a Story*. 3 vols. pp. 791—92.
NN *Strange Work: a Novel*. By Thomas Archer. 3 vols. p. 792.

Dec. 26

The Laws and Bye-Laws of Good Society: a Book of Etiquette.
The Art of Dressing Well.
How to Dress Well. By C. T. pp. 876—77.
Portraits of Celebrated Women. By C. A. Sainte-Beuve.
A Memoir of Lady Anna Mackenzie. By Alexander Lord Lindsay.
Studious Women. Translated from the French of Monseigneur Dupanloup. By R. M. Phillimore.

A Woman's Views of Women's Rights.
pp. 881—82.

1869

Jan. 2
Tricotrin: the Story of a Waif and a Stray.
By Ouida. 3 vols. pp. 15—16.
OLT *The Harp of the Valley.* By W.
Stewart Ross. p. 19.

ANOTHER BATCH OF GIFT BOOKS
*Tinykin's Transformations: A Child's
Story.* By Mark Lemon pp. 19—20.
Two Years of School Life, by Madame de
Presserné, edited by the Author of 'The
Heir of Redclyffe.' p. 20.
*The Loves of Rose-Pink and Sky-Blue;
and other Tales told to Children.* By
William F. Collier, LL. D. p. 20.
Queer Discourses on Queer Proverbs, by
Old Merry. p. 20.
*Lily and Nannie at School, a Story for
Little Girls.* By Annie L. Buckland p. 20.
'Now or Never'. An Autobiography, by
Charles A. Beach. p. 20.
*Story of the Kings of Judah and Israel
Written for Children.* By A. O. B. p. 20.
Our White Violet, by Kay Spen, with il-
lustrations, by T. L. Wales. p. 20.
Mince-pie Island by Robert St. John Cor-
bet. p. 20.
'Grandmamma': a Tale for Children. By
Emma Davenport. p. 20.
Cloudland and shadowland. By J.
Thackeray Bunce. p. 20.
The Stolen Cherries. By Emilia Marryat
Norris, p. 20.
*Stories from Germany—1. Goldseekers
and Breadwinners,* by Franz Hoffman; 2.
*The Cobbler, the Clerk, and the Lawyer,
of Liebenstein,* by Gustav Nieritz, p. 20.
The Sister's Year. p. 20.
Snowed Up; or, Lost in the World. Edited
by Miss E. M. Stewart.
One Year; or, a Story of Three Homes. By
F. M. P. p. 20.

Jan. 16
NN *On the Edge of the Storm.* By the

Author of 'Mademoiselle Mori.' [Miss
Margaret Roberts] p. 88.

AMERICAN BOOKS
Chronicles of St. Mary's. By S. D. N. p.
92.
*Marrying by Lot: a Tale of the Primitive
Moravians.* By Charlotte B. Mortimer. p.
92.

Jan. 23
NN *Leonora Casaloni: a Novel.* By T. A.
Trollope. 2 vols. p. 125.
NN *Doctor of Beauweir: an
Autobiography.* By the Author of 'Shirley
Hall Asylum,' 'De Profundis,' & c.
[William Gilbert] 2 vols. p. 125.
NN *The Chaplet of Pearls; or, the White
and Black Ribaumont.* By the Author of
'The Heir of Redclyffe.' [Charlotte
Yonge] pp. 125—26.

Jan. 30
NN (whole section) *Wife and Child.* By
Miss Whitty. pp. 169—70.
NN *The Fight of Faith: a Story.* By Mrs.
S. C. Hall. 2 vols. p. 170.
NN *Mad: a Story of 'Dust and Ashes.'* By
George Manville Fenn. p. 170.
NN *Dr. Harcourt's Assistant: a Tale of the
Present Day.* By Mrs. Hibbert Ware. pp.
170—71.

Feb. 20
NN *Society in a Garrison Town: a Novel.*
By the Author of 'Myself and my
Relatives.' [Anne J. Robertson] 3 vols. p.
273.
NN *Singlehurst Manor: a Story of Coun-
try Life.* By Emma Jane Worboise. p. 273.

Feb. 27
NN *Mea Culpa.* By Amelia Perrier. 2 vols.
p. 305.
OLT *A Book for Governesses.* By One of
Them. [Emily Peart] p. 309.

March 6
Orval; or, the Fool of Time. By Robert
Lytton. pp. 335—36.

March 13

Clara; or, the Children's Token. By Margaret L. Langford. p. 373.

Fellowship: Letters addressed to my Sister Mourners. pp. 373—74.

March 27

RECENT POETRY

Lady May: a Pastoral by Georgiana Lady Chatterton.

Poems by Menella Bute Smedley.

Twilight Hours: a Legacy of Verse. By Sarah Williams.

Fret Not, and other Poems. By Henry Bateman.

Sacred Lyrics. John Guthrie, M. A. pp. 436—37.

April 10

NEW POETRY

The Golden Chain of Praise: Hymns. By Thomas H. Gill. p. 500.

The Fountain of Youth, and other Poems; extracted from Sketches by the Wayside. By the Rev. Herbert Todd. p. 500.

Carmina Varia; being Miscellaneous Poems. By Justin Aubrey. p. 500.

Primitiae. By Zachary Edwards. p. 500.

The Cornish Ballads, and other Poems, of the Rev. R. S. Hawker. pp. 500—01.

Poems. By George Francis Armstrong. p. 501.

The Nine Days' Queen: a Dramatic Poem. By Mrs. Henry Prideaux. p. 501.

Basilissa, the Free of a Secret Craft: a Poem. By Compton Reade. p. 501.

Elfrida. By Robert B. Holt. p. 501.

Hope's Happy Home, and other Poems. By Kenneth M'Lachlan.

Jocelyn. By M. de Lamartine. Translated into English Verse by H. G. Evans and T. W. Swift. p. 501.

Poems. By J. B. Selkirk p. 501.

Wanderings in Verse. By One who Lost his Way. p. 501.

The Three Fountains: a Faery Epic of Eubaea. By the Author of 'The Afterglow.' p. 501.

A Child's Poetic Thoughts. p. 501.

Lays of my Boyhood. By Henry Meakin. p. 501.

Holly Berries; or, Double Acrostics from the Poets. Edited by A. P. A. p. 501.

Children of the Sun, & c.: Poems for the Young. By Caroline M. Gemma. pp. 501—02.

The Bab Ballads,—Much Sound and Little Sense. By W. S. Gilbert. p. 502.

April 17

NN *Hester's History: a Tale.* Reprinted from 'All the Year Round.' 2 vols. pp. 533—34.

NN *Lorna Doone: a Romance of Exmoor.* By R. D. Blackmore. 3 vols. pp. 534—35.

April 24

NN *Harry Egerton; or, the Younger Son of the Day.* By G. L. Tottenham. 3 vols. p. 567.

NN *On Smoking and Drinking.* By James Parton. pp. 567—68.

May 8

NN *Love the Avenger.* By the Baroness Blaze de Bury. 3 vols. p. 632.

NN *Erick Thorburn.* [Mary Bramston] 3 vols. p. 632.

May 29

NN *Old-Town Folks.* By Harriet Beecher Stowe. 3 vols. p. 727.

True Love. By Lady Di Beauclerk. p. 728.

June 5

(opens issue) *Walter Savage Landor: a Biography.* By John Forster. 2 vols. pp. 755—57.

June 19

NN *Madame Silva's Secret.* By Mrs. Eiloart. 3 vols. p. 823.

NN *Mary Stanley; or, the Secret Ones.* 3 vols. p. 824.

July 3

NN *Faithless; or, the Love of the Period: a Story of Real Life.* By Spes. 2 vols. p. 11.

NN *Netherton on the Sea: a Novel.* [Elizabeth M. Alford] 3 vols. pp. 11—12.

NN *Twice Refused: a Novel.* By Charles E. Sterling. 2 vols. p. 12.

NN *Wise as a Serpent.* By J. A. St. John Blythe. 3 vols. p. 12.

July 10
NN *The Three Graces*—[*Les Trois Graces*, par Amédée Achard]. pp. 44—45.

July 17
NN *Only an Earl.* By the Countess Pisani. 3 vols. p. 76.
NN *My Insect Queen: a Novel.* By the Author of 'Margaret's Engagement.' 3 vols. p. 76.
NN *Too True: a Story of To-Day.* p. 77.

NEW POETRY
Poems and Romances. By George Augustus Simcox. p. 78.
Dione, and other Poems. p. 78.
Margaret Ericsen's Choice, and other Poems. By E. A. M. L. pp. 78—79.
Italy: Original Poems and Translations. By F. W. Irby. p. 79.
Idonia, and other Poems. By James Burney. p. 79.
Few Leaves. By G. L. Larkins. p. 79.
Iona, and other Sonnets, & c. By Wade Robinson. p. 79.
Short Poems of Sacred Travel, Miscellaneous and in Memoriam by William Griffiths, M. A. p. 79.
Granny's Tale. By James R. Withers. p. 79.
Proposals for, and Contributions to, a Ballad History of England, and the States sprung from her. By W. C. Bennett. p. 79.
The Vision of Socrates, and other Poems. By Charles Wood Chapman. p. 79.
Bardrick, the King of Teign: a Lay of South Devon. In Ten Cantos. By E. Potts. p. 79.
Acrostics from across the Atlantic; and other Poems, Humerous and Sentimental. By a Gothamite p. 79.
Western Windows; and other Poems. By John James Piatt. p. 79.

July 24
(opens issue) *The Life of Madame Louis de France, Daughter of Louis the Fifteenth.* By the Author of 'Tales of Kirkbeck.' pp. 103—04.

EXTRAORDINARY TRAVELS
Voyages and Travels of Capt. Hatteras—[*Voyages et Aventures de Capitaine Hatteras*]. Par Jules Verne. p. 111.
Five Weeks in a Balloon: Travels of African Discovery by Three Englishmen.—[*Cinq Semaines en Ballon: Voyages de Découvertes en Afrique par Trois Anglais.* Par Jules Verne].
The Children of Capt. Grant: a Voyage Round the World—[*Les Enfants de Capitaine Grant: Voyage autour du Monde*] Par Jules Verne. p. 111.

July 31
(opens issue) *Woman's Work and Woman's Culture: a Series of Essays.* Edited by Josephine E. Butler. pp. 135—36.

Aug. 14
NN *Only a Woman's Love: a Novel.* By Lord Desart. 2 vols. p. 208.

Aug. 21
(opens issue) *Robert Owen, the Founder of Socialism in England.* By Arthur John Booth, M. A. pp. 231—33.

Aug. 28
The Wedding Day in all Ages and Countries. By Edward J. Wood. 2 vols. pp. 268—69.

Oct. 9
NN (whole section) *A County family: a Novel.* By the Author of 'Lost Sir Massingberd,' & c. [James Payn] 3 vols. pp. 461—62.
NN *Ann Severin.* By the Author of 'Le Récit d'une soeur.' 3 vols. p. 462.

NOVELS AND NOVELETTES
The Cage of Honour: a Tale of the Great Mutiny. By the Author of 'The Eastern Hunters.' 3 vols. p. 526.

Dec. 18
CHILDREN'S BOOKS
Fairy Flowers, for the Young and Good. Object Lessons: the Child's own Alphabet.

The One-Syllable Alphabet: Nouns in Rhyme, with about Three Hundred Pictures.
Cousin Charley's Step by Step to Learning, with the Hide and Seek Alphabet. By Edward N. Marks.
'Puzzle Monkeys:' Acrostics in Prose and Verse. By E. L. F. H.
Our Nurse's Picture Book. p. 818.

Dec. 25
NW *Forgotten by the World.* In 3 vols. p. 870.

1870

Jan. 1
NW *The Magical Eye-Glass.* By A. S. F. P. p. 21.

Jan. 8
BOOKS OF TRAVEL
A Search for Winter Sunbeams. By Samuel S. Cox.
Notes of England and Italy. By Mrs. Hawthorne p. 58.

Jan. 15
Autour d'une Source. By Gustave Droz. p. 93.
OLT *Fairy Fancies, from the German.* By Lizzy Selina Eden. pp. 93—94.

Jan. 22
OLT *Proverbs and Comediettas.* Written for Private Representation. By Percy Fitzgerald, M. A. p. 124.
Drawing Room Plays and Parlour Pantomimes. Collected by Clement Scott. p. 124.

Jan. 29
OLT *Notes on Burgundy.* By Charles Richard Weld. Edited by his Widow.
The Good St. Louis and his Times. By Mrs. Bray, p. 158.

Feb. 12
OLT *Brittany and its Byeways.* By Mrs. Buy Palliser. p. 228.

March 5
NW *Almost Faultless: a Story of the Pres-ent Day.* By the Author of 'A Book for Governesses.' [Emily Peart] p. 321.
NW *The Dead Lake, and other Tales.* By Paul Heyse. Translated by Mary Wilson from the German. p. 321.
OLT *Reptiles and Birds: a Popular Account of their Various Orders.* By Louis Figuier.
Wonders of the Deep: a Companion to 'Stray Leaves from the Book of Nature.' By M. Schele de Vere. p. 324.

March 12
OLT *Not an Actress. A Stage-door-keeper's Story.* By John Daly Besemeres. p. 354.

March 26
NW *Heirs of the Soil.* By Mrs. Lorenzo N. Nunn. pp. 419—20.
OLT *The Happy Boy: a Tale of Norwegian Peasant Life.* By Björnstjerne Björnson. Translated from the Norwegian by H. R. G. p. 420.

April 16
OLT *Cecy's Recollections. a Story of Obscure Life.* By Mary Bramston. p. 515.

BOOKS FOR THE YOUNG
George Cruikshank's Fairy Library—The Loving Ballad of Lord Bateman. p. 515.
The Story of Two Lives. By Winifred Taylor. pp. 515—16.
The Lost Father; or, Cecilia's Triumph: a Story of our own Day. By Daryl Holme. p. 516.
Rupert Rochester, the Banker's Son: a Tale. By Winifred Taylor. p. 516.
Mistletoe Grange: a Royal Road to Wrinkles. p. 516.

April 30
OLT *Essays and Stories.* By the late G. W. Bosanquet. p. 579.

May 7
OLT *Supplementary Stories and Poems.* By Edward Yardley. p. 612.
OLT *The Alexandra: a Gift Book to the*

Alexandra Orphanage for Infants, Hornsey Rise. Edited by Thomas Archer. p. 612.

May 14
Sketches of Life and Sport in South-Eastern Africa. By Charles Hamilton. Edited by F. G. H. Price.
Narrative of a Spring Tour in Portugal. By the Rev. Alfred Charles Smith, M. A. p. 639.

May 28
France. By M. Prévost Paradol, de l'Académie Française. pp. 706—07.

June 18
BOOKS FOR THE YOUNG
An Old-Fashioned Girl. By Louisa M. Alcott.
The Young Mountaineer.
Oakdale Grange. By Thomas Simmons.
A Tale of the French Revolution. By the Rev. F. Osbern Giffard, M. A.
The Lost Legends of the Nursery Songs. By Mary Senior Clark.
Fairy Tales and Sketches by Hans Christian Andersen. Translated by Caroline Peachey, Augusta Plesner, H. Ward, and Others, p. 803.

June 25
The Fellah. By Edmond About. Translated by Sir Randal Roberts, Bart. p. 832.
OLT *German Tales*. By Berthold Auerbach. With an Introduction by Charles C. Shackford. p. 834.

July 2
BOOKS FOR THE YOUNG
Stories from Waverley; from the Original of Sir Walter Scott. By S. O. C. p. 16.
The Population of an Old Pear Tree; or, Stories of Insect Life. From the French of E. Van Bruyssel. Edited by the Author of 'The Heir of Redclyffe.' [Charlotte Yonge] pp. 16—17.
A Storehouse of Stories. Edited by Charlotte M. Yonge. p. 17.

July 9
OLT *The Household Fairy*. By the Lady Lytton. p. 47.

BOOKS FOR THE YOUNG
My Schoolboy Friends: a Story of Whitminster Grammar School.
The Modern Playmate: a Book of Games, Sports, and Diversions for Boys of all Ages. Compiled and Edited by the Rev. J. G. Wood, M. A.
By the Road-side. By John C. Freund.
Five Weeks in a Balloon: a Voyage of Exploration and Discovery in Central Africa, from the French of Jules Verne.
The Royal Merchant; or, Events in the Days of Sir Thomas Gresham, Knight. By William G. Kingston.
The Nations Around. By A. Keary.
A Poet Hero. By the Countess Von Bothmer.
Before the Conquest; or, English Worthies in the Old English Period. By W. H. Davenport Adams.
Jessie Grey; or, the Discipline of Life: a Canadian Tale. By L. G.
Katie Johnstone's Cross: a Canadian Tale. By A. M. M. pp. 48—49.

July 16
Thomas Chalmers: a Biographical Study. By James Dodds. p. 76.
OLT *A Winter's Journey to Rome and Back*. By William Evill. p. 79.
OLT *Sketches from the Border Land; or, a Daughter of England*. p. 79.
OLT *Lifting the Veil*. p. 79.
OLT *Three Weddings*. By the Author of 'Dorothy.' [Mrs. Margaret Agnes Paul] pp. 79—80.

July 23
BOOKS FOR THE YOUNG
Les Aventures de Robin Jouet. Par Emile Carrey. p. 115.
Cinderella: a Play in Rhyme for Children. By M.M. p. 115.
The Silver Bells: an Allegory. p. 115.

Aug. 6
The Life of Madame de Beauharnais de Miramion, 1629—1696. By M. Alfred

Bonneau. Translated by the Baroness de Montaignac. pp. 170—71.
NW *Lizzie Wentworth: a Story of Real Life*. By Benjamin Wilson, M. A. p. 176.

Aug. 13
OLT *Footprints of Former Men in Far Cornwall*. By R. S. Hawker, Vicar of Morwenstow. p. 209.

Sept. 3
Evenings with the Sacred Poets. By Frederic Saunders. pp. 300—01.

Oct. 1
NEW POEMS
Poems from the German of Ferdinand Freiligrath. Edited by his Daughter. p. 429.

Dec. 3
BOOKS FOR THE YOUNG
Aunt Judy's Christmas Volume for 1870.
Drifting and Steering: a Tale for Boys. By Lynde Palmer.
The Wonderful Pocket, and other Stories. By Chauncey Giles.
The Magic Shoes, and other Stories. By Chauncey Giles.
The Gate of Pearl. By Chauncey Giles.
Bible Wonders. By Richard Newton, D. D.
Blanche Gamond, a French Protestant Heroine.
Little Blue Mantle; or, the Poor Man's Friend: a True Story. p. 720.

Dec. 10
BOOKS FOR THE YOUNG
Routledge's Christmas Annual.
Aunt Judith's Recollections: a Tale of the Eighteenth Century. By the Author of 'Missionary Anecdotes,' & c.
Sunday Echoes in Week-day Hours. By Mrs. Carey Brock.
Little Effie's Home. By the Author of 'Bertie Lee.'
All's Well that Ends Well: a Tale for Children. By M. M. S.
Milly's Errand; or, Saved to Save. By Emma Leslie.

Dec. 24
Collects of the Church of England. p. 840.
A BATCH OF CHILDREN'S BOOKS
Esther West, a story by Isa Craig-Knox.
Hearts of Oak: Stories of Early English Adventure, related by W. Noel Sainsbury.
Old Merry's Annual. pp. 840—41.

Dec. 31
Adventures of a Young Naturalist. By Lucien Biart p. 886.
The Countess Gisela. p. 886.
Stephen Scudamore the Younger. By Arthur Locker p. 886.
Marmaduke Merry the Midshipman. By Mr. Kingston. p. 886.
Old Barnaby's Treasure. By Mrs. J. M. Tandy. p. 886.
Hetty's Resolve. By the Author of 'Under the Lime Trees' p. 886.
Pictures of Cottage Life in the West of England. By Margaret E. Poole. p. 886.
Lottie's White Frock, and other Stories. p. 886.

1871
March 11
BOOKS FOR THE YOUNG
Little Rosy's Pictures. By Lorenz Frölich.
Aunt Louisa's Home Companions.
Tales of the Civil Wars. By the Rev. H. C. Adams, M. A.
Stories About. By Lady Baker.
At the Back of the North Wind. By George Macdonald. p. 303.

April 8
BOOKS FOR THE YOUNG
Ranald Bannerman's Boyhood. By George Mac Donald.
The Boy in Grey. By Henry Kingsley.
Evenings at the Tea.
Old Merry's Travels on the Continent.
The Story of Madge and the Fairy Content. By Blanchard Jerrold.
Love and Duty; or, the Happy Life. By Anne J. Buckland.
The Story of Captain Cook's Three Voyages round the World. Told by M. Jones.

The Golden Gate, and other Stories. By Henry G. B. Hunt.
The Old and the New Home: a Canadian Tale. By J. E. p. 431.

April 15
BOOKS FOR THE YOUNG (whole section)
My Apingi Kingdom. By Paul Du Chaillu.
A Parisian Family. Translated from the French of Madame Guizot de Witt, by the Author of 'John Halifax.'
Silken Cords and Iron Fetters. By Maud Jeanne Franc.
The King of Topsy-Turvy. By Arthur Lillie.
Our Domestic Pets. By the Rev. J. G. Wood, M. A.
At the South Pole. By William H. G. Kingston.
One Trip More, and other Stories. By the Author of 'Mary Powell.' [Miss Anne Manning]
The Happy Nursery. By Ellis A. Davidson.
The young Artist: a Story of Christmas Eve. By the Author of 'The Basket of Flowers.' pp. 462—63.

May 20
Spring Comedies. By Lady Barker. pp. 618—19.

July 22
The Art of Amusing. By Frank Bellew. pp. 110—11.
OLT *Chamber Dramas for Children.* By Mrs. George Mac Donald. p. 111.

Aug. 26
NW *The Outbreak of the French Revolution, related by a Peasant of Loraine.* By MM. Erckmann-Chatrian. Translated by Mrs. Cashel Hoey. 3 vols. p. 271.

Sept. 2
BOOKS FOR THE YOUNG (whole section)
When I was a Little Girl. By the Author of 'St. Olaves.' p. 304.
Little Pussy Willow. By Harriet Beecher Stowe.

Stories for Darlings. By the Sun.
The Magic Spectacles: a Fairy Story. By Chauncey Giles.
The Mine; or, Darkness and Light. By A. L. O. E. [Miss Sarah Tucker]
The Grey House on the Hill. By the Hon. Mrs. Green.
Little Black Cap, and other Stories.
The Giant. By the Author of 'A Fairy Tale for the Nineteenth Century.' Edited by the Author of 'Amy Herbert.' [Elizabeth Sewell] pp. 304—05.

Sept. 9
BJÖRNSON'S TALES
The Fisher Girl.
The Newly-Married Couple.
Love and Life in Norway. p. 335.

BOOKS FOR THE YOUNG
The Cousin from India. By Georgiana M. Craik.
The Story of a Moss Rose. By Charles Bruce.
Violet Rivers. By Winifred Taylor.
Pink and White Tyranny. By Mrs. Harriet Beecher Stowe.
Little Sunshine's Holiday: a Picture from Life. By the Author of 'John Halifax, Gentleman.' [Dinah Mulock Craik]
Heroines in Obscurity. A Second Series of Papers for Thoughtful Girls. By Sarah Tytler.
The Home at Heatherbrae: a Tale. By the Author of 'Everley.'
Autobiography of a Lump of Coal; a Grain of Salt; a Drop of Water; a Bit of Old Iron; a Piece of Flint. By Annie Carey.
My New Suit; and other Tales. By H. A. F.
Little Elsie's Summer at Malvern. By the Hon. Mrs. Clifford Butler.
The Bible Opened for Children. By Mary Bradford. pp. 336—37.

Sept. 16
The Selected Writings of John Ramsay, M. A. With Memoir and Notes, by Alexander Walker. pp 363—64.

Sept. 23

BOOKS FOR THE YOUNG (whole section)

Sowing the Good Seed: a Canadian Tale. By Alicia.

Alice Herbert, and Emily's Choice. By E. V. N.

Short Stories for Young People. By Mrs. F. Marshall Ward.

Off to Sea; or, the Adventures of Jovial Jack Junker on his Road to Fame. By W. H. Kingston.

Four Messengers. By E. M. H.

Aunt Mabel's Prayer. By Mrs. Henderson.

Lilliput Lectures. By the Author of 'Lilliput Levee.'

Margaret: a Story of My Life from Five to Twenty-five.

The Pet Lamb. By the Author of 'The Basket of Flowers.'

The Boot on the Wrong Foot, and other Tales.

Child Life. Adapted from the German of Rudolph Reichenam, by Crichton Campbell.

Campanella; or, the Teachings of Life. By Mrs. Jerome Mercier.

Martin the Weaver; or the Power of Gold. From the French, by Mr Campbell Overend.

Labour Stands on Golden Feet. By Heinrich Z. Schokke. pp. 400—01.

Nov. 4

OLT *Flower, Fruit, and Thorn Pieces.* By Jean Paul Frederick Richter. p. 593.

Nov. 11

OLT *Under the Blue Sky.* By Charles MacKay. p. 622.

Nov. 18

CONTEMPORARY FRANCE

Mes Semblables. Par Jacob de la Cottiee. p. 652.

CHRISTMAS BOOKS

Moonshine: Fairy Stories.

Routledge's Every Boy's Annual.

A Village Maiden. By the Hon. Augusta Bethel.

My Young Days. p. 654.

Dec. 9

CHRISTMAS BOOKS

Old Merry's Annual.

Boy Life among the Indians. By the Rev. R. F. Goulding.

A Tale of a Nest.

The Oak Staircase. By M. and C. Lee.

Aimee; a Tale of the Days of James the Second.

Alda Graham and her Brother Philip. By E. M. Morris.

The Journey to the Centre of the Earth.

Mrs. Isoult Barry 'her diurnal book.'

Distant Cousins. By the Author of 'What Makes Me Grow.'

The Young Franc-Tireurs. By G. A. Henty.

Sacred Allegories. By the late Rev. E. Munro.

The Old Maid's Secret. By E. Marlitt.

Master John Bull. By Ascot R. Hope.

Stories of French School Life. By Ascot R. Hope.

The Vagabond. By Mrs. F. Marshall Ward. pp. 753—54.

Dec. 23

CHRISTMAS BOOKS

Aunt Judy's Christmas Volume for Young People.

Doll World; or, Play and Earnest.

The Home Theatre, by Mary Healy.

The Besieged City by Mrs. Cambell Overend.

Old Ways New Set by Mrs. Henry Mackarness.

My Wife and I; or, Harry Henderson's History by. Mrs. Beecher Stowe.

Mrs. Gibbon's Parlour Maid by M. G. Hogg.

Our Uncle's Home, and What the Boys Did There by Mother Carey.

Kirstin's Adventures, by the Author of 'Casimir, the Little Exile.'

Susanne De L'Orme: a Story of France in Huguenot Times, by H. G.

Round the World, and other Stories,—
The Children and the Sage, and other
Stories.
Louis Duval, and other Stories.
A Christmas Cake, in Four Quarters, by
Lady Barker.
The Children's Hour Annual.
Marion's Path Through Shadow to Sunshine by Mary Meeke.
The Mother's Book of Poetry, selected by
Mrs. Alfred Gatty.
*The Melville Family, and their Bible
Readings.* by Mrs. Ellis.
The Miner's Oath: and Underground, by
Dora Russell.
The Princess and the Goblin by Mrs. Mac
Donald.
A Storehouse of Stories, edited by
Charlotte M. Yonge.
The Magician's Own Book, edited by W.
H. Cremer.
and *The Merry Circle,* edited by Mrs.
Clara Bellew.
The Winborough Boys; or, Ellerslie Park,
by the Rev. H. C. Adams.
Peter Parley's Annual for 1872.
*Shoals and Quicksands: Sketches from
Passing Scenes,* by Sydney Bessett. pp.
835—36.

1872
March 16
OLT *The Service of the Poor.* By Caroline
Amelia Stephen.
The Streets and Lanes of a City. p. 335.

March 23
NW *The Story of the Plébiscite.* From the
French of MM. Erckmann-Chatrian. p.
367.

March 30
The Life of Thomas Cooper. Written by
Himself. pp. 397—98.

May 4
*Manners of Good Society; being a Book of
Etiquette.* pp. 555—56.

June 8
NW *Ekkehard: a Tale of the Tenth Cen-*

tury. By Joseph Victor Scheffel. 2 vols. p.
717.

July 27
*The Life of Saint Jane Frances-Fremyot
de Chantal.* By Emily Bowles. pp.
106—08.

Aug. 3
BOOKS FOR THE YOUNG
Is it True? By the author of 'John Halifax,
Gentleman.' [Dinah Mulock Craik]
Beauty and the Beast, and Tales of Home
by Bayard Taylor.
*The Friend in Need Papers; or, Sketches
from Daily Life.*
*Marvels from Nature; or, a Second Visit
to Aunt Bessie,* by Bertha E. Wright. pp.
145—46.

Sept. 7
BOOKS FOR THE YOUNG (whole section)
Little Plays for Little People. By Mrs.
Chrisholm.
Aunt Joe's Scrap Bag, by Louisa M.
Alcott.
The Slave, the Serf, and the Freeman,
translated and adapted by Mrs. Overend
Campbell.
Jean Jarousseau, the Pastor of the Desert,
by Eugène Pelletan.
*Jacqueline: a Story of the Reformation in
Holland,* by Mrs. Hardy.
Percy and Ida: a Story for Children, by
Katherine E. May.
Lame Felix: a Book for Boys full of Proverb and Story, by Charles Bruce. p. 303.

Sept. 14
NW *Six of One by Half-a-Dozen of the
Other: an Everyday Novel.* By Harriet
Beecher Stowe et al. pp. 332—33.

Sept. 21
OLT *Abbot's Crag: a Tale.* By M. C.
Rowsell. p. 365.

BOOKS FOR THE YOUNG (whole section)
The Adventures of a Brownie, as Told to

My Child, by the Author of 'John Halifax.' [Dinah Mulock Craik]

Philip Walton.

Picture Lessons, by the Divine Teacher, by Peter Grant.

Margaret Müller: a Story of the late War in France, by Madame Eugène Bersier, freely translated by Mrs. Carety Brock.

Little Pierre, the Pedlar of Alsace translated from the French by J. M. C.

The Pioneers by R. M. Ballantyne.

Little Lives, by the Author of 'My Young Days.'

Poems for My Little Friends, by Minna Wolff.

Italian Scenes and Stories, by the Author of 'What makes Me Grow?'

Twyford Hall; or, Rosa's Christmas Dinner, and What She did with It, by Charles Bruce.

Story of Conrad the Squirrel: a Story for Children, by the Author of 'Wandering Willie.' pp. 365—66.

Sept. 28

Difficulties of the Day. By the Rev. E. S. Ffouleks, B. D. pp. 392—93.

Nov. 2

OLT *Loves and Lives: an Unfinished Story.* By Ellis Ainsley. p. 560.

Nov. 16

CHRISTMAS BOOKS (whole section)

Every Boy's Annual for 1873, edited by Edmund Routledge.

My Sunday Friend Stories; Third Series—Festivals, by the Authoress of 'Helpful Sam.'

Blind Olive; or, Dr. Greyvill's Infatuation, by Sarson.

The Path She Chose, by F. M. S.

The Norsemen in the West; or, America before Columbus.

The Orphans, by E. C. Phillips. pp. 632—33.

Dec. 7

CHRISTMAS BOOKS (whole section)

Dogs; their Points, Whims, Instincts, and Pecularities, illustrated and edited by H. Webb.

Parables of Life, by the Author of 'Earth's Many Vocies.'

May's Garden, and where the Flowers went.

Castle Cornet, by Louisa Hawtrey.

Mary: a Tale of Humble Life.

New Stories on Old Subjects.

Sea Kings of the Mediterranean, by the Rev. George Fyler Townsend.

Ling Bank Cottage: a Tale for Working Girls, by the Author of 'Lenten Lessons,' & c. p. 731.

Dec. 14

CHRISTMAS BOOKS (whole section)

Sea Gull Rock, translated from the French of Jules Sandeau by R. Black.

Marcella of Rome, a Tale of the Early Church. By Frances Eastwood.

The Boy's Watchword by Jessie Harrison.

Robin Tremayne by Emily Sarah Holt.

Stories of Success by James F. Cobb.

Stranger than Fiction.

Little Mother, by the Author of 'Little Rosie's Travels.'

The Village Beech Tree; or, Work and Trust.

The Widdow and the Rabbits, a Fairy Legend, by a Ferret.

Grandmamma's Relics, and her Stories about Them, by C. E. Bowen.

Tales at Tea-time, Fairy Stories, written by Mr. E. H. Knatchbull-Hugersen, M. P.

The Little Wonder Horn, by Jean Ingelow.

Buds and Blossoms, Stories for Children.

Peter Parley's Annual.

Father Time's Story-Book for the Little Ones, by Kathleen Know.

Hymn Stories by Edis Searle.

The New Year's Bargain, by Susan Coolidge.

Busy Bee.

Swift and Sure; or, the Career of Two Brothers, by Alfred Elwes.

Wrecked, not Lost by the Hon. Mrs. Dundas. pp. 766—67.

Dec. 21
CHRISTMAS BOOKS
Jessie's Work by Mary E. Shipley.
The Modern Sphinx.
Not Forsaken by Agnes Giberne.
The Round Robin edited by Old Merry.
The Twins of St. Marcel par Mrs. A. S. Orr.
Women of the Last Days of Old France by the Author of 'On the Edge of the Storme' & c.
The Three Midshipmen. By W. H. G. Kingston.
The Great Battles of the British Navy pp. 808—09.

1873
Jan. 4
BOOKS FOR CHRISTMAS (whole section)
George's Enemies, by Ascott Hope.
The Sea and the Savages, by Harold Lincoln.
Camping Out edited by C. A. Stephens.
Out at Sea, and other Stories, by Two Authors.
Chances and Changes by Beatrice Alsager Jourdan.
Aunt Judy's Christmas Volume, 1872, edited by Mrs. Alfred Gatty.
Meridiana, by Jules Verne.
Marigold Manor, edited by the Rev. A. Sewel, M.A.
The Miner's Son, and Margaret Vernon, by M. M. Pollard.
Sunday Chats for Sensible Children, by Clara C. Mateau.
The Runaway: a Story for the Young by the Author of 'Mrs. Jerningham's Journal' pp. 16—17.

Feb. 22
CHILDREN'S BOOKS
Ps and Qs; or, the Question of Putting Upon. By Miss Yonge.
The Good Voices. By the Rev. Edwin A. Abbot.

Summer Holidays. By E. Rosalie Salmon.
A Flat Iron for a Farthing. By J. H. Ewing.
Holiday Stories for Boys and Girls. By Lady Barker.
Letters of Marque, and Tales of the Sea and Land.
Favel Children. By Ellen L. Brown.
Sleepy Forest, and other Stories for Children. By Eustace R. Conder, M. A.
A Boy's Adventures in the Wilds of Australia. By William Howitt. pp. 244—45.

May 31
BOOKS FOR THE YOUNG
Christian Melville. By the Author of 'Matthew Paxton'.
Thrust Out, and Old Legend. By the Author of 'Drifted and Sifted,' & c.
The Noble Printer and his Adopted Daughter. Translated from the German by Campbell Overend.
Zina; or, Morning Mists. By the Author of 'The Wish and the Way,' & c.
Penelope. By Mrs. Stanley Leathes.
Echoes. By E. M. H. An Illustration by E. J. Poynter, R. A.
Twilight and Dawn by E. M. H.
Ribbon Stories. By Lady Barker.
Festival Tales. By John Francis Walker.
The Young Squire; or, Peter and his Friends.
Lily Hope and her Friends: a Tale. By Hetty Bowman.
In the Golden Shell. By Linda Mazzini. pp. 692—93.

June 14
OLT *Palmetto Leaves* by Harriet Beecher Stowe. p. 759.

June 21
How to Dress on 15 l. a Year. By a Lady. p. 785.

July 26
TWO AMERICAN TALES
The Other Girls. By Mrs. T. D. Whitney.

Work: a Story of Experience. By Louisa M. Alcott. p. 111.

Aug. 2
OLT *Adventures of a Protestant in Search of Religion* by Iota.
The Chateau Morville; or, Life in Touraine, from the French, by E. R. pp. 145—46.

Aug. 23
SOME ACCOUNT OF A PERSIAN POEM
Analysis and Specimens of the Joseph and Zulaikha Poem. By the Persian Poet Jami. pp. 237—39.

Sept. 6
BOOKS FOR THE YOUNG
How Frank began to climb the Ladder by Charles Bruce.
Twilight and Dawn, by the Author of 'Four Messengers,' & *Friendly Fairies, or Once Upon a Time.*
Hoity Toity, the Good Little Fellow, by Charles Camden.
Humbert Montreuil; or, The Huguenot and the Dragoon, by Francisca Ingram Ouvry p. 302.

Oct. 4
(opens issue) *Henry Fothergill Chorley: Autobiography, Memoir, and Letters.* Compiled by Henry G. Hewlett. 2 vols. pp. 425—27.

Nov. 8
CHRISTMAS BOOKS
From the Earth to the Moon. By Jules Verne. Translated from the French, by Louis Mercier and Eleanor E. King.
Allegories and Tales, by the Rev. William Edward Heygate.
Rockbourne: a Tale. By Marion Eliza Weir.
The Boy with an Idea. By Mrs. Eiloart.
Isabel's Difficulties, Or, Life on the Daily Path. By M. R. Carey.
Cris Miller. By Mrs. F. M. Marshall Ward.
Children of the Olden Time. By Mrs. Henry Mackarness.

Feathers and Fairies. By the Hon. Augusta Bethel.
Home Life in the Highlands. By Lilias Graeme.
The Children of the Parsonage. by the Author of 'Gerty and May,' & c. pp. 594—95.

Dec. 13
CHRISTMAS BOOKS
Lob Lie-by-the-Fire. By Juliana Horatia Ewing.
Blind Mercy. By Gertrude Crockford.
The Old Fairy Tales. Collected and Edited by James Mason.
Harry's Big Boots. By E. Gay.
The King's Servants. By Hesba Stretton.
Giles Minority. By Mrs. Robert O'Reilly.
Hope's Annual; The Night before the Holidays.
Geordie Purdie in London. By Daniel Gorrie.
Ned's Search. By M. H. Holt.
Aunt Ann's Stories. Edited by Louisa Loughborough.
An Earl's Daughter. By M. M. Pollard.
Sweet Violets and other Tales. By Mrs. Mackarness.
'My Kalulu,' Prince, King, and Slave. By H. M. Stanley. pp. 769—70.

Dec. 20
CHRISTMAS BOOKS
Aunt Judy's Christmas Volume for 1873. Edited by Mrs. Alfred Gatty.
Pet; or, Pstimes and Penalties. By the Rev. H. R. Haweis, M. A.
The Fur Country. Translated from the French of Jules Verne, by N. D'Anvers. p. 813.

Dec. 27
CHRISTMAS BOOKS (whole section)
Miss Moore: a Tale for Girls. by Georgiana M. Craik.
Young Prince Marigoold. By John Francis Maguire.
Fitful Gleams from Fancy Land. By Edith Milner.

The Lowells: a Story of the Danish War. By Mrs. Webb Peploe.
Doda's Birthday. By Edwin J. Ellis.
Elisie's Choice: a Story. By the Author of 'May's Garden.'
Tom: the History of a Very Little Boy. by H. Rutherford Russell.
Lonely Queenie and the Friends She Made. By Isobel. pp. 869—70.

1874

Jan. 3
BOOKS FOR CHILDREN
The Little People; and other Tales. By Lady Pollock, W. K. Clifford, and Walter Herries Pollock.
The Stories they Tell Me; or, Sue and I. By Mrs. Robert O'Reilly.
The Violets of Montmartre. By Madame Eugene Bersier.
A Needle and Thread: a Tale for Girls. By Emma J. Barnes.
Thwarted; or, Ducks' Eggs in a Hen's Nest. By Florence Montgomery.
The Robin's Nest by a Clergyman's Wife.
Easydale: a Story. By Edis Searle.
Sweet Flowers. By Mrs. Mackarness.
Eighty Years Ago. By H. Cave. p. 19.

Jan. 31
BOOKS FOR CHILDREN
Peter Parley's Annual for 1874.
True to the End. By the Rev. Dr. Edersheim.
Nothing to Nobody. By Brenda.
Verena. By Emily Sarah Holt.
The Three Sisters. By Mrs. Perring.
Bed-Time Stories. By Louise Chandler Moulton.
Blanche and Beryl. By Madame de Stolz.
Ned's Search. By M. H. Holt.
What Katy did at School. By Susan Codridge.
The Story of Waterloo. pp. 158—59.

May 23
BOOKS FOR THE YOUNG
The African Cruiser. By S. Whitchurch Sadler.
Brave Hearts. By Robertson Gray.

Live Dolls. By Annabella Maria Browne.
Lady Willacy's Protégées. By Agnes Grey.
Clemene: a Sketch. By the Author of 'Echoes,' & c.
Under the Southern Cross. By the Author of 'The Spanish Brothers.'
A Lily among Thorns. By Emma Marshall.
Ashley Priors; or, the Beauty of Holiness. pp. 694—95.

Sept. 19
Birds, their Cages and their Keep. By K. A. Buist. pp. 377—78.

BOOKS FOR THE YOUNG
The Tiny Library.
Beatrice Aylmer, and other Stories. By Mary M. Howard.
Old-Fashioned Stories. By Thomas Cooper.
Drusie's Own Story. By Agnes Giberne.
Heart's Ease in the House. By Emma Jane Worboise p. 381.

Nov. 14
CHRISTMAS BOOKS
Floating City by Jules Verne.
River Legends by the Right Hon. E. H. Knatchbull-Hugessen, p. 641.

Dec. 19
CHRISTMAS BOOKS
Boons and Blessings. By Mrs. S. C. Hall.
Good and Bad Managers. By Ellen Barlee.
The Little Lame Prince and his Travelling Cloak. By the Author of 'John Halifax, Gentleman.' [Dinah Mulock Craik]
Floss Silverthorne. By Agnes Giberne.
Fairy Gifts; or, a Wallet of Wonders. By Kathleen Know.
Life at Hartwell. By Katherine E. May.
Max Wild, the Merchant's Son.
Stories told in a Fisherman's Cottage.—Three Wet Sundays with the Book of Joshua. By Ellen Palmer.
Christmas at Annesley. By Mary E. Shipley.
Cotton. By S. W.
Boys and Girls. By M. Bramston.

A Month at Brighton, and what Came of It. By Mary E. Shipley.

An Inherited Task, Or, Early Mission Life in South Africa. By Charles H. Eden.

Riversdale. By C. E. Bowen.

The Slave-Dealer of Coanza. By S. W. Sadler.

Robin the Bold. By the Author of 'Life Underground.'

A Faithful Servant. By Jean Baptiste Clèry.

Snowdrop, and other Tales.—Wild Rose. By Mrs. Mackarness.

May's Own Boy. By the Author of 'Little Mother.'

Hope's Annual: the Day after the Holidays. pp. 827—28.

Dec. 26

CHRISTMAS BOOKS

Every Boy's Annual. Edited by Edmund Routledge.

Dog's Life.

Aunt Judy's Christmas Annual for 1874. Edited by H. K. F. Gatty.

Captain Jack.

Peter Parley's Annual for 1875.

This Troublesome World. By Lady Barker.

The Carved Cartoon: a Picture of the Past. By Austin Clare.

Lizzie Hepburn.

The Town-Crier. By Florence Montgomery.

Whispers from Fairy Land. By the Right Hon. E. H. Knatchbull-Huggesson, M. P.

Speaking Likeness. By Christina Rossetti.

With a Stout Heart. By Mrs. Sale Barker.

Paws and Claws. By the Authors of 'Poems written for a Child.'

Fleur-de-Lys: Leaves from French History. By Ester Carr.

The Fantastic History of the Celebrated Pierrot. By Alfred Assolant. And rendered into English by A. G. Munro. pp. 877—78.

Jan. 2

CHRISTMAS BOOKS

A Cruise in the Acorn. By Alice Jerrold (Mrs. Adolphe Smith).

The Princess of Silverland. By Emil Striveleyne.

Country Maidens. By M. Bramston.

Amongst the Maoris. By Emilia Marryat (Mrs. Norris).

What Might Have Been Expected. By Frank F. Stockton.

Mrs. Mouser; or, Tales of a Grandmother. By the Author of 'Aunt Annie's Stories.'

Sunday Echoes in Week-day Hours. By Mrs. Carey Brock.

True-hearted: a Book for Girls. By Crona Temple.

The Life of an Elephant. By the Author of 'The Life of a Bear.' p. 18.

March 20

BOOKS FOR THE YOUNG

Ciceley's Choice. By Mrs. Robert O'Reilly.

Wonder-world.

More Bed-time Stories. By Louise Chandler Moulton.

Pollie and Jack. By Alice Hepburn.

The Children's Band. By the Hon. Isabel Plunket.

A Year at School. By Tom Browne.

The Fables of AEsop. Translated by Samuel Croxall, D. D.

Hetty; or, 'Fresh Water-Cresses.' By Mrs. Henry Keary.

The Fairy Spinner. By Miranda Hill.

Mischief's Thanksgiving. By Susan Coolidge.

The Mirror of Truth. By Mrs. Hammerton. p. 392.

Oct. 23

NW *Eight Cousins; or, the Aunt Hill*. By Louisa M. Alcott. p. 539.

Nov. 13

CHRISTMAS BOOKS

Nothing but Leaves. By Sarah Doudney.

Laura Linwood. By the Author of 'The White Dove,' & c.

The Young Lady's Book. Edited by Mrs. Henry Mackarness. pp. 639—40.

Nov. 27
CHRISTMAS BOOKS
Tell Me a Story. By Ennis Graham.
Nine Little Goslings. By Susan Coolidge.
Higgledy-Piggledy. By the Right Hon. E. H. Knatchbull-Hugessen.
Aunt Judy's Christmas Volume. Edited by H. K. F. Gatty and J. H. Ewing.
Every Boy's Annual. Edited by Edmund Routledge.
The Adventures of Johnny Ironsides. By J. Girardin.
The Story of Sevenoaks. By Dr. J. C. Holland.

Dec. 11
CHRISTMAS BOOKS
Away on the Moorlands: a Highland Tale. By A. C. Chambers.
'Especially Those.' By Brenda.
Tales of Nethercourt. By the Rev. H. C. Adams. M. A.
Marty and the Mite-Boxes. By Jennie Harrison.
Rosamond Ferrars. By M. Bramston.
Joachim's Spectacles: a Legend of Florenthal. By M. and C. Lee.
Honour and Glory. By Jeanie Hering.
Miss Roberts's Fortune. By Sophy Winthrop.
The Old House on Briar Hill. By Isabella Grant Meredith.
Seven Birthdays; or, the Children of Fortune: a Fairy Chronicle. By Kathleen Know.
The Mysterious Island.—Dropped from the Clouds.—Abandoned.—The Secret of the Island. By Jules Verne. Translated by W. H. G. Kingston.
The Survivors of the Chancellor. By Jules Verne. Translated by Ellen Frewes.
The Modern Playmate. Compiled and edited by the Rev. J. G. Wood.
Minnie's Holiday. By M. Betham-Edwards.
Sunnyland Stories. By the Author of 'Aunt Mary's Bran Pie,' & c.

Fables. Illustrated by Stories from Real Life. By Mrs. George Cupples.
Little Rosy's Pets. By the Author of 'Little Rosy's Travels.'
The Field of Ice. By Jules Verne.
Seed to the Sower: Stories and Lessons for Sundays. By Crona Temple.
Evelyn Howard; or, Early Friendships. By Mrs. H. B. Paull.
Myrtle and Cypress. By Annette Calthrop. pp. 786—87.

1876

Jan. 15
BOOKS FOR BOYS
Augustine's Choice. By Louisa A. Moncriff. p. 87.

Jan. 29
Memoirs and Correspondence of Caroline Hershel. By Mrs. John Hershel. pp. 155—57.

April 8
BOOKS FOR CHILDREN
The History of the Fairchild Family; or, the Child's Manual. By Mrs. Sherwood.
Will Foster of the Ferry. By Agnes Giberne.
Eastern Tales. By Many Story Tellers.
War. By John Edgar.
Lily's Home in the Country. By Mrs. Sale Barker.
Rags and Tatters. By Stella Austin.
The National Nursery Book. pp. 495—96.

Aug. 12
BOOKS FOR CHILDREN
Houses and Housekeeping. By Lady Barker.
Rosamond Ferrars. By M. Bramston.
Fairy Guardians. By F. Willoughby.
Baron Bruno. By Louisa Morgan.
The Basket of Flowers.
Frank, Rosamond, Harry and Lucy. Re-edited and revised by Mrs. Valentine.
The Story of the Robins. By Mrs. Trimmer.
The Romans and Danes.
Silver Pitchers. By Louisa M. Alcott. pp. 205—06.

Aug. 26
Memorials of a Quiet Life. By Augustus J. C. Hare. p. 263.

Sept. 2
BOOKS FOR CHILDREN
Conquering and to Conquer. By the Author of 'Chronicles of the Schönberg-Cotta Family.'
The Christmas Mummers and Other Stories. By Charlotte M. Yonge.
Miss Hitchcock's Wedding Dress, by the Author of 'Mrs. Jerningham's Journal,' & c.
Jan of the Windmill. By Juliana Horatia Ewing.
The Old House on the Downs. By Volvo non Valeo. pp. 304—05.

Sept. 9
BOOKS FOR CHILDREN AND FAMILY NOTE BOOKS
The Star in the Dust-Heap. By the Hon. Mrs. Greene.
Wedding Chimes: Notes of Marriages of Relatives and Friends.
Immortelles: a Souvenir of Departed Relatives and Friends. p. 337.

Dec. 2
CHRISTMAS BOOKS
On a Pin-cushion. By Mary de Morgan.
The Pearl Fountain. By Bridget and Julia Kavanagh.
The Rose and the Lily. By Mrs. Octavian Blewitt.
Johnnykin and the Goblins. By Charles G. Leland. p. 721.

Dec. 9
CHRISTMAS BOOKS
Sacred Heroes and Martyrs. By J. T. Headley.
Terrapin Island. By Mrs. George Cupples.
The Home of the Wolverine and the Beaver. By Charles Henry Eden.
In the Marsh. By Bessie C. Curteis.
Erling; or, the Days of St. Olaf. By F. Scarlett Potter.
Round about the Minister Green. By Ascott Hope.

Sweet Little Rouges. By Elvina Corbould.
'Carrots': Just a Little Boy. By Ennis Graham.
Our Home in the Marsh Land. By E. L. E.
Seventeen to Twenty-one; or, Aunt Vonica. By M. M. Bell.
Fairy. By Lizzie Joyce Tomlinson. p. 760.

Dec. 30
CHRISTMAS BOOKS
The Clan of the Cats: True Stories about the Feline Animals.
Public and Private Life of animals. Adapted from the French of Balzac, Droz, Jules Janin, E. Lemoine, A. de Musset, George Sand, & c., by J. Thomson.
The Swan and her Crew. By Christopher C. Davies.
The Natural History Album. Printed in Kronheim's Oil Colours.
The Home Book for Young Ladies. Edited by Mrs. Valentine.
Merry Sunbeams: a Picture-Book for Boys and Girls. Richly Starlight Stories. By Fanny Lablache.
Around and About Old England. By Clara L. Mateau. p. 885.

1877
Jan. 6
BOOKS FOR CHILDREN
Only a Cat. Edited by Mrs. H. B. Paull.
Chats for Small Chatterers.
The Tower on the Tor: a Tale for Boys. By Richard Rowe.
The Cold Shoulder; or, Half-Year at Craiglea. By Robert Richardson, B. A.
Grey Towers; or, Aunt Hetty's Will. By M. M. Pollard.
Tales and Legends of Saxony and Lusatia. By W. Westall.
Tiny Houses and their Builders.
Dora: a Life Story. By S. L. Brand. pp. 15—16.

April 7
BOOKS FOR CHILDREN
Great St. Benedict's: a Tale. By Elizabeth Tomas.

150

Little Madeleine: a Story for Children. By Sarah M. S. Clarke.

A Child's Corner Book. By Richard Rowe.

My Godmother's Stories from Many Lands. By Eleanora Louisa Hervey.

Instinct or Reason? By the Lady Julia Lockwood.

The Little Head of the Family. From the French of Mdlle. Zènaide Fleuriot. pp. 445—46.

Aug. 11

BOOKS FOR CHILDREN

Household Tales and Fairy Stories.

Rose in Bloom. By Louisa M. Alcott.

The Lucky Bag. By Richard Rowe.

Scamp and I: a Story of City By-ways. By L. T. Meade.

The Little King. By S. Blandy. Translated from the French by Mary de Hauteville.

The Scholar's Handbook of Household Management and Cookery. By W. B. Tegetmeier.

Uncle John's First Shipwreck. By Charles Cruse.

The Ladies' Treasury for 1876. Edited by Mrs. Warren.

Joanna's Inheritance. By Emma Marshall.

The Barton Experiment. By the Author of 'Helen's Babies.' pp. 176—77.

Oct. 13

BOOKS FOR CHILDREN

Modern Magic. By Prof. Hoffman.

Grey Towers. By M. M. Polllard.

The Pampas. By A. R. Hope.

The Adventures of Tom Hanson. By Firth Garside, M. A.

A Sunshine in the Shady Place. By Edith Miller.

From New Year to New Year, and from All the World Round. By the Author of 'Copsley Annals,' & c.

Guiding Lights. By F. E. Cooke.

The feasts of Camelot. By Eleanora Louisa Hervey.

For Old Sake's Sake. By Stella Austin.

Our Ruth: a Story of Old Times in New England. By Mrs. Prentiss.

Rest on the Cross. By Eleanora Louisa Hervey. pp. 465—66.

Nov. 10

CHRISTMAS BOOKS

Owen Hartley. By William H. G. Kingston.

Drifted Away: a Tale of Adventure.

Two Voyages, and What Came of Them. by the Author of 'Motherless Maggie.'

The Snowball Society: a Story for Children. By M. Bramston.

The Snow Fort and the Frozen Lake; or, Christmas Holidays at Pond House. By Eadgyth. *Our Valley.* p. 596.

Nov. 17

CHRISTMAS BOOKS

Aunt Judy's Christmas Volume for 1877. Edited by H. K. F. Gatty.

Our Trip to Blunderland. By Jean Jambon.

Talent in Tatters. By Hope Wraythe.

Little Talks with Little People.

Little May's Friends. By Annie Whittem.

Stories of Girlhood. By Sarah Doudney.

Jungle, Peak, and Plain. By Gordon Stables, M. D. R. N. pp. 627—28.

Nov. 24

OLT *Common-sense Housekeeping.* By Phillis Browne. p. 661.

Dec. 1

CHRISTMAS BOOKS

The Children's Picture Annual. By Mercie Sunshine.

Field Friends and Forest Foes. By Phillis Browne.

Childhood.

Peep Show: a Pleasure Book for the Young.

Paulina's Ambition: a Story. By Edis Searle.

Told by the Sea. By F. Frankfort Moore.

All in a Garden Green. By Elizabeth C. Traice.

The Christmas Story-Teller. By Old Hands and New.

The Three Wishes. By M. E. B. p. 697.

Dec. 22
CHRISTMAS BOOKS
Little Wide Awake. By Mrs. Sale Barker.
Aunt Emma's Picture Book.
Good out of Evil. By Mrs. Surr.
Our Little Sunbeam's Picture Book. By Mrs. Semple Garrett. p. 813.

1878

Jan. 12
BOOKS FOR CHILDREN
The Daisy Playmate.
Little Rosy Cheek's Story Book. By Mrs. Sale Barker.
Rosabella: a Doll's Christmas Story. By Auntie Bee.
Women worth Emulating. By Clara L. Balfour.
Black Harry; or, Lost in the Bush. By Robert Richardson.
A Story of a Wooden Horse. By Emile Bayard.
God's Silver; or, Youthful Days. By the Hon. Mrs. Greene.
The Magic Valley; or, Patient Antoine. By E. Keary.
The Girl's Home Book; or, How to Play and How to Work. pp. 53—54.

Jan. 26
BOOKS FOR THE YOUNG
Jack Granger's Cousin. By Julia A. Mathews.
The Settler and the Savage. By R. M. Ballantyne.
The Fifth Continent. By Charles H. Eden. pp. 120—21.

Feb. 9
COOKERY BOOK
Common-Sense Cookery, by A. T. Payne.
Cassell's Dictionary of Cookery.
Every-Day Meals. p. 187.

March 2
BOOKS FOR THE YOUNG
Leila on the Island and at Home. By Ann Fraser-Tytler.
Old Pictures in a New Frame. By Douglas Straight.
Martin Noble. By John G. Watts.

My Boyhood: a Story-Book for Boys. By H. C. Barkley.
Seven o'Clock. By Janie Brockman.
The Nightcap Series. By Aunt Fanny. *Old Nightcaps, New Nightcaps, Little Nightcaps, Fairy Nightcaps.* Illustrations.
Little Tales for Tiny Tots. p. 284.

March 16
BOOKS FOR THE YOUNG
Gideon Brown. Edited by Charles Mackay.
The Old Looking-Glass. By Maria Louisa Charlesworth.
Polly Wyatt; or, Virtue is its own Reward.
The Cuckoo Clock. By Ennis Graham.
The Holiday Album for Children. p. 364.

April 6
BOOKS FOR THE YOUNG
The Bella and her Crew. By Harriet S. Hill.
Margaret Woodward. By the Author of 'Sydonie's Dowry,' & c.
Children's Toys, and some Elementary Lessons in General Knowledge which they Teach.
The Original Robinson Crusoe. By the Rev. H. C. Adams. M. A.
Story after Story of Land, Sea, Man, and Beast. By the Author of 'Cheerful Sundays.'
The Hill Side Children. By Agnes Giberne. p. 443.

April 27
BOOKS FOR THE YOUNG
Princes and Princesses. By H. E. and E. E. Malden.
Sunshine Jenny, and other Stories. By Mrs. G. S. Reaney.
Alfie the Street Boy; or, Hardly Won. By A. Stuart King.
Uncle Philip. By Stella Austin.
The Boys of Westonbury. By the Rev. H. C. Adams.
Lilly's Visit to Grandmamma. By Mrs. Sale Barker. pp. 540—41.

Nov. 9
Records of a Girlhood. By Frances Ann Kemble. 3 vols. pp. 590—92.

Dec. 7
CHRISTMAS BOOKS
Harty the Wanderer. By Farleigh Owen.
The Day of Wonders. By Mrs. M. Sullivan.
Left Alone. By Francis Carr.
Vain Ambition. By Emma Davenport.
Children's Hour. By Charles Bruce.
Golden Childhood.
Dora's Boy. By Mrs. E. Ross.
Aunt Judy's Christmas Volume. p. 723.

Dec. 21
CHRISTMAS BOOKS
Every Inch a King. By Mrs. J. Worthington Bliss.
Clever Boys.
Among the Welsh Hills. By H. G. Halifax.
Job Singleton's Heir. By Emma Marshall.
Kaspar and the Summer Fairies. By Julia Goddard.
The Ladder of Cowslips. By the late Lady Kay Shuttleworth. Edited by her Daughter.
What the Swallows told Me. By L. P. Mohun Harris.
Little Bess. By Mary W. Ellis. p. 802.

Dec. 28
CHRISTMAS BOOKS
The Magic Flower-Pot and Other Stories. By Edward Garrett.
Mary Mordaunt. By Annie Gray.
Monksbury College. By Sarah Doudney.
Archie Dann's Stories as Told by Himself.
The Young Deserter.
Englefield Grange. By Mrs. H. B. Paull.
Left to Themselves: a Boy's Adventures in Australis. By Augusta Marryat.
Straight Paths and Crooked Ways. By Mrs. H. B. Paull.
Who shall Win? By the Author of 'The Young Missionaries.'
Aunt Annette's Stories to Ada. By Annette A. Salaman. p. 852.

1879
Jan. 4
BOOKS FOR CHILDREN
One New Year's Night. By Edward Garratt.

Worth Doing. By Jamie Brockman.
Peter Parley's Annual for 1879.
Cloverly. By Mary R. Higham.
Lost: a Tale of the English Lakes. By S. M.
Gracie and Grant. By the Author of 'Ben and Kit.'
St. Quentin's, and Other Stories. p. 18.

Jan. 18
BOOKS FOR CHILDREN
Uncle Joe's Stories. By the Right Hon. Knatchbull-Hugessen, M. P. p. 86.

May 24
BOOKS FOR CHILDREN
Looking Back. By Mary E. Shipley.
The Rector's Home. By Agnes Giberne.
Routledge's Every Girl's Annual. Edited by Miss Alicia A. Leith.
Chats about Birds. By Mercie Sunshine.
The Girl's Own Annual, 1879. Edited by J. W. Darton.
Drawing-Room Amusement and Evening Party Entertainments. By Prof. Hoffman.'
'Grandmother Dear.' By Mrs. Molesworth.
Dick Sands, the Boy Captain. By Jules Verne.
Lily's Dilemma. By Anna Longmore. p. 661.

July 12
BOOKS FOR CHILDREN
The Black Crusoe. From the French of Alfred Seguin.
Pierrot, Humbly Born but Noble of Heart. By S. de K.
Queen Dora. By Kathleen Knox.
Life and Adventures in Japan. By E. Warren Clark.
Fairy Tales. By a Soldier of the Queen. p. 46.

Aug. 9
BOOKS FOR CHILDREN
Mary's Holiday Task. By Georgina M. Moore.
Victoria-Bess. By Brenda.
The Good-natured Bear, & c. By R. Hengist Horne.

The Girl's Own Toymaker. By E. Landells and his Daughter, Alice Landells.
Basil Grey; or, Tried and True. By the Rev. W. J. Bettison.
Needlework; Schedule III. By E. A. Curtis.
The Eskdale Herd-boy. By Lady Stoddart.
The Scottish Orphans.
Keeper's Travels in Search of his Master.
Memoir of Bob, the Spotted Terrier.
Mrs. Leicester's School. By Charles and Mary Lamb.
The History of the Robins. By Mrs. Trimmer.
The Adventures of the Bodley Family. By the Author of 'Dream Children.' pp. 172—73.

Nov. 22
CHRISTMAS BOOKS
Aunt Judy's Christmas Volume for 1879. Edited by H. K. F. Gatty.
Silver Linings. By Mrs. Reginald Bray.
Northcote Memories. By the Author of 'The Copsley Annals.'
Young Days: a Monthly Illustrated Magazine for the Young.
Ways and Tricks of Animals. By Mary Hooper.
The Bird and Insects' Post Office. By Robert Bloomfield. p. 659.

Dec. 6
CHRISTMAS BOOKS
Jimmy's Cruise in the Pinafore, & c. By Louisa M. Alcott.
John Smith. By Geraldine Butt and J. G. Butt.
Johan the Maid, Deliverer of England and France. By the Author of 'Chronicles of the Schönberg-Cotta Family.'
In New Granada; or, Heroes and Patriots by W. H. G. Kingston.
Little Hinges. By Madeleine Bonavia Hunt.
Post Haste. By R. M. Ballantyne. p. 725.

Dec. 13
CHRISTMAS BOOKS
The Children's Picture Annual. By Mercie Sunshine.

Parted: a Tale of Clouds and Sunshine. By N. D'Anvers.
Model Yachts and Model Yacht Sailing. By James E. Walton.
Honor Bright. By the Authors of 'Two Blackbirds,' & c.
The Begum's Fortune. By Jules Verne. Translated by W. H. G. Kingston.
The Old Ship. By H. A. Forde.
The Young Carpenters of Freiberg. Translated from the German by J. Latchmore, jun.
Golden Childhood.
Phil's Champion: an Irish Story. By Robert Richardson, M.
The Siege of Vienna: a Story of the Turkish War in 1683. Translated from the German by J. Latchmore, jun.
Adventures in Western Africa. By the Rev. H. S. B. Yates.
The Langdales of Langdale End. By the Author of 'Valeria.'
True to his Colours; or, the Life that Wears Best. By the Rev. T. P. Wilson.
Jane Taylor: her Life and Letters. By Mrs. H. C. Knight. pp. 760—61.

Dec. 20
CHRISTMAS BOOKS
Spindle Stories; or, New Yarns from Old Wool. By Ascott R. Hope.
Little Wideawake: an Illustrated Magazine for Good Children. Edited by Mrs. Sale Barker.
Every Boy's Annual. Edited by E. Routledge.
Other Stories. By the Right Hon. E. H. Knatchbull-Hugesson.
The Roll of the Drum. By R. Mountenay Jephson.
The Floating Light of Ringfinnan and Guardian Angels. By L. T. Meade.
A Houseful of Children. By Mrs. D. P. Sanford.
Chatterbox. Edited by J. Erskine Clarke, M. A.
Sunday Reading for the Young.
The Prize for Girls and Boys.

The Royal Umbrella. By Major Alfred F. P. Harcourt.

'Bunchy'; or, the Children of Scarsbrook Farm. By E. C. Phillips.

Kind Words: a Magazine for Young People.

Strahan's Grand Annual for the Young. 1879.

Little Folks: a Magazine for the Young.

An Involuntary Voyage. By Lucien Biart. Translated by Mrs. Cashel Hoey and Mr. John Lillie.

Peter Parley's Annual for 1880.

Hendricks the Hunter; or, the Border Farm: a Tale of Zulu Land. By W. H. G. Kingston.

Eminent Philanthropists, Patriots, and Reformers.

Friends over the Water. By M. Betham Edwards.

Crissy's Little Mother. By Emma Leslie. pp. 796—97.

Dec. 27
CHRISTMAS BOOKS
Rough the Terrier: his Life and Adventures. By Emily Brodie.

Jame Duke, Costermonger. By William Gilbert.

Gallery of Notable Men and Women. Compiled by the Editor of 'The Treasury of Modern Biography.'

Brave Janet, the Story of a Little Girl's Trials and Victories. By Alice Lee.

True as Steel. By Madame Colomb.

Her Benny: a Story of Street Life. By Silas K. Hocking.

Young Heads on Old Shoulders. By Ascott R. Hope.

Alice, and other Fairy Plays for Children. By Kate Freiligrath-Kroeker.

The Beautiful Face: a Tale. By Elizabeth Harcourt Mitchell.

Careless Kyts, and other Stories. By Charles Marshall.

Kitty and Bo.

St. Nicholas' Even, and other Tales. By Mary C. Rowsell.

Lady Sybil's Choice: a Tale of the Crusades. By Emily Sarah Holt.

Barton Ferris: a Tale of Village Life and Work. By Benjamin Clarke.

The Broken Looking-Glass; or, Mrs. Dorothy Cope's Recollections of Service. By Maria Louisa Charlesworth.

Stories for Mamma's Darlings. By Amanda Matorka Blankenstein.

The Leisure Hour, 1879. pp. 847—48.

1880

May 15
BOOKS FOR CHILDREN
Muriel Bertram: a Tale. By Agnes Giberne.

Nellie Arundel: a Tale of Home Life. By C. S.

Pat: a Story for Boys and Girls. By Stella Austin.

The Young Buglers: a Tale of the Peninsular War. By G. A. Henty.

The Spanish Cavalier; or, De Soto the Discoverer. By J. S. C. Abbott.

Dot and her Treasures. By L. T. Meade.

Lady Rosamond's Book; or, Drawings of Light. The Stanton-Corbet Chronicles. By L. E. Guernsey.

The Hamiltons; or, Dora's Choice. By Emily Brodie.

At the Lion. By the Author of 'An Elder sister.'

July 3
BOOKS FOR CHILDREN
The Otter's Story, and other Stories. By the author of 'Friends in Fur and Feathers.'

Jemima: a Story of English Family Life. By Adelaide.

The Tapestry Room: a Child's Romance. By Mrs. Molesworth. p. 14.

July 10
OLT *A Year's Cookery.* By Phillis Browne. p. 47.

OLT *Breakfasts and Luncheons at Home,* by Short. p. 47.

OLT *The Marvellolus Little Housekepers.* By Ida Joscelyne. p. 47.

List of Works Cited

Abbatt, William, comp. *The Colloquial Who's Who: An Attempt to Identify the Many Authors, Writers and Contributors Who Have Used Pen-Names, Initials, etc. (1600—1924). Also a List of Sobriquets, Nicknames, Epigrams, Oddities, War Phrases etc.* 2 vols. New York: Argonaut Press Ltd., 1966.

"The Athenaeum Centenary." *Nation & Athenaeum*, Jan. 14, 1928, pp. 558—59.

[Austin, Alfred]. "The Vice of Reading." *Temple Bar*, 42 (1874), 251—57.

"The Author of *Heartsease* and the Modern School of Fiction." *Prospective Review*, 10 (1854), 460—82.

"The Author of 'John Halifax.' " *British Quarterly Review*, 44 (1866), 32—58.

Batho, Edith C. and Bonamy Dobrée. *The Victorians and After, 1830—1914.* London: Cresset Press, 1938.

Bentley, Richard II and F. E. Williams, comps. *A List of the Principal Publications Issued from New Burlington Street, 1829—1898.* London: Richard Bentley and Son, 1893—1920.

Bevington, Merle Mowbray. *The Saturday Review, 1855—1868.* New York: Columbia Univ. Press, 1941.

Bigland, Eileen. *Ouida: the Passionate Victorian.* London: Jarrolds Ltd., 1950.

Blunden, Edmund. "Some Early Glories." "The Athenaeum Centenary Supplement." *Nation & Athenaeum*, Jan 21, 1928, pp. 602—03.

Bourne, H. R. Fox. *English Newspapers: Chapters in the History of Journalism.* 2 vols. London: Chatto & Windus, 1887.

Braddon, Mary Elizabeth. *Aurora Floyd.* 2 vols. Leipzig: Tauchnitz, 1863.

—. *The Lady's Mile.* 2 vols. Leipzig: Tauchnitz, 1866.

Broughton, Rhoda. *A Beginner.* London: Bentley and Son, 1894.

[—]. *Cometh Up as a Flower: An Autobiography.* Leipzig. Tauchnitz, 1867.

[—]. *Not Wisely, But Too Well.* Leipzig: Tauchnitz, 1867.

B[uchanan], R[obert] W. "Society's Looking-Glass." *Temple Bar,* 6 (1862), 129—37.

Calder, Jenni. *Women and Marriage in Victorian Fiction.* London: Thames and Hudson, 1976.

Carroll, David, ed. *George Eliot: The Critical Heritage.* London: Routledge & Kegan Paul, 1971.

Colby, Robert A. " 'How It Strikes a Contemporary': The 'Spectator' as Critic." *Nineteenth Century Fiction*, 11 (1956), 182—206.

Colby, Vineta and Robert. *The Equivocal Virtue: Mrs. Oliphant and the Literary Market Place.* Hamden, Conn.: Archon, 1966.

[Craik, Dinah Maria]. *Christian's Mistake.* Leipzig: Tauchnitz, 1865.

[—]. *John Halifax, Gentleman*. 1856: rpt. London: Dent, 1969.

[—]. "To Novelists and a Novelist." *Macmillan's Magazine*, 3 (1861), 441—47.

Craik, G. L. *A Compendious History of English Literature*. 2 vols. London, 1861.

Craik, Georgiana M. *Mildred*. Leipzig: Tauchnitz, 1868.

Cruse, Amy. *The Victorians and Their Books*. London: Allen & Unwin, 1935.

Cushing, William. *Anonyms: A Dictionary of Revealed Authorship*. 2 vols. London: Sampson Low, Marston, Searle & Rivington, 1890.

—. *Initials and Pseudonyms: A Dictionary of Literary Disguises*. London: Sampson Low, 1886.

Dallas, Eneas Sweetland. *The Gay Science*. 2 vols. London: Chapman and Hall, 1866.

Dixon, Ella Hepworth. *"As I Knew Them"; Sketches of People I Have Met on the Way*. London: Hutchinson & Co. Ltd., 1930.

[Eliot, George]. "Art and Belles Lettres." *Westminster Review*, 65 (1856), 625—50.

[—]. *"Rachel Gray."* *Leader*, Jan. 5, 1856, p. 19.

[—]. "Silly Novels by Lady Novelists." *Westminster Review*, NS 10 (1856), 442—61.

Ellegård, Alvar. "The Readership of the Periodical Press in Mid-Victorian Britain." *Victorian Periodicals Newsletter*, 13 (1971), 3—22.

Elwin, Malcolm. *Victorian Wallflowers: Studies in Nineteenth Century English Literature*. London: Jonathan Cape, 1934.

Fahnestock, Jeanne Rosenmayer. "Geraldine Jewsbury: The Power of the Publisher's Reader." *Nineteenth Century Fiction*, 28 (1973), 253—72.

"Female Novelists. Mrs. Marsh-Caldwell." *New Monthly Magazine*, 96 (1852), 313—22.

Fritschner, Linda Marie. "Publishers' Readers, Publishers, and Their Authors." *Publishing History*, 7 (1980), 45—100.

Fryckstedt, Monica Correa. "The Hidden Rill: The Life and Career of Maria Jane Jewsbury." *Bulletin of the John Rylands University Library of Manchester*, 66 (1984), 177—203 and 67 (1984), 450—73.

—. "New Sources on Geraldine Jewsbury and the Woman Question." *Research Studies*, 51 (1983), 51—63.

Gettman, Royal A. *A Victorian Publisher: A Study of the Bentley Papers*. Cambridge: Cambridge Univ. Press, 1960.

Graham, Kenneth. *English Criticism of the Novel 1865—1900*. Oxford: Clarendon Press, 1965.

"A Great Sensation." *Saturday Review*, March 8, 1862, pp. 276—77.

Greenhut, Morris. "G. H. Lewes as a Critic of the Novel." *Studies in Philology*, 45 (1948), 491—512.

[Greg, W. R.] "The False Morality of Lady Novelists." *National Review*, 8 (1859), 144—67.

Griest, Guinevere L. *Mudie's Circulating Library and the Victorian Novel*. Bloomington: Indiana Univ. Press, 1970.

Hannay, James. *A Course of English Literature*. London, 1866.

"Heartsease: or, The Brother's Wife." *Fraser's Magazine*, 50 (1854), 489—503.

Howe, Susanne. *Geraldine Jewsbury: Her Life and Errors*. London: George Allen & Unwin Ltd., 1935.

Hubback, Mrs J. *The Old Vicarage. A Novel*. 3 vols. London: Skeet, 1856.

Hughes, Winifred. *The Maniac in the Cellar: Sensation Novels of the 1860s*. Princeton: Princeton Univ. Press, 1980.

[Hutton, Richard Holt]. "The Empire of Novels." *Spectator*, Jan. 9, 1869, pp. 43—44.

[—]. "Novels by the Authoress of 'John Halifax'." *North British Review*, 29 (1858), 466—81.

Jeaffreson, John Cordy. *A Book of Recollections*. 2 vols. London: Hurst and Blackett, 1894.

—. *Novels and Novelists from Elizabeth to Victoria*. London: Hurst and Blackett, 1858. Vol. II.

Jump, J. D. "Weekly Reviewing in the Eighteen-Fifties." *Review of English Studies*, 24 (1948), 42—57.

—. 'Weekly Reviewing in the Eighteen-Sixties." *Review of English Studies*, NS 3 (1952), 244—62.

Kaminsky, Alice R. "George Eliot, George Henry Lewes and the Novel." *PMLA*, 70 (1955), 997—1013.

Kavanagh, Julia. *Rachel Gray. A Tale Founded on Fact*. 1855. Leipzig: Tauchnitz, 1856.

[Keddie, Henrietta]. *Phemie Millar*. By the Author of 'The Kinnears'. 3 vols. London: Hurst and Blackett, 1854.

Keith, Sara. "The 'Athenaeum' as a Bibliographical Aid: Illustrated by 'Lady Audley's Secret' and Other Novels." *Victorian Periodicals Newsletter*, 8 (1975), 25—28.

—. "Mudie's Select Library. Principal Works of Fiction in Circulation in 1848, 1858, 1869." TS Ann Arbor, Michigan, 1955.

Kellett, E. E. "The Press." In *Early Victorian England 1830—1865*. Ed. G. M. Young. London: Oxford Univ. Press, 1934, II, 3—97.

Kennedy, James, et al., eds. *Dictionary of Anonymous and Pseudonymous English Literature*. 6 vols. By Samuel Halkett and John Laing. Edinburgh: Oliver and Boyd, 1926.

[Kinnear, A. S.] "Mr. Trollope's Novels." *North British Review*, 40 (1864), 369—401.

"The Lady Novelists of Great Britain." *Gentleman's Magazine*, 40 (1853), 18—25.

Lee, Holme (pseud. for Harriet Parr). *Gilbert Massenger*. London: Smith, Elder & Co., 1855.

[Lewes, George Henry]. "Vivian." "A Gentle Hint to Writing-Women." *Leader*, 1 (1850), 189.

[—]. "Criticism in Relation to Novels." *Fortnightly Review*, 3 (Dec. 15, 1865), 352—61.

[—]. "The Lady Novelists." *Westminster Review*, NS 2 (1852), 129—41.

—. *The Principles of Success in Literature*. 1865; rpt. Farnborough Hants.: Gregg International Publishers Ltd., 1969.

" 'A Life for a Life'." *Saturday Review*, Dec. 10, 1859, pp. 708—09.

[Manning, Anne]. *Some Account of Mrs. Clarinda Singlehart*. By the Author of 'Mary Powell.' London: Hall, Virtue & Co., 1855.

[Mansel, H.L.] "Sensation Novels." *Quarterly Review*, 113 (1863), 481—514.

Marchand, Leslie A. *The Athenaeum: A Mirror of Victorian Culture*. Chapel Hill: Univ. of North Carolina Press, 1941.

[Marsh (Caldwell), Anne]. *Margaret and Her Bridesmaids*. By the Author of 'Woman's Devotion.' 3 vols. London: Hurst and Blackett, 1856.

Masson, David. *British Novelists and Their Styles: Being a Critical Sketch of the History of British Prose Fiction*. Cambridge: Macmillan and Co., 1859.

Maurer, Oscar Jr. "Anonymity vs. Signature in Victorian Reviewing." *Studies in English*, 27 (1948), 1—27.

"Mr. Charles Reade's Novels: *The Cloister and the Hearth*." *National Review*, 14 (1862), 134—49.

"Mrs. Marsh Caldwell." *Dublin University Magazine*, 34 (1849), 575—90.

Murray, Vincent E.H. "Ouida's Novels." *Contemporary Review*, 22 (1873), 921—35.

"Novel-Reading." *Saturday Review*, Feb. 16, 1867, pp. 196—97.

"Novels and Life." *Saturday Review*, Feb. 13, 1864, pp. 188—89.

"Novels of the Day: Their Writers and Readers." *Fraser's Magazine*, 62 (1860), 205—17.

"Novels, Past and Present." *Saturday Review*, April 14, 1866, pp. 438—40.

[Oliphant, Margaret]. *Lucy Crofton*. By the Author of 'Margaret Maitland.' 1859; rpt. London: Hurst and Blackett, 1860.

[—]. "Modern Novelists—Great and Small." *Blackwood's Edinburgh Magazine*, 77 (1855), 554—68.

[—]. "Novels." *Blackwood's Edinburgh Magazine*, 94 (1863), 168—83.

[—]. "Novels." *Blackwood's Edinburgh Magazine*, 102 (1867), 257—80.

" 'The Ordeal of Richard Feverel'." *Saturday Review*, July 9, 1859, pp. 48—49.

Ouida (Marie Louise de la Ramé). *Idalia. A Romance*. 2 vols. Leipzig: Tauchnitz, 1867.

"Our Female Novelists." *Christian Remembrancer*, 38 (1859), 305—39.

Page, Norman, ed. *Wilkie Collins: The Critical Heritage*. London: Routledge & Kegan Paul, 1974.

Parr, Mrs. "Dinah Mulock (Mrs. Craik)." In Mrs Oliphant et al. *Women Novelists of Queen Victoria's Reign*. London: Hurst & Blackett, 1897, pp. 217—48.

Ray, Gordon. *Thackeray: The Age of Wisdom*. London: Oxford Univ. Press, 1958.

Robinson, E. Arthur. "Meredith's Literary Theory and Science: Realism vs. the Comic Spirit." *PMLA*, 53 (1938), 857—68.

Rosenmayer, Jeanne. "Geraldine Jewsbury: Novelist and Publisher's Reader." Diss. Univ. of London, 1970.

Rust, James D. "The Art of Fiction in George Eliot's Reviews." *Review of English Studies*, NS 7 (1956), 164—72.

S. A. B. *The 'Athenaeum' Exposed*. London, 1863.

Sadleir, Michael. *Things Past*. London: Constable, 1944.

Sergeant, Adeline. "Mrs. Crowe, Mrs. Archer Clive, Mrs. Henry Wood." In Mrs. Oliphant et al. *Women Novelists of Queen Victoria's Reign*. London: Hurst & Blackett, 1897, pp. 149—92.

"The Shadow of Ashlydyat." *Saturday Review*, Jan. 16, 1864, pp. 82—83.

Showalter, Elaine. *A Literature of Their Own: British Novelists from Brontë to Lessing*. Princeton: Princeton Univ. Press, 1977.

Smalley, Donald, ed. *Trollope: The Critical Heritage*. London: Routledge & Kegan Paul, 1969.

Stang, Richard. *The Theory of the Novel in England 1850—1870*. London: Routledge & Kegan Paul, 1959.

[Stephen, James Fitzjames]. "The Relation of Novels to Life." In *Cambridge Essays*. London: Parker, 1855.

Terry, R. C. *Victorian Popular Fiction, 1860—80*. London: Macmillan, 1983.

Thomas, Sir William Beach. *The Story of the Spectator, 1828—1928*. London: Methuen & Co., 1928.

Thomson, Patricia. *George Sand and the Victorians: Her Influence and Reputation in Nineteenth-Century England*. London: Macmillan, 1977.

Tillotson, Kathleen. *Novels of the Eighteen-Forties*. 1954; rpt. London: Oxford Univ. Press, 1962.

Trollope, Anthony. *An Autobiography*. 1883; rpt. London: Oxford Univ. Press, [1947].

—. "Novel Reading." *Nineteenth Century*, 5 (1879), 24—43.

—. "On English Prose Fiction as a Rational Amusement." 1870. In *Four Lectures*. Ed. Morris L. Parrish. London: Constable & Co. Ltd., 1938.

Walbank, F. Alan, ed. *Queens of the Circulating Library: Selections from Victorian Lady Novelists 1850—1900*. London: Evans Brothers Ltd., 1950.

Williams, Ioan, ed. *Meredith: The Critical Heritage*. London: Routledge & Kegan Paul, 1971.

Wolff, Michael. "Victorian Reviewers and Cultural Responsibility." In *1859: Entering an Age of Crisis*. Eds. Philip Appleman, William A. Madden and Michael Wolff. Bloomington: Indiana Univ. Press, 1959, pp. 269—89.

Wolff, Robert Lee. *Gains and Losses: Novels of Faith and Doubt in Victorian England*. London: Murray, 1977.

—. *Sensational Victorian: The Life and Fiction of Mary Elizabeth Braddon*. New York: Garland Publishing Inc., 1979.

[Worboise, Emma]. *The Wife's Trials. A Tale*. London: Thickbroom Brothers, 1858.

Yonge, Charlotte. *Heartsease; or, the Brother's Wife*. 2 vols. Leipzig: Tauchnitz, 1855.

Index